PRAISE FOR
A LIFELONG CALL TO LEARN

"This is an exceptional resource—comprehensive in its identification of best practices in today's educational contexts and in its exploration of how lifelong learning has evolved over the past fifty years. After finishing this book, readers will view 'continuing education' in new ways, whether they participate in lifelong learning opportunities or plan them."

> *Kenneth J. McFayden, Professor of Ministry and Leadership Development at Union Theological Seminary and Presbyterian School of Christian Education and author of* Strategic Leadership for a Change: Facing Our Losses, Finding Our Future

"Essays in this collection mine the rich legacy and outline possible future directions for the continuing education movement. This book will inspire readers to make their own lifelong commitment to the lifelong learning enterprise."

> *Barbara Blodgett, Minister for Vocation and Formation, United Church of Christ*

"Striving to learn is to accept an invitation to participate in a thoughtful human community by discovering a transforming power within us in relation to others. Robert Reber and Bruce Roberts urge us to cultivate excellent religious leaders who can contribute to spirituality in a global context by bringing diverse perspectives on continuing education."

> *HiRho Y. Park, Director of Continuing Formation for Ministry, General Board of Higher Education and Ministry*

A Lifelong Call to Learn

A Lifelong Call to Learn

Continuing Education for Religious Leaders

Revised and Expanded Edition

Robert E. Reber and D. Bruce Roberts

THE
ALBAN INSTITUTE
Herndon, Virginia
www.alban.org

The Alban Institute
2121 Cooperative Way, Suite 100
Herndon, VA 20171

Scripture quotations, unless otherwise noted, are from the New Revised Standard Version of the Bible, copyright © 1989, Division of Christian Education of the National Council of Churches of Christ in the United States of America, and are used by permission.

Cover design by Spark Design.

Library of Congress Cataloging-in-Publication Data

A lifelong call to learn : continuing education for religious leaders / Robert E. Reber and D. Bruce Roberts, editors.
    p. cm.
Includes bibliographical references.
ISBN 978-1-56699-399-9
1. Clergy--Post-ordination training. 2. Theology--Study and teaching (Continuing education) I. Reber, Robert Eldred, 1937- II. Roberts, D. Bruce, 1939-
BV4165.L54 2009
230.071'1--dc22
                        2009042260

10   11   12   13   14   VP   5   4   3   2   1

Contents

122066

Part III: Innovations in Continuing Theological Education

Part IV: Development, Management, and Promotion of Programs

Why This Book?

More than nine years have passed since the publication of the first edition of this book, which focused on continuing theological education for church professionals, whether clergy or laity. Much has happened since that time. Increasingly, theological schools and conference and retreat centers are giving attention to the ongoing education of religious leaders. Judicatories, congregations, entrepreneurs, and professional societies are sponsoring continuing education programs. In many respects, this education activity reflects what is going on in the larger society where attention and considerable resources are being devoted to continuing education for professionals as well as a myriad of other types of adult education courses, workshops, seminars, and conferences for the general public.

This revised edition focuses on the broad arena of continuing education for religious professionals and laity. The contributors offer a variety of perspectives that have emerged from years of experience and reflection on their work with clergy and laity in a variety of programs. As directors of continuing education programs, teachers in adult and professional education, and lifelong learners, all eagerly share their insights and invite you to be part of the journey of lifelong education. There is no greater educational need in the life of congregations and religious organizations today than having a committed, informed, and continually educated leadership. We trust that this book will encourage the emergence of new and helpful understandings and practices related to life-long learning in the years to come.

Overview of Contents

The first section of this book is devoted to historical perspectives and educational contexts. Four chapters address questions such as:

- What is the current state of professional and continuing theological education?
- What is its mission and purpose?
- What historical developments have led up to the present situation?
- What are the current contexts in which lifelong learning is taking place?
- Who has been providing continuing education for clergy and laity?
- Who has been participating and who has been overlooked?

The next section focuses on theory and research in professional continuing education. Attention is given to a more systemic view of continuing education for religious leaders, and, more specifically, where and how do religious leaders learn.

The third section discusses innovations in delivery of continuing education and explores the implications of the laity's involvement in continuing education programs that link faith and daily life, taking seriously the growing religious pluralism in this country. Consideration is given to such questions as who is and should be involved in continuing theological education, what the content of future programs might be, and projections for the use of computers and the Internet for learning and for connecting learners.

The fourth section focuses on the development, management, and promotion of programs. Ronald Cervero and Donald Guthrie assert in chapter 17 that continuing education belongs at the center of the institutional mission of congregations and seminaries. The chapters that follow take up practical concerns, such as program planning, design and evaluation, marketing and promoting programs; creating hospitality and a welcoming environment for the whole person; and negotiating the difficulties of risk and managing risk for continuing education centers and programs.

The final chapter focuses on directions for the future and raises questions that need to be addressed by all of us who are committed to lifelong learning. Also, the questions point to a number of areas that require ongoing research. The future agenda for theological schools, continuing education programs, and conference and retreat centers is considerable. We who are committed to lifelong learning in religious communities have a lot of catching up to do living in a highly interconnected world. However, if each of us is willing to take on one of the areas identified in the concluding chapter and partner with others, amazing progress can be made.

Acknowledgments

Only because of the collaboration and encouragement of many colleagues and friends has this volume come to print. Several have given unstintingly of their time and have contributed chapters. We are deeply grateful to the many members of the Society for the Advancement of Continuing Education for Ministry (SACEM) who kept insisting that we needed to revise the original book published in 2000. At SACEM's annual gatherings we have been stimulated by discussions with directors of continuing education and lifelong programs from all over North America, from mainline Protestant, Evangelical, and Roman Catholic seminaries and conference and retreat centers. Many ideas, practices, and new and emerging models for ongoing learning have been tested with old-timers and newcomers to the field. We owe considerable thanks to the Sustaining Pastoral Excellence Program of the Lilly Endowment that has funded numerous projects in continuing theological education for clergy across the country during the past eight years. Many have been peer learning programs that are referred to in chapters in this book. Our experience as consultants and evaluators of several projects has informed and enriched our approach to what this book might contain and has introduced us to new leaders in continuing theological education.

Finally, we wish to express our thanks to two institutions that provided us in recent years an arena for our own work as continuing theological educators, Auburn Theological Seminary in New York City and Christian Theological Seminary in Indianapolis. Both provided generous support, time, and space, and continue to affirm the importance of lifelong learning and its centrality to the life of religious institutions and the church in particular. Also, this volume would not have been possible without the interest and commitment of the Alban Institute to publish and promote it.

Contributors

JUSTUS N. BAIRD is a rabbi and the director of the Center for Multifaith Education at Auburn Theological Seminary in New York City, where he works to prepare religious leaders for a religiously diverse world. He is the cofounder of Questia, a successful and far-reaching academic online library and the spiritual leader for the Reform Jewish Community of Barnegat on the New Jersey shore.

RONALD M. CERVERO is professor and head of the Department of Lifelong Education, Administration, and Policy at the University of Georgia. Three of his books have won national awards: *Effective Continuing Education for Professionals; Working the Planning Table: Negotiating Democratically for Adult, Continuing, and Workplace Education;* and *Planning Responsibly for Adult Education: A Guide to Negotiating Power and Interests.*

WARD CORNETT III is director of continuing education at Trinity Lutheran Seminary, Columbus, Ohio, and was for six years director of continuing education for Region 6 of the Evangelical Lutheran Church in America. Ordained in 1979, he previously served congregations in Washington, D.C., Pittsburgh, and St. Joseph, Michigan.

DENT DAVIS is the former dean and vice president for lifelong learning and member of the faculty at Columbia Theological Seminary in Decatur, Georgia. An ordained Presbyterian pastor for thirty years, he has been a retreat leader and consultant for more than seventy-five churches and judicatories. His academic background is in adult education and spiritual formation.

TIM DOLAN is the director of the Institute for Clergy and Lay Leadership Development at Whitworth University in Spokane, Washington. He also serves as director of the Master of Arts in Theology program and teaches in the theology department. Prior to coming to Whitworth in 1998, he served as a pastor for nearly seventeen years in two congregations.

LAURIE J. FERGUSON is a psychologist, coach, and Presbyterian minister. She consults with the Auburn Coaching Institute. She was the director of coaching for the New York Sabbatical Institute, a project of Auburn, New York, and Union Theological Seminaries. She has a private coaching practice and consults with different judicatories and denominations for training in coaching skills.

DONALD GUTHRIE is associate professor of educational ministries at Covenant Theological Seminary in St. Louis. He has served in various capacities at Covenant, including the Doctor of Ministry program director, field education program director, and vice president for academics. His research interests include vocational discipleship, intergenerational learning, and small groups.

A. CHRISTOPHER HAMMON serves as the administrator of the Wayne E. Oates Institute Online Learning Center, which has been offering online lifelong learning for ministers in the form of conferences, workshops, seminars, and certificate programs since 1998. He has been a leading voice in using media for lifelong learning for ministry for almost three decades, and is a member of the affiliated faculty for the Doctor of Ministry program at Drew University's Theological School in New Jersey.

EILEEN MACHOLL is director of finance and administration at Auburn Theological Seminary in New York City and is responsible for the areas of accounting, finance, personnel, technology, insurance, and facilities. She holds graduate degrees from Columbia and Fordham Universities. She has dedicated her career to the integration of practical and creative support for professionals in the fields of education, cross-cultural understanding, theology, and the arts.

PENNY LONG MARLER is professor of religion at Samford University in Birmingham, Alabama. A sociologist of religion, her scholarly interests include contemporary American religion and especially the relationship between church and society. Her recent research has focused on the impact of peer learning on pastoral leaders and their congregations. She is coauthor of *Being There: Culture and Formation in Two Theological Schools* and author of numerous scholarly articles and essays.

JANET L. MAYKUS is principal for the College of Pastoral Leaders and director of Christian leadership education at Austin Presbyterian Theological Seminary. She is the editor of the annual publication *Communitas* and producer of the seminary's *Need to Know* audio series. She is an ordained minister in the Christian Church (Disciples of Christ) and was previously the director of Hospice Austin's department of spiritual care and bereavement.

MARVIN L. MORGAN is minister of pastoral care and counseling for First Congregational United Church of Christ in Atlanta, and faith communities coordinator for United Food and Commercial Workers Union, assigned to the Justice@Smithfield Campaign, Lumberton, North Carolina. He has been pastor of congregations for more than thirty-five years while also directing continuing theological education at the Interdenominational Center in Atlanta for fifteen years. He was moderator of the UCC General Synod 27 in 2009.

CAROLYN HENNINGER OEHLER is the former executive director of Scarritt-Bennett Center, a conference, retreat, and educational center in Nashville. She is a writer, teacher, and seminar leader. Recent publications include "Lucy Rider Meyer" in *Women Building Chicago 1790–1990: A Biographical Dictionary*, "Steps Toward Building Wholeness: Learning and Repentance," and "The Journey Is Our Home."

ROBERT E. REBER is an adult educator, consultant, and coach, currently president pro tem of Bexley Hall Seminary, Columbus, Ohio, and formerly dean of Auburn Theological Seminary for sixteen years. He is the coeditor with D. Bruce Roberts and contributor to *A Lifelong Call to Learn: Approaches to Continuing Education for Church Leaders*; author of *Linking Faith and Daily Life: An Educational Program for Lay People*; and articles on professional and adult continuing education. For more than thirty years he has developed educational programs for laity and clergy.

D. BRUCE ROBERTS is professor emeritus of congregational education and leadership and served as director of the Indiana Clergy Peer Group Study Program at Christian Theological Seminary. He is coeditor with Robert E. Reber and contributor to *A Lifelong Call to Learn: Approaches to Continuing Education for Church Leaders* and author of articles on congregational leadership and adult education. As a United Methodist pastor, he served churches in Delaware and Massachusetts.

MARK ROUCH was for ten years director of the Intentional Growth Center, Lake Junaluska, North Carolina. He was a United Methodist pastor and director of continuing education, the United Methodist Church Board of Ordained Ministry. A founding member and former president of the Society for the Advancement of Continuing Education for Ministry, he was the author of one of the first books on continuing education for ministry, *Competent Ministry: A Guide to Effective Continuing Education.*

SALLY SIMMEL presents, consults, and writes in areas of laity, peace, the environment, and travel. She coordinates programs at a retreat center in Arizona and is active in a global network of lay retreat and educational centers. She was director for ministry in daily life of the Evangelical Lutheran Church in America from 1988 to 2004 and is the past president of the ecumenical Coalition for Ministry in Daily Life.

FREDERICK W. WEIDMANN is the former director of the Center for Church Life and professor of biblical studies at Auburn Theological Seminary. He was responsible for developing and directing the educational leadership programs for clergy, lay leaders, and an interested public, including the Auburn Coaching Institute, which works with leaders and ministers to renew and enhance their vision, actualize their mission and values, and thrive. He is coeditor with D. Seiple of *Enigmas and Powers: Engaging the Work of Walter Wink for Classroom, Church and World.*

PART I

Historical Perspectives
and Educational Contexts

CHAPTER 1

From Yesterday to Today in Continuing Theological Education

Mark Rouch
(Mark Rouch died in 2006. The chapter has been updated by Robert E. Reber.)

"Let me show you my favorite nude." My parents were even more startled than I by this suggestion from our pastor. The setting, however, was New York City's Metropolitan Museum of Art and the "nude," as it turned out, was a lovely piece of Greek sculpture. I was fifteen and we were attending the New York World's Fair. Our pastor and his wife were in Manhattan because he was enrolled in Union Theological Seminary's summer school. The year was 1940.

This personal incident illustrates that long before a widespread movement in support of continuing education programs for ministry gained momentum, there were individual clergy who took responsibility for their continued learning and agencies that provided outstanding program opportunities.

However, in the early 1960s in Protestantism and the 1970s in Roman Catholicism, a continuing education movement began that was to have far-reaching effects in the United States and Canada—and beyond. Never centered in a single organization—in fact, never tightly organized at all—it nevertheless has been a self-conscious movement involving a network of people focused upon a common enterprise and centered in several organizational structures.

The publication in 1960 of Connolly Gamble's "Continuing Theological Education of the American Minister" provided the spark that began the movement.[1] Prior to that time the growth of continuing education programs[2] had accelerated, including such pioneering ventures as the Tower Room Scholars at Union Theological Seminary in Richmond, Virginia, developed by Gamble, and the Institute for Advanced Pastoral Studies, Bloomfield Hills, Michigan, founded by Reuel Howe.

Gamble reported, however, that a surprising amount of continuing education was being developed. A questionnaire had been sent to five hundred agencies. Their response indicated that ninety-five seminaries, thirty-five colleges and universities, fifteen conference centers, and ten pastoral institutes offered some sort of continuing education programs for clergy. These findings created a lively discussion among church leaders and led to a series of events that resulted in the founding of the Society for the Advancement of Continuing Education for Ministry in 1967.

The Society for the Advancement of Continuing Education for Ministry

In 1964 the Department of the Ministry of the National Council of Churches convened a consultation at Andover Newton Seminary with Gamble as chair. Representatives came from a large number of groups, including seminary faculties, denominational offices, independent continuing education agencies, government agencies, and many others. The consultation was described as "the most widely diversified group ever to focus upon the continuing education of a single profession."[3]

The consultation recommended that the National Council of Churches Department of the Ministry (NCCDOM) establish a committee on continuing education. The committee was organized and for the next several years became an active arena of discussion of issues and new developments in the field. Another recommendation was to call a second consultation.

That consultation met in 1965 at the Center for Continuing Education of the University of Chicago. Some one hundred continuing educators assembled to consider emerging issues and developments. One recommendation from this consultation was to hold a series of learning events especially for continuing educators in ministry. This led to the third major event antecedent to formation of the Society for the Advancement of Continuing Education for Ministry (SACEM).

Planned by the NCCDOM Committee on Continuing Education, a seminar for continuing educators was held the following year at the Kellogg Center for Continuing Education, Michigan State University. Developed in cooperation with the staff of the center, it was a lively learning event that expanded the awareness of many of those attending. At the close, the group convened itself as a business session and decided that a society of continuing educators for ministry should be formed. A committee was named to draw up a set of bylaws, recommend a name, and bring a report to a second seminar the following year.

In 1967 at the Center for Continuing Education, Syracuse University (in sweltering heat with no air conditioning), SACEM was established during the business meeting when the committee's report was accepted. Bylaws were adopted and the name selected, with one emendation, from the committee proposal. Proposed was Society for the Advancement of Continuing Education of the Ministry. "The" was dropped to become "Continuing Education for Ministry"—a small but highly significant change. The majority sentiment was that the new society should focus on the whole ministry of the church, including the work of nonordained professionals in ministry, as well as laity.

A fourfold statement of purpose was adopted and remains unchanged to this day, guiding the work of SACEM. In summary, the four tasks are:

- to regularly bring together people concerned for ministry so that they might share ideas and grow as professionals in the field

- to identify issues that affect the advancement of continuing education for ministry and to develop strategies to address them
- to advocate continuing education for ministry
- to conduct, and encourage others to conduct, relevant research

Thus, SACEM was under way. A board was elected and Connolly Gamble enthusiastically selected as the first president. The first annual general meeting of the society was held in 1968 in Clayton, Missouri, a suburb of St. Louis, with a focus on the case study method in continuing education.

Each year since, a general meeting of the Society has been held in widely diverse locations, each with a theme focused on some significant concern of the Society. Planning committees have included members from the area where the meeting has been held, members of the SACEM board, and, in more recent years, denominational continuing education officials. Meetings have been planned as learning events for those attending, but networking and the informal exchange of ideas have always been significant functions.

Soon after its establishment, the Society decided that at least part-time executive leadership would be needed, and Gamble was chosen for this position. Continuing his work at Union Theological Seminary, and later as a member of the American Baptist continuing education staff, he served as part-time executive secretary of SACEM until 1987. In that year, Patricia Cremins, then on the continuing education staff of the University of Hartford, assumed the position. At the dinner honoring Gamble at the annual meeting in 1987, tribute was paid to his creative work with the Society. In 1989, it became necessary, for financial reasons, to discontinue the executive secretary position, at least temporarily, and to divide responsibilities among members of the board. This plan continues to this day.

From early on, Canadian educators were involved in SACEM. Robert Oliver, director of continuing education, Toronto School of Theology, became a member in the late 1960s and was elected to the board in 1971, later serving as president in 1975–76. In 1980 a major consultation of Canadian leaders was called by the Coordinating Committee on Theological Education in Canada. The committee decided that "SACEM should be the continuing foundation for an enlarged and enhanced effort in Canada which could extend the work already begun under its leadership."[4] By that time, however, Canadian participation in SACEM and its leadership had become a *de facto* reality, and an annual meeting had been held at the Ontario Institute for Studies in Education (OISE) in Toronto in 1977.

Not all of SACEM's one hundred sixty-nine charter members retained their membership; nevertheless, the membership remained strong and fairly stable until the late 1980s when the Society began to see a marked decline. Because the organization's major financial support came from membership fees, the decline in membership created serious financial problems, which was a major consideration in the decision to discontinue the executive secretary position.

The low point in terms of membership, finances, and morale was in 1990. At that time, several decisions were made that had long-range implications for the organization and effected a turnaround in its membership and finances. The first involved not only discontinuing the executive secretary position but also distributing responsibilities among members of the board. Fearful at first, the group soon began to feel new enthusiasm as it engaged in the new tasks, and a fresh esprit de corps developed.

A second decision was to seek closer relationships with denominational continuing education personnel. Included was the hope that denominational groups of continuing educators might be called together for meetings in conjunction with the SACEM annual meetings. This plan worked well; concomitantly, membership began to grow and finances strengthen.

Disseminating information has been one of the major services SACEM has provided to its members and others through the years. For three years, the Committee on Continuing Education of the NCCDOM published compendious listings of continuing education programs. SACEM took over the project in 1972 and published study guides for five regions of the United States, which included information concerning program agencies, the kinds of continuing education programs they offered, and how to contact them. Some fifty thousand were distributed each year. In 1976 a simpler format was adopted. The publication of the guides was discontinued in 1985.

When Connolly Gamble became executive secretary, he began publishing a newsletter that contained information about members' activities; listing of new members; and word of new relevant publications, including those by SACEM members. In 1983 the newsletter was replaced by *The Continuing Educator*, a journal that continues to provide substantive articles, reports of annual meeting presentations, and book reviews. Another information service that has been gaining increasing importance since its inception in recent years is a SACEM website on the Internet.

Educational events for members, in addition to the annual meeting, is another service provided by the organization. In 1972 a seminar called "The Effects of Justice, Liberation, and Development for Continuing Education for Ministry" was held. Between 1976 and 1978 four seminars on "Motivation for Continuing Education" were held in several regions of the United States, and members of National Organization for Continuing Education of Roman Catholic Clergy (NOCERCC) were part of the planning committee. In 1978 an event entitled "New Perspectives on Adulthood" took place. Sessions for new practitioners in continuing education have been held in connection with recent SACEM annual meetings, both to orient them to SACEM and to provide basic training for their work.

Another major activity of SACEM has been support of research by its members and the fostering of research by others in accord with its fourth basic purpose. Attention is given to that activity in connection with a broader discussion of research below.

SACEM has actively pursued connections with other organizations devoted to continuing education for ministry. The officers and executive secretary of SACEM have maintained active contact with a number of these organizations. They include the Association for Clinical Pastoral Education (ACPE); Association of Theological Schools (ATS); Action Training Coalition (ACT); Ecumenical Continuing Education Team; Association for Creative Change; and others.

Perhaps the most significant of these contacts has been with NOCERCC.[5] Its founding in 1973 was one of the landmark events in the continuing education for ministry movement.

The global economic crisis that began in the fall of 2008 has had a severe impact on theological education and continuing education for clergy and laity. Some seminaries and centers downsized and some closed. Face-to-face programs and conferences were cut back because of lack of travel funds for participants. The SACEM annual meeting in 2009 had less than half the usual number of participants.

National Organization for the Continuing Education of Roman Catholic Clergy

As with SACEM, NOCERCC did not appear on the scene full blown; significant antecedents led to its formation. Vatican II had seen and enunciated a new vision of the church, which led to profound changes in the church's organizational life. Out of that ferment, two organizations were formed in the United States that were to have significant impact on the continuing education movement: the National Council of Catholic Bishops (NCCB) in 1966 and the National Federation of Priests' Councils (NFPC) in 1968.

In 1972 the NCCB issued "The Program of Continuing Education for Priests," which outlined the importance of continuing education for priests, urged each diocese to appoint a director of continuing education, and recommended the formation of a national organization to coordinate continuing education developments. Also in that year, the NFPC charged its own continuing education committee to prepare for a national meeting to form an ongoing organization. The leaders of both groups have insisted that the occurrence of the two events in the same year was purely coincidental.

In February 1973 more than one hundred diocesan directors of continuing education and others met at the University of Notre Dame and, following serious discussion, decided to form an organization on the spot, adopted bylaws, and elected a board and officers. Thus, NOCERCC became a reality.

The first president was the Reverend Joseph Voor of the Louisville Archdiocese. Early in his presidency, Father Voor contacted SACEM and was elected to its board for the years 1973–1976. In a personal letter to this writer, Father Voor said, "My involvement with SACEM was my first venture into ecumenism as called for by Vatican II and really helped me to realize that we are brothers in Christ."

Thus began a lively contact, which continued for a number of years. Gamble attended the NOCERCC board, at their invitation, nine of his ten years as SACEM executive secretary; NOCERCC president the Reverend Jim Dunning met with SACEM in 1977, and conversations began that led to a joint meeting of the two boards in 1978. After the mid-1980s, contact between the two organizations waned, probably more through preoccupation with their own affairs than any explicit intent. SACEM minutes reflect at several points a desire to resume contact.

Striking similarities have existed between the two organizations. Both have held annual meetings focused on relevant themes. In fact, the lists of subjects addressed at the meetings of the two organizations are so similar that, with substitution of certain clerical terms, they could be interchangeable. Both have published newsletters regularly. Both have struggled to maintain steady membership numbers, although because of the organization's structure in relation to dioceses, maintaining memberships has perhaps been easier for NOCERCC. In 1998 NOCERCC reported membership of one hundred fifty-three U.S. dioceses from among one hundred seventy-seven. Opening the organization to representatives from religious communities and retreat centers has added to the membership potential. The parallel continues with NOCERCC employment of a part-time executive director, the Reverend James Dunning, in 1979. However, in the case of NOCERCC, the position has become full time, in contrast to SACEM, which eliminated the position.

The Adult Education Movement

One antecedent common to both SACEM and NOCERCC is the adult education movement. Perhaps it would be more apt to refer to it as "fertile soil" rather than as "antecedent." With roots in Europe, the adult education movement in the United States began in the late nineteenth century with the Chautauqua movement, the YMCA, extension services of land-grant universities, and other agencies and movements. By the 1960s the movement had become widespread in the United States and Canada, millions of adults were involved in educational programs, and departments of adult education established in many major universities. Seminal leaders in this period, such as Malcolm Knowles at Boston University and North Carolina State University, Alan Knox at Columbia University, Cyril Houle at the University of Chicago, and Alan Tough at the Ontario Institute for Studies in Education (OISE) in Toronto, had considerable influence on the continuing education for ministry movement. They presented papers at consultations, leaders in the movement studied with them, and their books and articles were widely read. In addition, their work fed the movement indirectly through their influence within the wider adult education movement. In short, the continuing education for ministry movement would have been inconceivable aside from the adult education movement.

Research

From very early in the continuing education for ministry move-
ment until the present, research has played a significant role.
Gamble's 1960 study was the first significant effort. In 1964 the
Ministers Life and Casualty Union cosponsored with the NCC-
DOM the Clergy Support Study. The study was repeated in 1969,
but this time included additional questions concerning continu-
ing education. The responses were analyzed and reported by the
Ministry Studies Board.

In 1965 the Association of Theological Schools and the NCC-
DOM jointly created the Ministry Studies Board (MSB), and at
the beginning in 1966 Edgar Mills became director. Until 1972,
when it merged with the NCCDOM, the board carried out a significant amount of research, much of which was published in
books and documents that had major impact on the movement.
One such book was *Stress in the Ministry* by Mills and John Koval,
published in 1971. Another was *Ex-Pastors: Why Men Leave the
Parish Ministry*.[6] Between 1967 and 1969 the MSB also published
twelve issues of a monograph series entitled "Ministry Studies."
The MSB, with Mills's leadership, provided sound, scientifically
based social research. Its demise was a loss to the field.

From the beginning, SACEM has had an active committee on
research, which has supported research by SACEM members as
well as promoted relevant research by others, including doctoral
candidates. Research supported by SACEM has fallen largely into
several categories—clergy participation in continuing education,
both the degree of participation and the settings; the effect of their
participation; and the needs clergy experience related to continuing education.

One major research project carried out by SACEM focused on
needs assessment instruments and processes and is discussed below. (See "Needs Assessment.") In 1984 a major study was made
of continuing education involvement of some fifty-four hundred

clergy in twelve denominations. A study was made of clergy who had earned the Doctor of Ministry degree, the results of which were reported to the annual meeting in 1982. More recent studies include continuing education in colleague or peer groups and spiritual growth needs of clergy in midlife.

Tracing two major strands of development will complete this survey of continuing education: (1) the agencies that have provided resource services, primarily programs, and (2) individuals as they have engaged in their own continuing education.

Educational Resource Agencies

The first strand includes denominational judicatories, seminaries, independent agencies, associations of program centers, and action training centers. The second includes individual use of career development centers, programs on spiritual formation, and self-directed studies that include reading, writing, and skill development.

Denominational Judicatories

In the 1960s and 1970s national denominational agencies provided a substantial number of program opportunities, but considerably fewer have been offered since then. One pioneering denominational program was the Young Pastors Schools sponsored by the United Presbyterian Church (USA) in which clergy, during the first few years after seminary, participated in a succession of three five-day seminars, the third with their spouses. The seminars offered a great deal of openness and freedom to examine the personal and professional issues they had encountered during this entry period. The Lutheran Church of America sponsored five-day seminars in various parts of the country, providing opportunities for clergy to engage in theological reflection in a small-group setting in which personal and relational issues could be examined openly. In 1987

NOCERCC sponsored a series of seminars, "A Shepherd's Care: Reflections on the Changing Role of the Pastor."

In the 1960s and 1970s, the major denominations all had at least one full-time staff person in continuing education, and in a few cases, more than one. These staff members were drawn together in various groups, such as the NCCDOM Continuing Education Committee and SACEM. In the late 1960s, they decided to form their own group meeting called the Ecumenical Continuing Education Team, which convened annually and allowed them to share ideas, to shape their own learning events, and to support each other in what was sometimes a lonely job. As long as denominations had full-time staff members, the team remained strong. As staffs shrank and many had multiple responsibilities, the team met less frequently and with fewer participants. In 1987 a small group gathered for the last time in conjunction with the SACEM annual meeting.

Gradually denominational programming has shifted to middle judicatories, but this has not reversed the trend toward reduced programming. A few judicatories, such as the United Methodist North Indiana Annual Conference, still offer a range of opportunities. One reason for reduced program sponsorship has been the shifting of available funds to scholarship assistance to enable clergy to participate in continuing education programs of their own choosing.

Seminaries

In the beginning of the movement, seminary programs multiplied rapidly. Most seminaries of major Protestant denominations employed full- or part-time directors and almost without exception had faculty committees of continuing education. As the Doctor of Ministry degree has gained prominence and many seminary budgets have become more limited, programming has gradually waned. A number of seminaries, however, continue to provide full, well-rounded programs: Princeton Theological Seminary;

Duke Divinity School; Garrett-Evangelical Seminary; New Brunswick Theological Seminary; and others.

Several institutions that offer active continuing education programs fall into this category, but with a difference. Two are Auburn Theological Seminary in New York City and Hartford Seminary Foundation in Connecticut. Auburn has not offered degrees since it moved to the campus of Union in New York City in 1939; Hartford offers a limited degree program, but no longer offers a basic seminary degree. Both agencies sponsor continuing education based on research and analysis of the needs of the church and its ministry. A third institution in this category is the Scarritt-Bennett Center in Nashville. For many years, as Scarritt College, it had been a degree-granting institution primarily for lay professional workers in the United Methodist Church. Early in the 1970s, it began a transition, first with the establishment of a Center of Continuing Education directed by Robert E. Reber. Finally ending its degree program in 1988, it has become a center sponsored by the Women's Division of the United Methodist Board of Global Ministries, which offers learning events for both clergy and laity.

Most seminary programming has been designed to draw the participant to the school for a period of time; however, some schools have made provision for faculty to meet with groups in the field. Another exception to residence programs deserves special mention. A few schools simply provide enrollees with books on library loan, accompanied by a study guide. The user enrolls in a particular guide and books are sent to him or her successively, according to the guide's design. The original program was developed by Gamble at Union in Richmond; at its height, it made available some seventy-five guides. The other major program was at Perkins School of Theology, Southern Methodist University. The Perkins program made it possible for a study group to contract for the use of a guide, and at the end of the period of study, Perkins would provide a professor to meet with the group for a day. Both programs have been discontinued.

The Doctor of Ministry Degree

One of the pioneer ventures in continuing education in the early 1960s was the Doctor of Scientific Theology degree and a comparable master's degree at San Francisco Theological Seminary, designed primarily by Henry Adams. The degree was promoted as a break with traditional theological degree programs and shifted the arena of learning from academy to the parish or other venues of ministry. One of Henry Adams's frequently expressed phrases was "learning ministry from the practice of ministry." From the beginning, a backlog of people waited for admission into one of these degree programs.

Other seminaries quickly saw the potential of such a degree program and announced what came to be known as the Doctor of Ministry degree. At a consultation of United Methodist continuing educators in 1973, Marvin Taylor, then a staff member of the ATS, announced that 70 percent of ATS-accredited seminaries either were offering or had definite plans to offer the degree.

Enrollees increased along with the number of programs. In 1988, 6,077 students were enrolled; in 1992, 7,274; in 1998, 8,356, and in 2007, 9066. As of this writing, more than one hundred accredited schools offer a Doctor of Ministry degree.[7]

The value of the Doctor of Ministry degree as continuing education has been the subject of ongoing discussion among continuing educators. Critics claim that the temptation of status resulting from the title of "doctor" interferes with the educational value of such programs. Others assert that once one is enrolled in a program, one finds that the possibility of adjusting the learning program to changing needs is too limited, and the financial cost is often too heavy. On the other hand, advocates reply that the programs are helpful because they focus on questions of professional practice, encourage planned continuing education to reach well-defined goals, and, in most cases, utilize peer group approaches that often become an important means of support for participants. Whatever the pros and cons, the Doctor of Ministry degree continues to attract a number of clergy for at least a portion of their continuing education.

Independent Agencies

Independent institutions and retreat centers have served a relatively small percentage of those seeking continuing education. Yet, some of these offer the most creative programming. A primary instance was the Institute for Advanced Pastoral Studies, mentioned above as one of the early pioneer institutions. Another, although with some denominational affiliation, was the Disciples Divinity House at Yale, directed by Parker Rossman. Still a third was the Interpreter's House at Lake Junaluska, North Carolina, directed by Carlyle Marney. These three programs have gone by the wayside partly because the competition for warm bodies and continuing education dollars has increased and partly because they were too dependent upon a charismatic individual for their survival.

Others remain strong and well rounded. Kirkridge, located in the beautiful Delaware River Valley of eastern Pennsylvania, has since its founding offered creative and cutting-edge continuing education for both clergy and laity. The Alban Institute, in Herndon, Virginia, features experimental programming, the results of which have been written, published, and offered to the church. The Institute has maintained a staff of program leaders available to assist groups wanting to use the programs it has developed. Still another is Pendle Hill near Philadelphia, with a strong Quaker history and tradition, offering both short-term and semester study periods. Used widely by members of the Society of Friends, Pendle Hill has also provided an unusual opportunity for clergy and laity of other denominations, including Roman Catholics, to experience continuing education designed to touch both mind and spirit. There are other such centers.

Associations of Program Centers

Perhaps the most widely used program agencies in this category have been centers for clinical pastoral education (CPE). Initiated by Anton Boisen and others in the early 1900s, these programs were originally based almost entirely in medical institutions and were primarily for the benefit of seminarians. Gradually, however, more and more centers became oriented to the needs of those out of seminary and engaged in ministry. Over the years clinical pastoral educators and centers had congealed into four basic groupings, but in 1967 came together to form the Association of Clinical Pastoral Education (ACPE), which has remained the central agency for furtherance of the movement and accreditation of educators and centers. Records have not been kept by the Association of the total number of practicing church professionals in CPE programs at any one time, but they are known to be in the thousands. At the time of this writing, there are four hundred and eighty-one accredited centers, almost all of which include enrollees engaged professionally in ministry. Although in the beginning the venue and focus of all programs was hospitals and other medical institutions, the range of institutions over the years has expanded greatly, including several in urban centers in which the primary venue is the parish.[8]

Spiritual Formation and Spiritual Growth Centers

Centers for spiritual formation and growth are discussed in connection with a shift in the perception of the nature of ministry described under "Individual Involvement in Continuing Education" below.

Action Training Centers

In the 1960s many church leaders, including some continuing educators, believed that the church was not making an adequate response to the nation's social crises, especially in urban areas. One result was the establishment of what came to be known as action training centers. The training they provided involved, among other things, a plunge into deteriorated areas of cities. Participants were given a small amount of money and sent out on their own for several days, then to return to reflect on the experience and its implications for ministry. At the height of this movement, some twenty centers were located in various parts of the United States. In 1968, at the instigation of some of their directors and several interdenominational church groups, Protestant and Roman Catholic, a meeting was held at which the Action Training Coalition was formed. Gradually, as the church turned its attention to other concerns, the number of centers decreased until at present, to this writer's knowledge, no programs remain. However, a limited number of theological schools and church organizations are engaged in important efforts to address urban issues and ministry. Many congregations have developed significant outreach programs focused on hunger, the homeless, unemployment, health concerns, and education.

Many agencies not mentioned here have offered continuing education opportunities to people in ministry: colleges and universities; public libraries; human relations training agencies, such as those that sprang from the National Training Laboratories; and others.

Individual Involvement in Continuing Education

A second major strand of development in continuing education is the individual's own involvement. Before looking at this matter statistically, it is important to see it in the larger context of a shift in the understanding of the nature of ministry that has taken place within the period of this continuing education survey.

Early in the 1960s much attention was given by leaders in continuing education to the concept of ministry as a profession.

Leaders in adult education, such as Cyril Houle at the University of Chicago, were focusing on the nature of the continuing education of professionals. Thinking also of continuing education for ministry in those terms was natural. In 1968 Abingdon Press published a book by James Glasse entitled *Profession: Minister*. In that same year, Edgar Mills presented a major paper on ministry as a profession to a United Methodist consultation on continuing education. In my book, *Competent Ministry: A Guide to Effective Continuing Education*, published five years later, I interpreted competence largely in terms of professional practice based on the historic understanding of the professional as one who masters a particular area of knowledge and skill and makes that expertise available to a particular segment of society.[9]

The concept of career is closely related to the concept of profession, and in this period much attention was given to the dynamics of ministerial career, informed by such career psychologists as Donald Soper at Columbia University. One outcome of this concern was the career-stage seminars developed by the United Presbyterian Church (USA), the United Methodist Church, and others.

Out of this focus on career a group of agencies known as Church Career Development Centers were established. Edward Golden, director of the United Presbyterian Interboard Office of Personnel Service, envisioned "the possibility of career centers where testing and counseling services could enable ministers to take charge of their own careers and make more informed career decisions."[10] A pilot center was established in Princeton, New Jersey, with Thomas Brown, a trained career counselor (later president of SACEM) as director. The project was successful and became the first of a group of Church Career Development Centers across the United States. These centers were brought together in the Church Career Development Council (CCDC) in 1969 in Philadelphia. The Council had both denominational and center directors as members and became the primary agency to further the movement and to accredit both the centers and their counseling staffs.

The centers have served the purpose not only of providing counsel concerning future career direction but also of enabling participants, especially those who had decided to remain in a ministerial career, to develop more effective personal continuing education programs. In fact, the American Baptist Centers for Ministry, which were members of the CCDC, had individuals in the same staff who provided career counseling and others available for continuing education counseling. "Ministry Development Council" has replaced "Church Career Development Council" as the name of the umbrella organization, reflecting to a degree the shift in thinking about the nature of ministry.

Over time, the emphasis on ministry as a profession lessened. A substantial number of church leaders, including continuing educators, began to fear that the true nature of ministry was being eroded by professionalism and that the emphasis on career and career dynamics was leading to careerism. (In this writer's view, nothing in the true understanding of either profession or career leads necessarily in that direction. Rather, the shift probably was fostered more by increased membership and competitiveness among clergy.)

As focus on profession waned, a new emphasis on spirituality in ministry began to emerge. This shift was probably caused by the rise in a new, general interest across churches in spiritual growth, or spiritual formation.

In response to this shift, a number of centers and programs have been established that focus on spiritual formation. One of the first and most prominent is the Shalem Institute in Washington, D.C., directed by Tilden Edwards, an early member of SACEM and its board. Epiphany Associates was established in 1979, with centers in both Pittsburgh and Indianapolis. The Academy of Spiritual Formation is sponsored by the United Methodist Church with centers in Alabama, California, and Wisconsin. There are others, some sponsored by Roman Catholics, some by Protestants, but all ecumenically open. No figures are available for the number of clergy who have participated in this group of programs, but they would be in the thousands.

Numerically, clergy participation in their own continuing education is difficult to estimate. However, there is little question that over the period covered in this chapter's historical survey the numbers have increased dramatically. The Clergy Support Study of 1973 showed that 34 percent of those responding had taken part in a continuing education event of at least three days within the previous two years; Gamble's 1982 study showed that 75 percent of those responding had engaged in learning away from home in the year surveyed. While the figures are not exactly comparable, they show an encouraging increase. What the figures would be today is unknown because no national study has been done.

In *Competent Ministry*, I defined *continuing education* as "an individual's personally designed learning program which begins when formal education ends and continues throughout a career and beyond. An unfolding process, it links together study and reflection and participation in organized group events."[11] When continuing education is viewed broadly in this way, the question of the number of those participating changes. I continue to believe that while the number who enroll each year in one kind of continuing education program or another may be quite high, the number who engage in a well-planned program of learning designed to meet their needs is much lower. Exceptions to this, of course, would be those enrolled in a Doctor of Ministry degree or in a structured learning program such as CPE, or engaged in one of the thousands of peer groups that have been formed (see chapter 6, "Peer Groups Matter") or in a personal learning plan. One hopes that patterns of planned learning established in such programs might continue after they have ended.

One organization that has urged the planning of a personal program of learning for its members is the Academy of Parish Clergy. The late Granger Westberg wrote an article published in *The Christian Century* in the mid-1960s entitled "Why Not an Academy of Parish Clergy." He had proposed an organization founded on the pattern of the Academy of General Practice for physicians, and in 1968 in Houston, Texas, such an academy was organized. Based on the concept that the clergyperson should take responsibility for his or her own continuing education, rather than being dependent on schools or denominational agencies, the Academy developed suggestions and procedures for enabling this to happen, including a needs assessment process to be conducted with the help of a chosen colleague in ministry and in the congregational setting. The Academy has never claimed a large percentage of the total number of ordained clergy as members, but has been a distinct and important voice in the continuing education movement.

Needs Assessment

As the idea that continuing education should be understood as the individual's participation in a personally planned learning program became more widespread, it became evident that developing an individual's learning program on the basis of well-defined learning needs was important. Accordingly, groups and individuals began to develop needs assessment instruments and procedures that were quite widely used in the 1970s and 1980s. One of the most ambitious and extensive research projects carried out by SACEM focused on analysis of the various needs assessment instruments to determine which were the most effective. Among other things, the research determined that the most beneficial were those in which the clergyperson was the sole beneficiary. The study also determined that the degree of follow-through, once needs were determined, was enhanced by support of judicatory officials and colleagues.

Currently, evidence suggests that, in the context of peer learning groups and individual and group coaching, attention in varying degrees is given to needs assessment. Programs of individual assessment have faded in part because of the national impact of the Lilly Endowment's Sustaining Pastoral Excellence Program that has involved thousands of clergy in peer groups during the past eight years. Also, the new emphasis on coaching for clergy is another major resource that was almost nonexistent ten years ago.

The constraints of a chapter such as this have required that many developments in continuing education for ministry be either shortchanged or omitted. It should be realized also that while much of the above has focused on organizations, the real history of the movement has been in the creative and devoted effort given to it by many, many individuals.

When Shakespeare in *The Tempest* has Antonio say, "What's past is prologue," he obviously is not referring to affairs such as those described here. Nevertheless, one might hope that his words apply. It is fitting that this chapter come at the first of this book, not only to provide background but also to make evident what rich soil has been prepared for future growth. And, indeed, the chapters that lie ahead show what new life and energy—and new horizons—are now present in this movement. Surely, "what's past is prologue."

Notes

1. Published by Union Theological Seminary, Richmond, VA.

2. From this point, when the term *continuing education* is used, it denotes "continuing education for ministry," unless otherwise noted.

3. Unattributed quotation from Connolly Gamble, "The SACEM Story" (unpublished paper, 1987), 5. This extensive paper, commissioned and distributed by SACEM, has been an invaluable resource in preparing this chapter and is a significant document for SACEM's history from its inception to 1987. Used by Connolly Gamble's permission.

4. Ibid., 44.

5. Much of the information concerning NOCERCC is taken from Joseph M. White, "A Work Never Finished" (Schiller Park, IL: J. S. Paluch, 1997).

6. Edgar Mills, Gerald Jud, and Genevieve Burch, *Ex-Pastors: Why Men Leave the Parish Ministry* (Philadelphia: Pilgrim Press, 1970).

7. Figures have been updated from the ATS website as of March 2009.

8. Charles E. Hall, "Head and Heart: The Story of the Clinical Pastoral Education Movement," *Journal of Pastoral Care Publications* 1 (1992), 164. This book is a helpful resource for the history of the movement, written by one who was, for many years, executive of the ACPE.

9. Mark A. Rouch, *Competent Ministry: A Guide to Effective Continuing Education* (Nashville: Abingdon Press, 1974). See especially chapter 3.

10. James Gunn, "CCDC: The Beginning" (unpublished paper, Church Career Development Council, 1984). At the time of writing, Gunn was the executive for professional church leadership, the National Council of Churches (formerly NCCDOM).

11. Rouch, *Competent Ministry*, 16–17.

CHAPTER 2

Educating Out of the Future: Where Are We Headed in Continuing Theological Education?

Robert E. Reber

The ambiguity of this chapter's title is deliberate and expresses the ambivalence I feel about the directions in which continuing and adult theological education programs seem to be heading. We leaders in continuing theological education can educate church leaders for the future or we can educate them without regard for the future and therefore find our efforts increasingly irrelevant and out of touch with life and ministry in the world and the church. We are, in fact, doing both. On the one hand, some programs take seriously what is emerging in the life of the world and the church and the implications this has for continuing education. On the other hand, one can also identify programs that ignore what is ahead and focus only on the immediate, if pressing, demands of the present, resulting in a simplistic, short-term approach.

I remember well my first meeting of the Society for the Advancement of Continuing Education for Ministry (SACEM) in 1972. The director of professional medical education of a leading medical school in the United States gave the opening address. His thesis was that there was not a shred of evidence to suggest that mandatory continuing education of physicians leads to any qualitative difference in the practice of medicine. His comment continues to haunt me after thirty-seven years, especially since some have sought through legislation to make continuing education mandatory, an effort that has been misguided and has failed for the most part. To a large extent, I think his judgment reflects the past and current state of much continuing education for religious professionals. In fact, a more recent study found that "70 to 75 percent of members of three professions who participated in formal educational programs reported little or no change after the implementation of mandatory continuing education." The participants were physicians, health care professionals, and certified public accountants. Author and researcher Ronald Cervero says that "although mandatory continuing education is touted as an effective way to foster participation, the evidence shows a relatively weak effect."[1]

Thirty years ago, Mark Rouch, who for a number of years was the national staff person at the Board of Higher Education and Ministry of the United Methodist Church and worked full time on continuing education for clergy, gave a lecture. The title of the address was "Continuing Education as a Subversive Activity." Rouch maintained that "all education is, by its nature, subversive—continuing education no less than any other education. In fact, when true to itself, continuing education may be the most subversive of all." He said that our business is to subvert, "to destroy" in terms of the Latin root, to turn upside down "every fragmented, inadequate view of truth. Looked at another way, our business is to subvert every block to human growth in those persons for whom we have responsibility in education for ministry." Obviously, Rouch's commitment to continuing education as a subversive activity is based on an assumption that continuing education for ministry can make a difference. I believe this also. That is why I have devoted much of my professional life to continuing theological education for clergy and laity.

However, I live constantly with the question, Are our efforts in continuing education for clergy and laity bringing about any qualitative difference in the lives of people, and in the practice of ministry and mission in congregations and other diverse settings? We have a responsibility to ask ourselves this question. The answers may not be clear and may be hard to get, but we owe it to ourselves to continue asking. Considerable resources have been made available by denominations, judicatories, seminaries, congregations, foundations, and individuals. The least that we can do is to be honest about what we know and do not know, or refuse to find out, and hold each other accountable.

Clearly, a tension exists between my ideal, following Rouch, that education subverts our inadequate understandings and the reality, described by Cervero and the keynote speaker, that continuing education has no measurable influence on performance. I ask you to keep this tension in mind as I address three questions in the remainder of this chapter:

- What is the current state of continuing theological education for clergy and laity?
- What should the future be?
- What are questions that all continuing theological educators need to struggle with?

My answers, of course, unavoidably will reflect my own experiences. Your perspective may be different, and I invite you to keep your experiences in mind as we explore ideas about how to educate out of the future.

What Is the Current State of Continuing Theological Education for Clergy and Laity?

First, continuing theological education is still at a real disadvantage in the church's educational ecology. It is still not a part of the top educational priorities of most, if not all, denominations, judicatories, and seminaries in the United States and Canada. In fact, recognition of its importance has been slipping in recent years. Consider that twenty-five years ago most mainline denominations had a full-time staff person responsible for continuing education for ministry at the national level. Now only one, the Evangelical Lutheran Church in America, has a full-time person. In addition, directors of continuing education continue to be the last hired and the first to go at many seminaries. They are probably the most marginalized group within the institution, and often the only staff members whose courses must pay for themselves. Continuing education for clergy and laity is the least subsidized educational enterprise in all of seminary education and church education in general.

Second, the Lone Ranger image continues to dominate the field of continuing education. We continuing theological educators are still asked to believe that pastors or lay leaders, who come to one-day to one-week events offered by our institutions and centers, will bring about change, both personally and corporately. We expect that an individual can return to home base and make a difference. Lack of accountability, recognition, and reward for participation in continuing education for clergy and laity further reinforces this Lone Ranger image.

Third, the offerings in continuing education are becoming shorter and shorter across the United States and Canada. Ten years ago centers offering five-day programs were the norm. Today most programs are limited to forty-eight hours or fewer. Longer programs do not guarantee that participants learn more. However, I am convinced that longer programs do offer a greater possibility for sustainable growth. Many forces encourage shorter programs: lack of recognition and reward, a quick-fix mentality, resistance to give much time, family pressures when both spouses are working outside the home, financial strain, and so forth.

Fourth, continuing education offerings tend to focus more on the how-to and promise practical helps. This is what folks will buy and is in part driven by pressing needs and a desire to make an immediate difference in facing new situations personally, in the congregation, and, to some extent, in society. On the one hand, the demand for readily applicable programs is quite understand-able and deserves a sympathetic hearing. All of us are driven by a sense of immediacy and want the programs we attend to make an immediate difference in some aspect of our professional and per-sonal lives. On the other hand, a dangerous and highly functional-ist view of church life and ministry may result. Serious questions about the nature and purpose of the church, ministry, and mis-sion must be addressed, but require more substantive reflection and offer less immediate gratification. In short programs, issues of how people learn and how systems change tend to be ignored. So, caught in this cycle, continuing education offerings get narrower and narrower in focus and, in the end, continuing theological ed-ucators cannot deliver what we promise: a qualitative difference in the lives of people and their practice of ministry and mission.

Fifth, in continuing education for clergy and laity, we tend to offer what we think is best for the constituencies to be served. By "we," I mean directors of continuing education, seminary faculty, and independent centers. We believe that we should offer what our experience, study, scholarship, and commitment tell us may be best in terms of leadership and the content and practice of con-tinuing education programs for clergy and laity. People come to centers for relatively short periods to participate in programs that we publicize. Sometimes we go out to local communities where groups of clergy and church professionals gather, programs that occasionally include laypeople. It is the exception to the rule, how-ever, when representatives of the constituencies to be served are involved in planning the particular programs to be offered. Most likely, this does not happen because nobody wants to pay for the staff time to do it, and we do not see the planning process itself as educational. Lack of local participation in planning is probably the major reason why programs are canceled.

Sixth, much of continuing education is market driven. What will "sell" is given top priority. This often comes from the de-mand that program income cover not only direct costs but also institutional overhead in terms of staff and facilities. I believe it is

accurate to say that continuing education for clergy and laity is
the only educational enterprise that is often asked to pay its own
way. With this limitation, it is tough to be creative, to take risks, to
be inclusive in terms of class and race, to move beyond big names
(who usually demand big fees), and to wrestle with what will
make a qualitative difference in the lives of people, institutions,
and societies.

Seventh, much of continuing theological education still tends
to be stuck in one type of educational format: lecture and questions and sometimes discussion. This approach is quite useful at
times but is too limiting when we consider how people learn and
the different types of learning that are needed—that is, knowledge, understanding, skills, attitudes, and values. Methods and
techniques should be related to the types of learning needed or
the objectives of any educational event.

Eighth, most people who spend time professionally directing
continuing education centers for clergy and laity do so by accident,
circumstance, and surprise. Some see it as a calling, but others
consider it a way station on the road to something else. Over the
years this has changed somewhat because of the work of professional organizations like SACEM or the National Organization for
Continuing Education of Roman Catholic Clergy (NOCERCC).
Also, the work of the American Association of Adult and Continuing Education has sought to bring standards of training and
professionalism to the field. Auburn Theological Seminary's former Colleague Program for New Directors of Continuing Theological Education certainly indicated an eagerness by seminaries
and independent centers and their new directors of continuing
education to change this. Funded by the Henry Luce Foundation,
this program provided on-the-job training for new directors over
a period of eighteen months. Participants came to four three-day
modules and worked intentionally on different issues in their
job settings. Even though denominations seem to be giving less
importance to continuing education for clergy, some seminaries
and independent centers are not. There is an interest in having

trained and professional directors. However, many places have a long way to go in developing mission statements and policies that place continuing theological education for clergy and laity at the heart of institutional life, and in taking responsibility to partner with clergy and laity for at least forty years of ongoing education.

Ninth, the past eight years have seen a major expansion of the peer group learning model for ongoing education for clergy. The Lilly Endowment has made millions of dollars available for funding peer groups across the United States to experiment with different approaches to sustaining pastoral excellence. Having been involved directly in five of these projects and in a national study of the Lilly program, I clearly see that major changes have taken place in the lives of clergy in a qualitative and quantitative manner (see chapter 6, "Peer Group Matters: The Impact of Leadership, Composition, and Cost"). The current state of continuing theological education is certainly being affected by this ten-year program of Lilly, as well the troublesome economic conditions in the United States and the world at this time.

What Should the Future of Continuing Education for Clergy and Laity Be?

My thoughts about the current state of continuing education for clergy and laity tend to be somewhat bleak. In relation to each of the nine points above, exceptions and signs of hope are evident. We must move into the future, keeping in mind our current weaknesses and keeping alive our hope.

First and foremost, continuing education in the future must regain its subversive quality. It should seek to subvert our limited, fragmented, and distorted views of truth. It should take on seriously the theological task of faith seeking understanding. I do not mean this in any narrow academic sense but in the larger sense of offering opportunities for pastors and laity to examine the life of faith from biblical, theological, historical, and missional perspectives. Education cannot be subversive unless it addresses the whole person and the context in which he or she lives, works, and ministers and invites people into situations where learning and growth are possible.

Second, continuing education for ministry should be front and center in the life of denominations, congregations, theological centers, and seminaries. This requires a careful examination of mission statements and policies of our institutions. If it is merely an add-on, it will be a weak and insignificant enterprise. I think all of us are being challenged to see how we can be theological resource centers for the church and the larger community. Yes, we have a primary responsibility for educating clergy and church professionals at the Master of Divinity level, but we also have a serious mandate to consider what resources we might bring to bear in the ongoing education of clergy and laity. Much of higher education is already doing this. The United States went through a major change in the 1970s when, for the first time in its history, more people above age eighteen than below enrolled in educational institutions of all kinds. This is a major reason for the growth of adult and continuing education programs in the context of higher education. Increasingly, a criterion for funding all sorts of schools may be, "To what extent does an institution serve members of society on a lifelong basis?" Should we not bring this same criterion to bear on our own institutions as educational centers in the life of the church?

Third, ecumenical and interreligious perspectives should inform our work in continuing education for clergy and laity. What opportunities are there for ecumenical and interreligious collaboration? In my experience, they are almost endless. Ecumenical and interreligious collaboration is vitally important to the future of continuing theological education and lifelong learning. The reasons we should *not* operate in isolation are many. We have a biblical and theological mandate to work toward, and manifest, the unity of the church and of humankind. Our parochialism betrays the gospel and mirrors rather than disputes the conditions of a fractured community, world, and church. If we believe that God wills the unity of the church and humankind, it should be evident in our work as individuals responsible for continuing theological education. We need to network with other churches, denominations, civic organizations, and educational institutions in order to have a clearer picture of the particular communities in which we have been called to work; to avoid unnecessary duplication and expenditure of resources; to build stronger educational programs that make a difference in the lives of laity and clergy; and to generate contacts and more effective ownership on the part of the constituencies we wish to serve.

At Auburn Theological Seminary where I worked, we took this mandate to work ecumenically and interreligiously with utmost seriousness. As staff, we collaborated with thirty-three different organizations and institutions in planning and carrying out our educational programs. I had no idea of the number until someone asked me this question and I sat down and counted them. We collaborated with other seminaries, ecumenical and interreligious organizations, universities, denominations, judicatories, congregations, and independent centers. In many cases, we have taken the initiative and in others our partners approached us. When an idea for a program popped into our heads, we asked, "Who else can we work with?" In an overall evaluation of Auburn's educational programs, the outside evaluator said, "My sense is that the central idea of Auburn is to serve as a broker among the many competing stakeholders in the ongoing societal conversations about the role that religion and spirituality can play in creating a better world for all peoples. In being a broker across multiple differences, Auburn sees that education is both a struggle for meaning and power."

I do not tell you this because Auburn is the best example or something that anybody else should imitate. Each situation is different. I contend, however, that none of us can afford to operate as the Lone Ranger and somehow think that we can sit in our offices, institutions, or centers and decide what is best for the church or for the larger community. We need partners. If you undertake the work of collaboration, doors will open that you never dreamed of and only a few will close.

We must be willing to risk with partners for the future. I believe that God is calling us to work and to educate across multiple differences in our communities and world. This may mean with other denominations; with people and organizations outside the church; with different religious communities that may be Jewish, Muslim, Hindu, or Buddhist; with different racial, ethnic, and socioeconomic groups; with people of different sexual orientations; and with different age groups, be they young, middle aged, or older adults. It is also time for us to come out of our religious hideaways and witness in public life to what our religious faith means and stands for. The stakes are too high in civil society to back off from the public square. The quality of life, civil discourse, and even the survival of the planet depend upon all of us doing our part educationally to bring about change in people's lives, in our churches, and in society at large.

Fourth, a systemic approach is required to move beyond apathy (sometimes resistance) and a lack of valuing the ongoing education of clergy and laity. Appreciation, affirmation, and reward are critical to changing the current climate. A 1997 report adopted by the Evangelical Lutheran Church in America, "Life-long Learning and Development for Faithful Leaders," makes a commitment to doing this: "The church envisions . . . an environment in which intentional continued learning and development are valued and expected, and the rostered [ordained ministers, associates in ministry, deaconesses, and diaconal ministers] leaders enjoy supportive partnerships with their congregations or agencies, colleagues, and the synodical and churchwide expressions of this church."[2]

To what extent are we as leaders in continuing theological education serving clergy and increasingly laity on a lifelong basis? Should this be based only on the ability to pay? I hope not. Again, this is a policy and resource issue that needs careful attention.

Many pastors and laypeople are looking for a structure to be provided in which they can engage in continuing education. Many are not going to take a sustained, disciplined approach to learning on their own. Those of us who provide continuing education opportunities need to take a more serious look at this matter. This was one of the key things identified in the Doctor of Ministry study that Auburn and Hartford seminaries carried out. Clergy in Doctor of Ministry programs tended to view as unsatisfactory short-term workshops, seminars, and courses they picked using a shotgun approach. They seek in Doctor of Ministry programs "an ordered progression of activities and a discipline that they find it difficult to provide for themselves in the midst of a demanding full-time job."[3] We who are directors of nondegree programs need to take note: Doctor of Ministry participants represent a sizable group of clergy who "find an ordered curriculum, the opportunity to submit work for evaluation, and the discipline of deadlines and requirements, to be important elements in continuing professional learning. Some of these features can be provided outside a degree context as well as within it."[4]

Fifth, I believe that continuing education for ministry must involve both clergy and laity. After all, ministry involves both groups and we need to offer educational programs that inform, enrich, and enable the ministry of all God's people. Again, programs that focus on particular needs of clergy, whether this is in worship, preaching, or other areas of professional development, are essential. This is also true of laity. For example, Auburn Seminary carries out extensive programs with health care professionals, lawyers and judges, middle managers, and chief executive officers of corporations. It has programs that help laity from many different walks of life consider and reflect upon what it means to live out one's faith in the workplace, at home, and in the larger community.

Sixth, to involve various constituencies in ongoing education for ministry clearly means that the delivery systems have to change. Programs offered Monday through Friday from nine to five are increasingly unattractive for clergy and even more so for laity. If we are to involve members of both groups, the times and days we choose and the formats we follow will have to vary. We also need to cultivate greater flexibility about where we hold programs. Everything will not take place on our turf or in our facilities. In collaboration with others, we may need to offer educational programs in closer proximity to where people work and live.

Seventh, the whole arena of electronic technology and the information super highway must be considered. More and more pastors and laypeople have personal computers and access to unlimited resources via the Internet. They are looking for educational programs that they can use in individual and group settings. Two examples of organizations producing quality materials on CDs are the American Bible Society and Harvard's Center for the Study of World Religions. The "electronic church," teleconferencing, and online programs on different topics already allow interaction between teacher and student. Those of us in more traditional religious institutions need to be aware of these developments or we will be left behind. The possibilities for both online and face-to-face education are enormous.

Eighth, I think the future of continuing education for clergy and laity should mean paying serious attention to the teaching-learning enterprise, no matter what the subject is. How do people learn? How are needs and interests assessed and tested? How does change take place in people or institutions? What does it mean for the congregation or local church to understand itself as the agency of education? Who is an effective teacher? If learning means change in knowledge, understanding, attitudes, values, and skills, what has to be part of the teaching-learning transaction? There are no easy answers, but we do know some things from research on how adults learn. We need to experiment with different models and evaluate our efforts.

Finally, with a major expansion in peer group learning and both individual and group coaching, we are beginning to see what significant learnings may take place in individuals and organizations. Evaluations are being carried out to provide documentation. A major one is the national study of Sustaining Pastoral Excellence programs that engage clergy in peer groups (see chapter 6, "Peer Group Matters: The Impact of Leadership, Composition, and

Cost"). Having been involved directly in five of these projects over several years, I have plenty of anecdotal evidence about transformational change in clergy and, to a lesser extent, congregations. This study and others to come need utmost attention by all of us so that we use whatever resources we have for lifelong learning in an informed and strategic way.

Despite the serious obstacles we face, I am convinced that ongoing education for ministry can make a qualitative difference in the lives of individuals, congregations, and organizations. Below are some questions that I hope we can struggle with together.

Questions for Our Future Work in Continuing Education

- *Why are clergy tending to read less and less in all areas?* This seems to be true in theological disciplines as well as reading novels, biographies, poetry, plays, and social and political analyses. Why are they giving less and less time to ongoing educational opportunities that have a sustained educational thrust over time?
- *How might we involve clergy and laity who don't participate in continuing education, whether in structured programs or their own independent study?* We tend to get the committed. What do we do about those who are hard to reach?
- *What can we do to move beyond the undue emphasis on the quick fixes or how-tos of congregational life?* Short workshops on fixing sermons, educational programs, congregational growth, and spirituality abound. I even saw a workshop advertised on "Preaching in Sound Bytes."
- *How might we focus more on critical issues about the quality of life on this planet and in the life of religious communities?* So few of our educational offerings take up questions about peace in the world, racism, sexuality, the feminist movement, the pollution of the environment, the quality of health care for all, economic justice the ecumenical movement,

and the growing religious pluralism in American society. Each of us could add issues to this list.

- *What do we need to do to strengthen and sustain ecumenical and interreligious collaboration with other similar-minded organizations?* What are the theological and ecclesial issues we should be addressing? How might our ecumenical commitments really be incarnational—that is, rooted theologically in what we do day in and day out?
- Given the current national study of peer groups and the Alban Institute Consultations on Lifelong Learning for Clergy in the Twenty-First Century, *how do we apply what we may be learning?*

The future of continuing education for ministry depends on changing the climate, the expectations, the values, and the rewards for lifelong learning in the church and the church's educational institutions. We must engage in strategic planning to accomplish this daunting agenda. Recognition of ongoing learning's importance must permeate every area of professional, denominational, and community life. We cannot just say it is good for others; we must also demonstrate in our own lives our involvement in lifelong learning for ministry and mission and our willingness to risk and take on the difficult issues facing us in the church and our society. Walter Brueggemann says that "theological education [and I would add continuing theological education] is not about reasonableness and skill and management, all of which may be necessary. Rather, it is about power, insight, vision, courage and freedom of another kind, wrought precisely against the rulers of this age. It is now a question in the church whether faith and resources are available for a radically different reading of reality."[5]

Robert Greenleaf, in his book *Servant Leadership*, tells a story from his childhood about a dogsled race in his hometown. Most of the boys in the race had big sleds and several dogs. Greenleaf, only five years old, had a small sled and one dog. The course was one mile staked out on the lake. As the race started, the more powerful contenders quickly left small Greenleaf behind. In fact, he hardly looked like he was in the race at all. All went well with the rest until about halfway around. The team that was second started to pass the team in the lead. They came too close and the dogs got into a fight. Soon, the other dog teams joined in and little Greenleaf could see one seething mass of kids, sleds, and dogs about one-half mile away. So, he gave them all wide berth and was the only one who finished the race. Looking back as an adult, he concludes, "As I reflect on the many vexing problems and the stresses of our times that complicate their solutions, this simple scene from long ago comes vividly to mind and I draw the obvious moral: no matter how difficult the challenge or how impossible or hopeless the task may seem, if you are reasonably sure of your course—just keep going!"[6]

If we really believe that we may contribute to the lifelong education of clergy and laity, the unity of the church and humankind, and the quality of life on this planet, we must keep going.

Notes

1. Ronald M. Cervero, *Effective Continuing Education for Professionals* (San Francisco: Jossey-Bass, 1988), 73.

2. Evangelical Lutheran Church in America, Division for Ministry, "Lifelong Learning and Development for Faithful Leaders" (Chicago: Evangelical Lutheran Church in America, 1997), 2.

3. J. W. Carroll and B. G. Wheeler, "Doctor of Ministry Program: History, Summary of Findings, and Recommendations," in *Theological Education* (Spring 1987): 36.

4. Ibid.

5. Walter Brueggemann, *Hope within History* (Atlanta: John Knox Press, 1987), 13B14).

6. Robert K. Greenleaf, *Servant Leadership: A Journey into the Nature of Legitimate Power and Greatness* (New York: Paulist Press, 1977), 175.

CHAPTER 3

Building Systems of Continuing Education for the Professions

Ronald M. Cervero

A central feature of North American societies in the late-twentieth century was the professionalization of their workforces. One estimate is that nearly 25 percent of the United States workforce claims membership in a profession.[1] These professionals teach society's children, guide our businesses, manage and account for our money, settle civil disputes, diagnose and treat our mental and physical ills, fight our wars, and help mediate our relationship to God. Thus, it is important to keep our eye on what is truly at stake in continuing education. The bottom line of continuing education is to improve the practice of these teachers, physicians, managers, and clergy. Contrasting this bottom line with the picture of the most frequently encountered form of continuing education is instructive:

> [Continuing education] is dominated by the informational update. In what is typically an intensive two- or three-day short course, a single instructor lectures and lectures and lectures fairly large groups of business and professional people, who sit for long hours in an audiovisual twilight, making never-to-be-read notes at rows of narrow tables covered

with green baize and appointed with fat binders and sweating pitchers of ice water.[2]

This picture is as universally recognizable to people in any profession as it is criticized for being largely ineffective in improving the performance of these same professionals. Indeed, the familiarity of this picture would be funny if the importance of continuing education were not so great.

Historical Development of Continuing Professional Education

An incredible amount of resources, financial and human, are used to support three to six years of professionals' initial education. Until recently, however, little systematic thought was given to what happens for the following forty years of professional practice. Many leaders in the professions believed that these years of preservice professional education, along with some refreshers, were sufficient for a lifetime of work. However, with rapid social changes, explosion of research-based knowledge, and technological innovations, many of these leaders now understand the need to continually prepare people for forty years of professional practice through continuing education.[3]

Beginning in the 1960s, embryonic evidence for systems of continuing education began to appear. Perhaps the first clear signal of this new view was the publication in 1962 of a conceptual scheme for the lifelong education of physicians.[4] The 1970s saw the beginning of what is now a widespread use of continuing education as a basis for relicensure and recertification.[5] By the 1980s organized and comprehensive programs of continuing education were developed in engineering, accounting, law, medicine, pharmacy, veterinary medicine, social work, librarianship, architecture, nursing home administration, nursing, management, public school education, and many other professions.[6] During that decade, many professions developed their systems of accreditation for providers of continuing education.[7]

As the next millennium begins, the picture of "a single instructor lecturing and lecturing large groups of professionals" is still easily recognizable as the predominant form of continuing education. A similarly recognizable picture of a system of continuing education effective in today's complex world is not yet evident. The major reason for this lack of a unifying picture of effective continuing education is that the professions are in a transitional stage, experimenting with many different purposes, forms, and institutional locations for the delivery of continuing education. These systems, such as they are, are incredibly primitive.[8] I would characterize them as:

- devoted mainly to updating practitioners about the newest developments, which are
- transmitted in a didactic fashion and
- offered by a pluralistic group of providers (workplaces, for-profits, associations, and universities) that
- do not work together in any coordinated fashion and
- are almost entirely unconnected to previous levels of professional education.

Relatively speaking, these systems of continuing education are in their infancy. By way of analogy, at the end of the twentieth century continuing education was in the same state of development as preservice education was at the beginning of the twentieth century. Medical education serves a useful point of comparison. In his 1910 report on medical schools in Canada and the United States, Abraham Flexner found that only 16 of 155 schools expected that their incoming students would have any previous college education, and he recommended closing the schools that did not.[9] It is unlikely that anyone in 1910 would have predicted the structure of medical education today. Likewise, systems of continuing education will grow through this transitional period to achieve an equivalent coherence, size, and stature as the preservice stage of professional education. Indeed, the leaders of most professions would probably agree that what we hardly dare prophesy today will be seen by later generations as efforts to achieve a manifest necessity.[10] While these systems of continuing education are in transition, many choices must be made.[11]

Critical Issues for the Future of Continuing Professional Education

The task of building systems of continuing education is fundamentally more complex than what faced leaders earlier in the twentieth century as they successfully built the existing systems of preservice professional education. First, whereas preservice education takes place in a relatively short period of time, continuing education must help professionals for years of professional practice, which is characterized not only by constant change but also by competing values. Second, whereas preservice education is predominately controlled by universities and professional schools, multiple institutions offer continuing education, all of which claim to be the most valid and effective provider. Three critical issues must be addressed in building systems of continuing education.

Issue 1: Continuing Education for What? Struggle between Updating Professionals' Knowledge and Improving Professional Practice

The most fundamental issue is, what is the problem for which continuing education is the answer? If the picture painted at the beginning of the chapter is the answer, then it is clear that the problem has been conceived as *keeping professionals up-to-date on the profession's knowledge base*. In fact, keeping professionals up-to-date is as close to a unifying aim as continuing education has.[12] This educational model flows from the deeply embedded view that professional practice consists of instrumental problem solving made rigorous by applying scientific theory and technique.[13] This scientific knowledge is produced by theorists and researchers, and the foundation is laid in professional school, with additional building blocks added through forty years of continuing education. In a sense, continuing education becomes an extension of faculty members' lines of research. Yet most of the problems professionals face are not in the book. Schon's studies of professional practice led him to say:

> In the varied topography of professional practice, there is a high, hard ground overlooking a swamp. On the high ground, manageable problems lend themselves to solution through the application of research-based theory and technique. In the swampy lowland, messy, confusing problems defy technical solution. The irony of this situation is that the problems of the high ground tend to be relatively unimportant to individuals or society at large. . . . While in the swamp lie the problems of greatest human concern.[14]

What does it mean for education if we believe that professionals conduct most of their practice in the swamp of the real world? In response to this view, some professional schools have begun moving to more problem-centered curricula. For example, in providing the rationale for Harvard's new problem-centered, as opposed to subject-centered, medical school curriculum (one inspired by McMaster University), the president noted the growing change in perception of how physicians go about making their characteristic decisions of diagnosis and treatment: "Few doctors are now inclined to think of themselves as simply arriving at logically determined conclusions by applying scientifically tested truths to experimentally derived data. . . . Considerations of many kinds are often jumbled together to form a picture full of uncertainties, requiring the most delicate kinds of judgments and intuitions."[15]

Continuing education has a great advantage over other stages of professional education in seeking to promote effective practice. It occurs when professionals are most likely to be aware of a need for better ways to think about what they do. But if we are to exploit this natural advantage and move our systems beyond the update model, we need to find ways to better integrate continuing education, both in its content and educational design, into the ongoing individual and collective practice of professionals.

Issue 2: Who Benefits from Continuing Education? Struggle between the Learning Agenda and the Political and Economic Agendas of Continuing Education

In a sense, this issue is also about the purposes of continuing education. While the first issue dealt with the various educational purposes for continuing education, this issue recognizes the reality that continuing education is about many things in addition to professionals' learning. I believe that we all recognize that continuing education can and often does improve professionals' knowledge and positively affects our organizations and communities.[16] However, continuing education offers many additional benefits to individuals and organizations. Any director of continuing education for a professional school knows that she will be expected to generate surplus revenues to be used to support faculty members' travel, research, and instruction. Any director for a professional association knows that his programs will need to generate revenues to fund staff salaries in nonrevenue producing activities, such as lobbying, maintaining certification programs, and promoting the public image of the profession. Another example is that training programs are an important benefit that can help to retain employees, as one survey found: "Among the many benefits offered to their employees, continuing education is considered the most important after health insurance. More than 90 percent of the companies surveyed currently offer CE as an employee benefit and 97 percent plan to offer their employees this benefit by 2000."[17]

There is no reason to expect that education can, or even should, be immune from the political and economic agendas of our institutions and the wider society. To address these realities, the first question any continuing educator needs to ask is, what is the mission of my institution and where does continuing education fit in that mission? Second, whose interests will be served by offering continuing education and what are those interests? Finally, what are the political relationships at my institution and how will they enable or constrain implementing the vision for continuing education? This struggle between the learning and the political-economic agendas will always exist. However, by answering these three questions, we will be better able to negotiate a successful resolution to this struggle.

Issue 3: Who Will Provide Continuing Education? Struggle for Turf Versus Collaborative Relationships

Most continuing education is provided through some sort of collaboration between two or more institutions. A central finding of the body of research on this topic is that any understanding of collaboration for continuing education has to recognize the larger organizational goals being pursued through forming such relationships. For example, a study of collaborative programs in engineering found that while respondents believed the programs were needed to keep engineers up-to-date with new technologies, the university-corporation relationship was driven by larger institutional issues.[18] For corporations, the benefits included access to university students as employment prospects and more direct and regular access to university faculty and research. For universities, the programs provided a mechanism to secure research contracts and faculty consulting, provided a means to secure student internships, and generated profits to subsidize other institutional functions. In a similar vein, other research has found that a primary reason medical schools have extensive collaborative relationships with community hospitals is to increase the number of patient referrals to the university hospital, which results from faculty members speaking at these programs.[19]

While there is general agreement that collaborative programming is a good (even "politically correct") idea, the central question is always "Who's in charge?" This governance issue is negotiated in partnerships and the fundamental issues typically revolve around who controls the content of the program and how profits and losses will be shared. These enduring issues are being played out in the brave new world of technology-assisted instruction. The growth of distance education has raised the questions of who owns the course material created by professors and who should benefit from the profits gained by the sale of multimedia course materials and web-based courses. For example, in 1994 the extension program at UCLA signed a ten-year contract with the Home Education Network. The contract granted the company exclusive rights to distribute and market video recordings of UCLA's extension courses. In 1996 the contract was amended to include online courses as well. In May 1998 the company changed its name to OnlineLearning.net. The central question in this case is, who owns the content of those courses and who will share in the profits: UCLA Central Administration, its Extension Program, the faculty members, or OnlineLearning.net?[20]

Collaboration is a strategy that has been used extensively and will continue to be used to develop systems of continuing education.[21] However, astute leaders recognize that forming collaborative relationships is fundamentally a political process in which costs and benefits must be clearly weighed, including those involving organizational agendas other than those connected to the continuing education program. Thus, effective partnerships will develop not from a belief that collaboration is the right thing to do but from a definitive understanding of the goals to be achieved by the partnership, a clear recognition of the benefits to be gained by each institution, and the contribution of equivalent resources by each partner.[22]

A Concluding Note

The leaders of workplaces, professional associations, universities, and governments have both a tremendous opportunity and a clear responsibility to further develop the systems of continuing education systems for the professions. These three issues illuminate the

critical choices before institutional leaders and individual professionals in building these systems. As with any humanly constructed
system, the building of a coordinated system of continuing education for any profession is a political process. This process will be
marked by fundamental struggles over the educational agenda and
the competing interests of the educational agenda and the political-economic agendas of the multiple stakeholders for continuing
education. With this understanding, then, it is crucial that all of the
stakeholders participate in a substantive way in negotiating these
agendas for continuing education. For the immediate and long-
term negotiation of these struggles will define whether continuing
education can make a demonstrable impact on the quality of professional practice.

Notes

1. Ronald M. Cervero, *Effective Continuing Education for Professionals* (San
Francisco: Jossey-Bass, 1988).

2. Philip M. Nowlen, *A New Approach to Continuing Education for Business
and the Professions: The Performance Model* (New York: Macmillan, 1988), 23.

3. Cyril O. Houle, *Continuing Learning in the Professions* (San Francisco:
Jossey-Bass, 1980).

4. B. V. Dryer, "Lifetime Learning for Physicians: Principles, Practices, Proposals," *Journal of Medical Education*, no. 37 (1962).

5. Ronald M. Cervero and John F. Azzaretto, eds., *Visions for the Future of
Continuing Professional Education* (Athens, GA: Georgia Center for Continuing
Education, The University of Georgia, 1990).

6. Cervero, *Effective Continuing Education*.

7. W. Robert Kenny, "Program Planning and Accreditation," in *Problems
and Prospects in Continuing Professional Education*, ed. Ronald M. Cervero and
Craig L. Scanlan, New Directions for Adult and Continuing Education 27 (San
Francisco: Jossey-Bass, 1985).

8. Cervero and Azzaretto, *Visions for the Future*.

9. Abraham Flexner, *Medical Education in the United States and Canada*
(New York: Carnegie Foundation for the Advancement of Teaching, 1910).

10. Houle, *Continuing Learning in the Professions*, 302.

11. William H. Young, *Continuing Professional Education in Transition*, 5th
ed. (Malabar, FL: Krieger, 1998).

12. Nowlen, *New Approaches to Continuing Education*.

13. Donald A. Schon, *Educating the Reflective Practitioner: Toward a New Design for Teaching and Learning in the Professions* (San Francisco: Jossey-Bass, 1987).

14. Ibid., 3.

15. Derek Bok, "Needed: a New Way to Train Doctors," *Harvard Magazine* (May–June 1984), 37–38.

16. Karl E. Umble and Ronald M. Cervero, "Impact Studies in Continuing Education for Health Professionals: A Critique of the Research Syntheses," *Evaluation and the Health Professions* 19, no. 2 (1996): 148–74.

17. University Continuing Education Association, *Lifelong Learning Trends: A Profile of Continuing Higher Education*, 5th ed. (Washington, DC: University Continuing Education Association, 1998), 31.

18. A. H. Colgan, "Continuing Professional Education: A Study of Collaborative Relationships in Engineering Universities and Corporations" (PhD diss., University of Illinois at Urbana-Champaign, 1990).

19. Ronald M. Cervero, "Collaboration in University Continuing Professional Education," in *Realizing the Potential of Interorganizational Cooperation*, ed. H. W. Beder, New Directions for Continuing Education 23 (San Francisco: Jossey-Bass, 1984); Roger G. Maclean, "Negotiating between Competing Interests in Planning Continuing Medical Education," in *What Really Matters in Adult Education Program Planning: Lessons in Negotiating Power and Interests*, ed. Ronald M. Cervero and Arthur L. Wilson, New Directions for Adult and Continuing Education 69 (San Francisco: Jossey-Bass, 1996).

20. Lisa Guernsey and Jeffrey R. Young, "Who Owns On-line Courses?" *The Chronicle of Higher Education*, June 5, 1998, A21–A23.

21. Ronald M. Cervero, "Cooperation and Collaboration in the Field of Continuing Professional Education," in *Professional Workers as Learners*, ed. E. S. Hunt (Washington, DC: U.S. Department of Education, 1992).

22. Cervero, *Effective Continuing Education*; M. M. Collins, "Exploring Professional Associations' Perceptions of Institutions of Higher Education as Potential Partners" (PhD diss., The Pennsylvania State University, 1998).

CHAPTER 4

Collaboration in Continuing Theological Education: Creating Communities of Moral Deliberation

Ward Cornett III

Continuing theological education for clergy and church leaders in North America consists of a diverse range of opportunities and possibilities. Traditionally, the focus of continuing theological education has been on programs that served the needs and interests of clergy involved in the daily work of parish ministry. Today we in churches understand the arena of continuing theological education in a much larger sense—as a contribution to the congregation's work in dialogue with the culture in which it is located. An important aspect of this work is to structure continuing theological education programs as collaborative enterprises with various other sectors of society. Such collaboration or partnering will result in the creation of communities of moral deliberation.

Throughout its history, the church has struggled to define its relationship to society. An isolationist or sectarian position is, for most Christians, unworkable because they and their church communities are too fully integrated into the surrounding culture. Conversely, a posture of uncritical accommodation of culture and society is also unacceptable. The challenge for the church and many religious institutions is to assume an active but critical engagement in the world around it. The collaborative enterprise of continuing theological education is one way in which the church can actively engage the world.

Active Engagement between Church and World

Collaboration in continuing theological education challenges the church to rethink its traditional boundaries and its natural tendency to turn inward, especially in difficult times, in order to engage the larger culture in which the church is located. The world is multicultural, multiracial, and religiously pluralistic. Our society is served by governmental agencies, businesses, nonprofit organizations, varieties of religious organizations, social service and healthcare organizations, professional associations, businesses, industry, and community service organizations. Our culture is also politically diverse, ranging from ideological extremes of the far left to the far right with a broad middle ground. A wide range of organizations, reflecting that political diversity, routinely engage in major research that becomes the basis for public and political advocacy on behalf of their constituencies.

Collaborative efforts in continuing theological education invite the Christian community and different faith traditions to build bridges into the community and undertake learning partnerships with organizations, agencies, institutions, and individuals beyond the boundaries of the religious community. Collaboration suggests that continuing theological education can be planned and facilitated in partnership with other groups in society that may contribute to the ongoing conversation within the religious community. Likewise, those groups will benefit from their participation in educational projects conducted in collaboration with religious communities.

The rationale for creating a broader arena for discussion through collaboration is affirmed by the psalmists who suggest that anything and everything is subject to theological analysis. To quote Psalm 24, "The earth is the LORD's and all that is in it"

(24:1a). Psalm 8 reminds us that God has created humanity a little lower than the angels and given us dominion over the works of God's hands. The psalmists provide a clear mandate to be about the business of the world. From a theological perspective, nothing in all of creation is out of bounds for discussion. God has endowed humanity with responsibility for everything that exists. The church's service in the world can be greatly enhanced as the faithful become more familiar with the rich diversity of God's creation. Christian vocation is the call to engage the world wherever we are located.

Theology is always contextual. Therefore, it must naturally be in conversation with its respective cultural setting. Canadian theologian Douglas John Hall commends the North American church to a "genuine give-and-take, in which the world is permitted to speak for itself."[1] Only in this way can the disciple community learn something of the spirit of the times, or zeitgeist. By listening to the "host culture," the community can come to a better understanding of the forces at work upon the human spirit. "The disciple community sees its socio-historical habitat, not only as a field to be investigated, but as a partner in the investigation—and therefore as a contributor to the theological task itself."[2] Through contextual analysis, the church can find common cause with the culture.

Contextual theology can take a variety of forms, beginning with the basic task of listening to and observing the surrounding culture in order to inform the church's teaching, preaching, and witness. Another form of contextual theology is the exercise of collaboration in continuing theological education. Representatives of various community organizations or institutions and leaders in continuing theological education sitting down together to plan and produce an educational event is collaboration that puts theology to the test of listening to the culture. This is fundamental to theological education and the life of discipleship. Hall states with force and clarity the need for such an undertaking: "The church can become a theologically alive and obedient disciple community only as it permits its thinking to be receptive to and re-formed by the realities of the world."[3]

The collaborative effort can be mutually beneficial to participants in a given project. For the church's purposes, it is immediately beneficial to the enterprise of continuing theological education. As Hall notes, contextual theology enlivens the church. The church can only be enriched in its understanding as a result of such an enterprise.

The collaborative model represents what the church has always done: engage in public witness. Historically, the church has carried out a public witness through its social ministry and ongoing work for justice for the poor, the oppressed, and exploited peoples. However, at the beginning of the new millennium, issues of justice have become much more complex, sometimes polarized, and not as easily addressed by the church without extensive specialized knowledge, expertise, and increased understanding of the issues at stake. The most legitimate prophetic witness in the North American church has been that which is best informed by the broadest possible knowledge of cultural trends and ideas. It is expressed within the framework of a civil society that exercises mutual respect and appreciation for diverse points of view. Certainly civil action has been part of the church's repertoire for effecting social change. It has played a role in the past in the civil rights movement and opposition to the Vietnam War. However, those events were high points of civil crisis that called for the use of extreme measures. In the more mundane day-to-day business of addressing the social problems of our time, carefully considered and measured civil exchange will have the most impact. The enterprise of collaborative continuing theological education is one arena where this exchange can take place.

The church has a unique relationship to its surrounding culture. It has no legal authority but significant moral authority exercised not as coercion but as persuasion. However, this authority is eroding as Christianity, specifically, and religious faith, more broadly, are marginalized and diminished in an increasingly secular, ethnically and religiously pluralistic culture. The church is also unique in that it is the one institution charged by public consensus, history, and tradition with the responsibility of promoting humane values. The church has been the repository of concern for human dignity, love and justice, hospitality to the stranger, care for the neighbor, and issues of community cohesion. Clearly, these are not simply private values, but matters of great public import. Ronald Thiemann contends that public theology is actually not a specialized discipline or a technical subspecies of theology. Rather, he says, it is guided by the Anselmian credo, "I believe in order that I may understand." Public theology, according to Thiemann, is faith seeking to understand the relationship between Christian convictions and the broader social and cultural setting in which the Christian community lives. To understand that relationship, the theological challenge is to offer a careful and detailed description of the entities in question. The goal is not to provide an overarching theory about church and world but to identify those places where Christian convictions intersect with practices that characterize contemporary public life. Thiemann has stated concisely the rationale for the collaborative model of continuing theological education.[4]

Collaboration involves bringing the religious perspective into the public and community arena. Especially troubling for church people today is that the religious community, its message, and its activities are becoming less significant in contemporary society. Numerous writers and scholars have documented the concern for both the fragmentation of the religious voice in the public arena and the complete dismissal of religion as a legitimate participant in the cultural and civic enterprise. Religion, as a significant voice in the public arena, suffers from a number of hindrances. First, the faith perspective is typically compartmentalized or privatized by religious people. The tendency is for the religious person to segregate the practice and understanding of religion from the rest of her or his life; that is, to confine religion within the walls of the church and the congregation's local ministries. Especially for Christians, this tendency reflects a shortcoming of religious education. Parishioners, typically, are not instructed or urged to think about their vocation or their place of work as the arena for living out their faith. Only in recent years has there been a movement toward a religious understanding of vocation or ministry in daily life. Otherwise, the normal practice is to leave our religious beliefs at home and at the church. Religious self-understanding and expressions of faith are not particularly welcome within the workplace and public arena, nor do many Christians readily share expressions of their faith perspective openly.

Stephen Carter has documented this tendency to privatize and compartmentalize religious faith in his book *The Culture of Disbelief: How American Law and Politics Trivialize Religious Devotion.* Carter deals extensively with a number of aspects of religion and culture, including the church-state debate, religious expression in the public schools, and the resurgence of Christian evangelical demands for recognition and rights. Although he is sympathetic to some of the difficulties Christian Evangelicals have experienced with attempts to curb their public expression of religious faith, Carter does not limit himself to the problems of only one particular religious movement. He is more broadly concerned about American culture and its inability to recognize the place and the importance of religion in the overall cultural scheme. Not only do law and politics trivialize religion but the culture itself also treats religion as if it has nothing substantive to contribute. Carter cites numerous examples of open hostility to religion and religious expression in American culture, including academic treatises that disparage religious belief. Various sectors of society have little tolerance for religious belief and expression. The wholesale indifference toward religion that is evident in other corners of American culture is just as harmful and insidious. Noting this tendency, Carter repeatedly makes reference to the idea of religion as a hobby. In other words, religion is understood as being primarily a private and personal matter that has little public or political consequence.[5]

The church as the embodiment of Christianity is, of course, only one expression of religion in the North American culture and in the global community. Into the 1970s Christians have lived a sheltered life in North America regarding religion. That is no longer possible today. As the result of extensive immigration of other faith traditions into the North American setting and growing global awareness, the general public has become acutely aware of the importance of other religious traditions, including Judaism, Islam, Buddhism, Hinduism, Sikhism, and Janism. The antidote for Carter's concern about trivializing religion in North American culture is for Christianity, especially through continuing education and lifelong learning, to become more inclusive and multifaith in program development. Because North America is a multifaith environment, it is incumbent upon the church to demonstrate that reality by the regular collaboration and inclusion of other faith traditions as part of continuing education and lifelong learning. That practice is certainly consistent with the idea of continuing education as a community of moral deliberation. The ethical and theological resources for engaging in moral deliberation and discernment are greatly expanded by engaging the interfaith community.

The public's attitude of indifference toward specific institutions of the church is also evident. Theological education is uniquely the province of the church, its judicatories, and its educational institutions, including church-related graduate schools of religion and theology and theological seminaries. These same institutions serve as venues for continuing education. A 1999 study conducted by Auburn Theological Seminary determined that many community leaders were simply unaware of the presence of seminaries in their communities. According to Barbara G. Wheeler, president of Auburn and director of the Auburn Center for the Study of Theological Education, "seminaries are virtually invisible to leaders of secular organizations and institutions, even those in the seminary's own city and region." Wheeler reports of one community activist who lives in a city with several seminaries who remarked, "The seminaries don't appear often on people's radar screens." A businessman in the same city said, "I don't know that anyone in this town knows that [the seminaries] are there." The study documents thoroughly the invisibility of theological seminaries and the more general tendency of religious leaders, including parish pastors and church-related institutions, to be increasingly disengaged from issues in the public realm.[6]

Part of the challenge in collaborative continuing theological education is convincing the secular community that the church has something important to contribute. Convincing the church that it has anything to gain by participating in the public arena through a collaborative approach to theological education is also a challenge. To make the case for collaborative theological education, the church must be clear in its rationale for such an undertaking. Otherwise, it will not be convincing to the world or to its own constituency.

Moral Deliberation and Individualism

Of course, more is at stake than the church's public witness and presence. For example, the church needs to support efforts to renew civic life, cultivate common ground for mutual conversation, and encourage the exchange of diverse viewpoints on a series of topics, including some that are highly controversial. Noted historian Arthur M. Schlesinger Jr. addressed social isolation and public fragmentation in his 1991 reflections on multicultural society, *The Disuniting of America*. He notes that the United States has been incredibly successful, up to now, at nurturing and maintaining an amalgamated society consisting of a rich diversity of ethnic origins—European, African, and now, South American. That unity has been served by the emphasis upon individual identity with the larger culture of the country, rather than with ethnic origin. Individuals desired to shed their ethnic identity and assimilate unnoticed into the American milieu, "to forge a new American culture."[7] This has been accomplished despite the "curse of racism" that has prevailed over centuries of American development. Schlesinger laments the fact that this assimilating capacity has diminished significantly as more people are finding their identity primarily within ethnic and linguistic subcultures. This occurs often at the expense of broader cultural and nationalistic sources of identity. The consequence of this trend is that tribalism will continue to grow and different groups in society will focus exclusively on their own interests and concerns.

In the book *Habits of the Heart*, sociologist Robert Bellah and his associates report the results of a series of in-depth interviews they conducted with a wide range of people. The interviews were designed to measure the degree of independence and individualism versus commitment to communitarian values. Following the interviews, the sociologists engaged in extensive analysis of the results. Part of the basis for their analyses was the nineteenth-century study of American culture and character, *Democracy in America* by Alexis de Tocqueville, from which Bellah derived his title, *Habits of the Heart*. De Tocqueville used the term to describe attitudes, notions, opinions, and ideas that "shape mental habits" and are "the sum of moral and intellectual dispositions of men in society." Mores, according to Bellah, seem to involve not only ideas and opinions but also habitual practices with respect to religion, political participation, and economic life. De Toqueville, writing in the 1830s, used a new term, *individualism*, to describe the way in which Americans lived, a way exemplified by Benjamin Franklin. Individualism is more moderate and orderly than egoism, which predates the use of individualism, but yields the same results. According to de Toqueville, "Individualism is a calm and considered feeling which predisposes each citizen to isolate himself from the mass of his fellows and withdraw into the circle of family and friends; with this little society formed to his taste, he gladly leaves the greater society to look after itself."[8]

Bellah reports that de Toqueville was especially interested in those forces that would work to return people from their isolation and into social communion. Immersion in private economic pursuits was one of the forces that drove people away from a life of civic responsibility and into their own privatized spheres. At the same time, civic responsibility and involvement in public af-

fairs was seen as the best antidote to individual isolation. De Toqueville was concerned that an overemphasis on individualism,
self-reliance, and economic affluence would result in the rejection
of their contemporaries, their ancestors, and their descendants.
"Each man," contended de Toqueville, "is thrown back on himself
alone, and there is danger that he may be shut up in the solitude
of his own heart."[9]

Bellah asserts that the growth of individualism is destructive
to the basic commitment to community values. He and his colleagues presuppose that community affiliation, whether in the
form of neighborhood, family ties, or institutional membership
(including the church), is an essential source of individual identity.
Their research uncovered increasing tendencies for individuals to
define themselves beyond the bounds of traditionally recognized
communities of moral deliberation, a place where they face more
uncertainty regarding their sense of self-worth. Consequently,
the only standard remaining against which one can be measured
are the measures established by the market economy: levels of income, consumption, and one's ability to conform to the means for
achieving that end. Bellah notes that this is the curious paradox of
nonconformity in American society. As individuals reject confor-
mity to traditional sources of community standards and personal
identity, they are simultaneously conforming to standards of status and achievement.[10] Living under such compulsion leaves little
room for attention to the common good, the needs of others, or
questions that would naturally evolve from the process of moral
deliberation. Bellah's work is somewhat dated, but the basic principles still apply, and perhaps even more so at the beginning of the
new millennium.

American society is becoming fragmented, highly individualized, and ghettoized into a diverse range of cultural enclaves,
including those created by disparities in wealth and income.
Witness the proliferation of privatized, gated communities and
other exclusive housing developments in the United States that
are accessible only to the very affluent. The exclusiveness of these

neighborhoods demonstrates the lengths to which individuals will go to avoid the costs of living in a broad-based, pluralist, and inclusive community. They illustrate further how difficult it is to find common ground for moral deliberation and discussion of the common good. Combined with the decline in political party affiliation, increasingly low voter turnout that began in the early 1950s, and a general decline in church participation, Bellah's concerns for the disintegration of communities of moral deliberation are only magnified.

Ultimately, the roots of this moral fragmentation go much deeper than Bellah's analysis. One of the foremost ethicists of this era, Alasdair MacIntyre, in his 1984 publication, *After Virtue*, addressed the moral crisis of the twentieth century. He asserts that the Enlightenment failed to find a common ground for exercising moral discernment and deliberation based on reason alone. MacIntyre understands this failure to have occurred because, in each era prior to the Enlightenment, all attempts to find a moral center only resulted in affirming the prevailing norms and values of the contemporary culture. Further, the Enlightenment project refused to deal with the teleological dimensions of human existence. In short, there was no acknowledgment of the duality of human nature. Enlightenment-era philosophers proceeded on the assumption of the basic goodness of human nature. Consequently, any effort to formulate moral injunctions failed because the effort was always disconnected from the teleological understanding. Instead of an understanding based on assumptions about the human condition, the tendency in formulating moral injunctions is to resort to arbitrary authority for justification.

For MacIntyre, arbitrary authority becomes the philosophy of emotivism, which is nothing more than the anarchy of the individual will, due to the lack of criteria for making moral or evaluative judgments. Emotivism depends on the use of the personal pronoun *I* as the individual engages in the expression of personal preference without regard to objective reason or attention to the facts. MacIntyre notes that moral discourse today is becoming increasingly shrill due to the lack of a coherent set of principles or an overarching framework in which to make ethical determinations. Participation in public discourse has become highly individualized, reflecting a fragmentation of public unity. Overall, MacIntyre was concerned in 1982 with the general disintegration of public moral authority.[11]

American culture, and indeed the whole world, is undergoing another dramatic change with the advent of the digital revolution and the burgeoning growth of the Internet. The Internet has already redefined the idea of community. Now, individuals who are relatively unknown to one another, separated by thousands of miles, and isolated in front of a computer screen can enter into discussion groups about virtually any topic in the world. In some sense, these new communities may be communities of moral deliberation. It is more likely they will reflect the characteristics of emotivism addressed by MacIntyre, the anarchy of the individual, and personal preference rather than any deliberative process.

Sociobiologist Edward O. Wilson argued ten years ago that the Internet in the twenty-first century will democratize knowledge. Those who merely possess knowledge alone will not run the world. As the result of science and technology, "access to factual knowledge of all kinds is rising exponentially while dropping in unit cost. It is destined to become global and democratic." Knowledge or information is increasingly available everywhere on television and computer screens. "We are drowning in information," he contends, "while starving for wisdom. What is needed will be people who have the ability to synthesize information, to put together the right information at the right time, think critically about it, and make important choices wisely."[12] This is the task of ethics, the task of religious leaders especially, and the challenge to communities of faith and to the arena of continuing theological education.

The question arises again as to who will participate in communities of moral deliberation. Will it be the church, corporations, government, scholars in research institutes, and self-appointed synthesizers of information? Is it possible that the arena of continuing theological education can play a role in facilitating this kind of conversation now that knowledge and information have become readily accessible? How can continuing theological education provide a forum for moral deliberation?

Toward the end of the first decade of the twenty-first century, the economy of the United States is weaker than it has ever been since the Depression. The United States is engaged in wars in Iraq and Afghanistan. Public morale is ponderous, if not despairing. The United States faces serious concerns in government, society, and the economy. There is great disparity in income and resources between the rich and everyone else, especially the poorest in society. We have not solved the problem of poverty, despite the earlier masquerade of welfare reform. The incidence of child poverty is higher in the United States than in any other Western industrialized country. Approximately 48 million U.S. citizens are without health insurance, many of them working people. Concerns about youth violence, crime, and excessively high levels of incarceration of our citizenry persist unresolved. Many in the scientific community have concluded that the world faces a global environmental catastrophe as the result of environmental degradation, global warming, and the loss of biological diversity. The threat of terrorism is always looming on the horizon. There could be no better time for the church, through continuing education and lifelong learning, to create and promote communities of moral deliberation!

The church addresses all of these concerns and more, at different levels and to different degrees. Continuing theological education is called to provide a forum for the church's ongoing engagement of these concerns as well as gather the scholars, community leaders, and political figures that have some say about how the decisions that will determine the future well being of much of humanity will be made.

If the collaborationist model of continuing education can serve any larger purpose, it is in the realization of truth borne through the process of discovery. Wilson, like MacIntyre, recognizes the failure of the Enlightenment to find a common ground for ethi-

cal discernment and truth seeking. Nevertheless, he describes the
Enlightenment with poetic appreciation. It was never, he says, a
unified moment, "less a determined swift river than a lacework of
deltaic streams working their way along twisted channels."[13] The
Enlightenment consisted of a variety of thinkers within the European academy, driven by the thrill of discovery and a shared
"passion to demystify the world and free the mind from the im-
personal forces that imprison it. They were driven by the thrill of
discovery. They agreed on the power of science to reveal an orderly, understandable universe and thereby lay an enduring base
for free, rational discourse."[14]

Continuing theological education, especially when done collaboratively, can provide a similar framework for free, rational
discourse and its consequent thrill of discovery. Those who participate in programs that foster moral deliberation are in a good
position to reflect upon the social currents of the day. When such
free, open, and rational exchange occurs, the result can be an experience of "consilience," the unity of knowledge. Wilson defines
consilience as a "jumping together of knowledge by the linking of
facts, and fact-based theory across disciplines, to create a common groundwork of explanation."[15] When the church engages the
world on common ground, seeking to listen to what the world is
saying as well as address the world with its message of hope, the
possibility exists for finding explanations for what ails humanity
and prescriptions for solving the problems.

Models of Collaboration in
Continuing Theological Education

The examples of collaborative programs are as numerous as the
sectors of society and issues to be addressed. This list offers a sample of the kinds of collaborative programs that can be developed
and, where possible, an identification of resources:

Building Communities from the Inside Out

Urban renewal and community redevelopment programs from the Institute for Policy Research at Northwestern University have been used extensively in communities around the country. The individuals responsible for this program format, John P. Kretzmann and John L. McKnight, are excellent speakers and resource people. Kretzmann has strong ties to the faith community and is available as a resource person for the church. This is a specific program initiative. But many more examples of community- and church-based organizing efforts exist across the country.

Funding of Nonprofit Social Service Organizations

Fund-raising is a critical issue for church-based social service organizations such as Lutheran Social Services, Catholic Charities, United Methodist children's homes. The first two organizations cited comprise the two largest private, nonprofit organizations in the United States with more than 50 percent of their multibillion dollar budgets coming from federal sources. This community issue has political, theological, and sociological dimensions.

Care of Creation

Numerous resources are present within the secular academy and the theological community for addressing environmental concerns. Various denominations have formulated public statements about the care of creation and Christian responsibility for environmental stewardship. One theologian who has given this the most attention is Larry Rasmussen, the Reinhold Niebuhr Professor Emeritus of Social Ethics at Union Theological Seminary in New York. Another highly qualified individual is David Orr, professor of environmental studies at Oberlin College. The Nature Conservancy, Defenders of Wildlife, and the Humane Society of the United States are all organizations that lend tremendous expertise to the challenge of engaging in moral deliberation. The Ohio State University Byrd Polar Research Center is a major institute for the study of climate change and global warming.

Global Hunger and Development

Bread for the World, Church World Services, Lutheran World Relief, and Catholic Relief Services are endowed with extensive expertise in addressing global hunger. In addition, business, including food producers and commodity brokers, needs to be part of any conversation on the future of the world's food supply. World Vision is the most extensive advocacy, education, and service organization in the world for addressing hunger and global development. It also has a much broader constituent base in North America that ranges from conservative evangelicals to liberal and mainline denominations. It is only natural that World Vision would become a major program resource for continuing education events that intend to reflect an element of moral deliberation.

As noted previously about the growing North American awareness of other faith traditions, it is critically important today that the church engage the resources of the interreligious community in the conduct of continuing education. There are two critical dimensions to engaging other faith traditions in collaboration in continuing education. One is the importance of drawing upon the rich intellectual and spiritual resources of other faith traditions. A second, perhaps little noted, is that the other faith traditions represent a global reach not always readily available in the church.

Global Peace and Justice

Peace and justice is a broad category, and one that reflects many of the areas of concern already raised, including hunger, development, care of creation, and respect for the dignity and rights of other peoples. It is incumbent upon the church through continuing education and collaboration to look broadly for resources and expertise to carry out programs that address the current international security crisis of war, violence, terrorism, and insecurity. Organizations such as the Council for a Parliament of World's Religions and World Conference of Religions for Peace reflect the inclusion of other faith traditions and address themselves to the crises of violence and war in the global community. The Carnegie Endowment for International Peace offers a range of resources and people who are well equipped to help the church address issues of war and peace and human rights. The United Nations Association has offices in a number of midsize to larger cities and provides resources and speakers to address global conflict. Likewise, the council on world affairs movement has a whole network of local offices. These organizations are well equipped with knowledge and expertise, and their mission is fostering global knowledge and awareness. The local council on world affairs is often ready to collaborate on bringing speakers into the community.

Interprofessional Educational Programming

Many mainline Protestant denominations expect their clergy and professional leaders to participate in continuing education. However, only in recent years have denominations begun to identify more clearly their expectations and accountability for participation in lifelong learning. That is not the case with other professions, which are accountable to state licensure boards, professional associations, and specific policies for a defined amount of continuing education in order to maintain professional certification. This is an important dimension of continuing theological education programs that involve collaboration with other organizations, agencies, and institutions. Professionals in many other fields, such as social work, education, and various health care fields, are required to earn Continuing Professional Education

(CPU) credits or contact hours. Attorneys must take Continuing Legal Education units (CLEs). Collaborative programs can then serve the needs of a number of constituencies at once.

Professional associations and state licensure boards normally have specific expectations for program offerings that will satisfy their requirements for continuing education contact hours. Including other professions in a continuing education offering creates the opportunity to engage in joint development of goals, objectives, and program format. Joint undertakings will challenge program planners to look critically at the needs and interests and professional development agendas of other professions and thus be exposed to different approaches to addressing human needs and solving the pressing social problems of our era.

The Future of Collaboration in Continuing Theological Education

It is important for continuing theological educators to recognize that, despite a reigning attitude of disparagement in the secular sphere, the church has something to contribute to the surrounding community. The secular realm will reap benefits as the church offers its resources as a historic community of moral deliberation. Secular society desperately needs a forum where moral discernment is appropriately exercised in a free and open exchange that includes diverse perspectives and the opportunity to engage critically across lines of difference.

The beginning of the new millennium represents a time of great challenge and opportunity for the church's educational enterprise, especially in the area of continuing theological education. Challenge and opportunity are offered because of the amount of rapid change underway in the church, the culture, and the world. At this writing, dramatic changes are under way in the field of education and, specifically, in the area of continuing education. For one thing, the term *continuing education* is being questioned. More and more people today describe their participation in such programs as a process of "lifelong learning" and "ongoing education."

Reflecting more than simply a name change, this new terminology denotes a change in attitude, outlook, and practice that is consistent with a dramatic paradigm shift under way in the arena of organized learning.

One significant change is related to educational technology. As digital technology continues to become less expensive and more accessible, it will increasingly become one of the tools available for congregations to use in their educational enterprise. One possibility for the future of continuing theological education is the blurring of distinctions between seminaries, continuing education centers, and congregations. Not only are congregations recipients of programming but they will also become program providers, resource centers, and collaborators in continuing theological education. As congregations become teaching congregations, the base for collaboration and partnership with a broad range of people will expand considerably. Within ten years it is likely that numerous congregations around the world, most graduate schools, seminaries, learning centers, businesses, and nonprofit organizations will be equipped with video conferencing capacity and the ability to share resources on the Internet. As this transition to digital connections occurs, opportunities for bridges within and among communities will multiply. In the very near future, collaboration in continuing theological education will not be the exception but the norm for program planning and presentation. It will occur with regularity in the digital realm and in face-to-face formats. Developing an understanding of the importance and potential of collaboration with a variety of partners in continuing education, as well as developing the skills to make the collaborative process productive, open, and inclusive, is crucial to the future vitality and relevance of conference centers, continuing education programs, and other institutions of theological education.

Notes

1. Douglas John Hall, *Thinking the Faith: Christian Theology in a North American Context* (Minneapolis: Fortress Press, 1989), 79.

2. Ibid.

3. Ibid., 85.

4. Ronald F. Thiemann, *Constructing a Public Theology: The Church in a Pluralistic Culture* (Louisville, KY: Westminster/John Knox Press, 1991), 21–22.

5. Stephen L. Carter, *The Culture of Disbelief: How American Law and Politics Trivialize Religious Devotion* (New York: Basic Books, 1993), 51–84.

6. Elizabeth Lynn and Barbara G. Wheeler, "Missing Connections: Public Perceptions of Theological Education and Religious Leadership," *Auburn Studies*, no. 6 (September 1999): 4.

7. Arthur M. Schlesinger Jr., *The Disuniting of America: Reflections on a Multicultural Society* (New York: W.W. Norton, 1992), 12, 13.

8. Cited in Robert N. Bellah, Richard Marsden, William M. Sullivan, Ann Swidler, and Steven M. Tipton, *Habits of the Heart: Individualism and Commitment in American Life* (Berkeley: University of California Press, 1985), 37, 38.

9. Ibid., 37.

10. Ibid., 149.

11. Alasdair MacIntyre, *After Virtue: A Study in Moral Theology* (Notre Dame, IN: University of Notre Dame Press, 1984), 6–61.

12. Edward O. Wilson, *Consilience: The Unity of Knowledge* (New York: Alfred A. Knopf, 1998), 269.

13. Ibid.

14. MacIntyre, *After Virtue*, 21.

15. Wilson, *Consilience*, 8.

PART II

Theory and Research in Continuing Education

CHAPTER 5

Motivated Learning and Practice: A Peer Group Model

D. Bruce Roberts

"Mainline" Protestant churches are experiencing a serious decline in membership in once vital congregations. Many observers of this situation agree with Loren Mead, congregational consultant and founder and past president of the Alban Institute, who describes the problem as a "storm buffeting the churches," which is very serious, indeed more serious than yet perceived: "The problems are not minor, calling for adjustments or corrections. They are problems that go to the roots of our institutions themselves. [It] is not something we fix. It is a state of existence in which we must learn to live.... The storm is so serious ... that it marks the end of 'business as usual' for the churches and marks a need for us to begin again building church from the ground up."[1]

Mead suggests that church leaders at all levels need to face the reality and mobilize all available resources toward transforming congregations. He wants to see "the structures that surround congregations—the judicatories, the national structures, the seminaries, and educational institutions—building skills in new ways, ready to help transform congregations from what they are to what they must be as centers of apostolic ministry."[2]

What are the appropriate responses needed in this situation? Edwin Friedman, the rabbi who applied family systems theory to congregational leadership, suggested that what is needed in situations of uncertainty and high anxiety is a "spirit of adventure. . . . For a fundamental reorientation to occur, that spirit of adventure which optimizes serendipity and which enables new perceptions beyond the control of our thinking processes must happen first."[3]

Innovation Needed

Leadership is needed that will be willing to risk exploring new structures, new ministries, new music, even new articulations of the ancient faith. Theological education at all levels, basic and continuing, is challenged to find ways of stimulating leadership that will foster innovations in congregations in order to learn and discover what will be effective bearers of the gospel message in our time.

A primary question for theological educators is how to deliver theological education in a way that addresses the need for innovation in congregational leadership. The need for innovation only arises in situations in which it is not clear what action to take in a given context. The problematic of the "old-line" denominational decline is the context requiring new approaches to congregational leadership and ministry. It is not clear that any one answer exists; it is not clear that national or regional judicatories or, particularly, seminaries have any answers to the problem, beyond an occasional exception. Much of what we have been doing for the past several decades—if not centuries—is not working now. I strongly suspect that if we want answers to our current situations, we will need to learn how to learn with interested groups and people; we will need to foster a climate of openness in order to sponsor innovations and experiments that will help us learn what kind of action and what kind of leadership can be effective in restoring sagging and boring churches. In effect, we will need to learn how to prepare leaders for ministries who know how to learn through their own practice in a specific context.

Continuing theological education is in a strong position to initiate experiments aimed at developing innovations in congregations. Pastors as well as judicatory leaders at all levels are looking for answers, and in some cases have funds that could be expended to help address the pain inherent in the situation. This chapter suggests ways of thinking about adult education, models for adult learning, and a particular model of peer group learning that provides one way of encouraging the kind of innovation and experimentation needed.

Perspectives on Adult Learning and Continuing Education for the Professions

In an article on continuing professional education, Ronald M. Cervero proposes that the goal of professional practice in any field is "wise action" and that, although formal knowledge gained in traditional academic settings is important, "knowledge acquired from practice is necessary to achieve [the goal of wise action]."[4] Based upon the importance of knowledge gained from practice, Cervero goes on to propose that "a model of learning from practice should become the centerpiece of systems of continuing education for the professions. . . . It is important . . . to involve groups of practitioners and a context of practice," because "learning advances through collaborative social interaction and the social construction of knowledge within a community of practitioners and a context of practice."[5]

Ample theoretical support for Cervero's proposals can be found in a number of sources, only a few of which will be used here. Jean Piaget, the Swiss genius, made a lifetime study of the way individuals learned to know. Since many movements in adult education are either based upon his ideas or are congruent with them, I will begin with a review of his work. Piaget suggested that a characteristic of humankind is that we organize our perceptions of reality in an attempt to understand. Of course, these organizations are always inadequate because they are limited by perspective, experience, and maturation. As we live with a particular cognitive organization, what Piaget called an "equilibration," we attempt to make that organization explain everything; we "assimilate" all data into it until there are so many questions and inconsistencies that we are forced to revise our understanding. Piaget called that reorganization of our worldview "accommodation," leading to a new balance or equilibration. Cognitive development for Piaget comprises the stages of progressively more adequate organizations of our perceptions in interaction with our world. The highest adult level, or equilibration, is the recognition that we are always working at assimilating data into our current worldview with the understanding that eventually we will have to accommodate, to develop a new equilibration or understanding. Adult knowing is a lifelong process of continuing to revise (accommodate) our current understanding (equilibration) into a more adequate and coherent way of organizing our perceptions.[6]

Peter Senge and his associates have given the phenomenon Piaget called cognitive organizations (or equilibrations) a different name, "mental models." Senge has identified five disciplines for creating a "learning organization," one of which is the process of identifying mental models: "Mental models are the images, assumptions, and stories which we carry in our minds of ourselves, other people, institutions, and every aspect of the world. Like a pane of glass framing and subtly distorting our vision, mental models determine what we see. Human beings cannot navigate through the complex environments of our world without cognitive 'mental maps'; and all of these mental maps, by definition, are flawed in some way."[7]

For Piaget and Senge, the flaws in our current mental maps create conflicts between our internal mental organization of the world and the external structures of reality. These conflicts make it necessary for all human beings to be lifelong learners; old ways of understanding become inadequate and we are forced to change (accommodate) in order to solve new problems or account for new information (a new equilibration).

What are the implications for professional education from this way of understanding human learning? In the *Science of Education and the Psychology of the Child,* Piaget raises questions about education, makes some suggestions for change, and talks about teacher (adult) education. He raised three fundamental questions:

1. What is the aim of teaching?
2. What should teachers teach?
3. How should teachers teach?[8]

In answering the first question, Piaget suggests that the primary goal of education is the facilitation of mature, reflective thought through the interaction of a maturing student with the physical and social environment. What we all need most to learn is how to learn, how to be self-directing and independent. Much of what is taught will be out of date in a short time, but creative, inventive, and critical minds will always be needed. For Piaget, the task of teaching is to facilitate creativity, "to form the intelligence rather than to stock the memory, to produce intellectual explorers rather than mere erudition."[9]

Since, for Piaget, learning grows at all levels through action, the training of teachers and other professionals must take on an action-reflection orientation. He advocated preparing teachers by involving them in research projects on how children learn, done under the supervision of a trained research assistant. This is the kind of professional education now being advocated by Cervero and others. Since adults learn through a dialectical interaction of their current understandings or mental models with the reality in situations of living or practice, it is important to set up professional continuing education in a way that engages that interactive process.

Piaget's understanding of the way adults learn is corroborated in the work of Patricia M. King, Karen Strohm Kitchener, and Parker Palmer.[10] In a study of how people develop critical thinking, intelligence, and reflective judgment, King and Kitchener reach conclusions similar to Piaget. People at the highest levels of what they call "reflective judgment" are lifelong learners: "Knowledge is the outcome of a process of reasonable inquiry in which solutions to . . . problems are constructed. The adequacy of those solutions is evaluated in terms of what is most reasonable or prob-able according to the current evidence, and it is reevaluated when relevant new evidence, perspectives, or tools of inquiry become available."[11]

Parker Palmer, in his book *The Courage to Teach*, echoes Piaget in suggesting people are able to learn and develop more adequate conceptions of reality only in intentional social interaction he calls "communities of truth." The hallmark of such a community is that "*reality is a web of communal relationships, and that we can know reality only by being in a community with it.*"[12] For Palmer and Piaget, the most mature form of knowing involves "*an eternal conversation about things that matter, conducted with passion and discipline* . . . as the passionate and disciplined process of inquiry and dialogue itself, as the dynamic conversation of a community that keeps testing old conclusions and coming into new ones."[13]

Piaget, Palmer, King and Kitchener, and Senge all understand adult learning to be a complex process that involves the willing-ness to have one's current worldviews challenged in a communal process in which the person attempts to understand a particular subject or context. For Palmer, the process involves

> sharing observations and interpretations, correcting and complement-ing each other, torn by conflict in this moment and joined by consensus in the next. The community of truth, far from being linear and static and hierarchical, is circular, interactive, and dynamic.
>
> At its best, the community of truth advances our knowledge through conflict, not competition. Competition is a secretive, zero-sum game played by individuals for private gain; conflict is open and some-times raucous but always communal, a public encounter in which it is possible for everyone to win by learning and growing. . . . Conflict is the dynamic by which we test ideas in the open, in a communal effort to stretch each other and make better sense of the world.[14]

Ample theoretical evidence supports the contention that pro-fessional education, both basic and continuing, is most effective when it involves actual practice as a basis for learning, reflection, and evaluation of other information and knowledge. It is in living and working that people experience the dissonance of old ways of thinking that no longer are adequate, that no longer solve problems but raise more questions. In what follows, I examine some of the models of adult education that have been developed and that embody the theoretical insights cited above.

Processes for Thinking-in-Action Adult Learning

There are many examples of learning in practice that are consistent with the above perspectives; most of them have been called by different names.

In the early part of the twentieth century, the Methodist Episcopal Church South developed a program for training Sunday school teachers that evolved into what was called "Laboratory Schools" by the Methodist Church after 1939. The training involved teachers and other leaders in processes of (1) diagnosing learning needs, (2) setting learning goals, (3) planning, (4) selecting resources for teaching or leading, (5) practicing the teaching or leading on an appropriate age-level group, and (6) seeking feedback and evaluating the results. By the decade of the 1950s the Laboratory School was a primary instrument of leadership development and produced several generations of people who were excited about laboratory learning and who passed that excitement on to members of congregations.

In 1970 Malcolm Knowles published *The Modern Practice of Adult Education: Andragogy Versus Pedagogy*, which proposed a process for adult education with essentially the same steps as the Methodist Laboratory Schools of half a century earlier.[15] Knowles called his process for adult learning "andragogy," involving seven steps:

"(1) establishment of a climate conducive to adult learning; (2) creation of . . . a structure for participative planning; (3) diagnosis of needs for learning; (4) formulation of directions of learning (objectives); (5) development of a design of activities; (6) operation of the activities; and (7) re-diagnosis of need for learning (evaluation)."[16] Note that the final step involves returning to the diagnosis of needs for learning involving a continuous lifelong cycle of learning.

A movement concurrent with Knowles's work (with which he was familiar) was developed by social scientists and came to be known as "The Laboratory Method." Leland Bradford, Jack Gibb, and Kenneth Benne, in *T-Group Theory and Laboratory Method: Innovation in Re-education*, report work by social scientists seeking to understand the way change takes place in individuals and in all kinds of human institutions. Bethel, Maine, became the center for many experiments and innovations in education for change. As Bradford, Gibb, and Benne express it:

> A laboratory curriculum is designed to help some unit of human organization assess its needs for change and to support that unit in inventing and testing ways in which changes may be achieved. The focal unit may be a single individual or a team of individuals. In either case, the desired direction of learning and change is toward a more integrative and adaptive interconnection of values, concepts, feelings, perceptions, strategies, and skills. . . .
>
> For the learners, every day in a laboratory is full of episodes of re-learning, of reorganization of previous learnings, of confrontations of old patterns with new possibilities. . . . The achievement of each learning objective ordinarily involves examination of the relationships between old and new experiences, between old and new learnings, and the arduous process of achieving some viable choice or synthesis between the old and the new.[17]

A laboratory curriculum reflects the idea that adult learning involves the process of what, in Piaget's terms, is equilibration, for King and Kitchener is reflective judgment, and for Palmer is the community of truth.

The laboratory style of learning has been utilized by Clinical Pastoral Education (CPE) and by theological field education. While CPE used a kind of laboratory method primarily in hospital settings, field education used parish settings for laboratory style learning. In the latter years of the 1960s, theological educators, partly in response to an exasperated constituency of local congregations that wanted better prepared leaders, moved from requiring theological students to have *field work* to having an experience of *field education*. While field work involved assigning students to work in a congregation or other appropriate work environment, field education worked at integrating the practice of ministry in a particular context with courses taken concurrently in the theological curriculum utilizing a trained facilitator called a supervisor, using the CPE terminology.

Field education, as a way of learning through the practice of ministry, anticipated work by Donald A. Schon (*The Reflective Practitioner: How Professionals Think in Action* in 1983) and by Ronald M. Cervero (*Effective Continuing Education for Professionals* in 1988). The basic idea for Cervero is to help "learners become researchers of their own practice"[18]—essentially the same purpose as theological field education. The process of theological field education involves a trained and experienced "supervisor" who leads a process of helping students identify learning needs, set learning objectives, identify and do appropriate work in ministry, and then reflect on what is being learned. Reflection on the practice of ministry includes several emphases, including theological perspectives in the situation, social analysis, personal emotional states, and perception of interpersonal dynamics. Students are asked to work in peer groups with a supervisor and to ask each other evaluative questions: What alternatives are there if you could do this work over again? What theological perspectives are present in the situation (including one's own)? What are the alternative next steps? Of the alternatives, which will you try in the near future? This style of reflection encourages experimentation and creative work in the practice of ministry.

New perspectives for adult education have grown out of the literature on organizational systems theory. Peter Senge, in *The Fifth Discipline: The Art and Practice of the Learning Organization*, advocates creating "learning organizations" that will integrate five disciplines: personal mastery, mental models, shared vision, team learning, and systems thinking. The discipline that captures most fully the kind of learning processes I am attempting to articulate here is that of team learning.

> The discipline of team learning starts with "dialogue," the capacity of members of a team to suspend assumptions and enter into a genuine "thinking together."
>
> The discipline of dialogue also involves learning how to recognize the patterns of interaction in teams that undermine learning. The patterns of defensiveness are often deeply engrained in how a team operates. If unrecognized, they undermine learning. If recognized and surfaced creatively, they can actually accelerate learning.
>
> Team learning is vital because teams, not individuals, are the fundamental learning unit in modern organizations. This [is] where the "the rubber meets the road"; unless teams can learn, the organization cannot learn.[19]

Senge distinguishes two key skills in the discipline of team learning: dialogue and discussion. Dialogue is the procedure in a team in which participants listen to each other carefully and note the dissonance in themselves without reacting; it is an exercise in hearing others, remaining nonreactive, and in observing one's own mental models and assumptions. By contrast, discussion is the presentation and defending of specific views and the movement toward a decision.[20] Although both dialogue and discussion are necessary to team learning, most people use discussion in advocating a position without the examination of their assumptions that comes in dialogue.

Dialogue is necessary, because no one perspective is adequate; we need a diversity of perspectives to help develop more competent solutions to a given problem. In this respect, Senge is consistent with cognitive developmental theory.

Another contemporary source of thinking about adult leadership and learning is Ronald A. Heifetz writing with Marty Linsky in *Leadership on the Line*. Heifetz and Linsky distinguish between "technical" and "adaptive" change. Technical change is primarily aimed at routine problems for which there is an available technical solution. Adaptive challenges are "problems that are not amenable to authoritative expertise or standard operating procedures."[21]

We call these adaptive challenges because they require experiments, new discoveries, and adjustments from numerous places in the organization or community. Without learning new ways—changing attitudes, values, and behaviors—people cannot make the adaptive leap necessary to thrive in the new environment.[22]

Heifetz's strategy for stimulating learning is primarily one of facilitative leadership, leadership that facilitates or even provokes the learning needed in a group or institution. That is, Heifetz does not want to provide easy answers (the title to his first book was *Leadership without Easy Answers*); rather, he advocates helping groups identify the adaptive challenges in their institutions and then create a climate for identifying alternative solutions by asking questions of people involved and by encouraging groups to take responsibility for experimentation that involves learning in a particular context.

This strategy is similar to Piaget's ideas that people learn best when they experience the dissonance of their own internal disequilibrium and to Senge's notions about dialogue. For Senge, learning in dialogue requires three basic conditions: "(1) 'suspend' ... assumptions, literally to hold them 'as if suspended before us'; (2) regard one another as colleagues; (3) there must be a 'facilitator' who 'holds the context' of dialogue."[23]

To suspend assumptions is tension producing; that is, we must know what we are assuming while staying open to testing our current understanding (mental model) against other perspectives. The "dis-ease" of that tension is exactly why we must, in Senge's words, "regard each other as colleagues," and, in Palmer's words, "create a community of truth" in order to produce what Knowles identifies as a "climate for learning." Senge argues that dialogue is a difficult discipline and that groups need a skilled process facilitator to help create and hold the climate of community conversation that leads to the deepest kind of learning.[24]

An example of research coherent with the perspectives cited so far is that reported in a 2002 book, *Primal Leadership*, by Daniel Goleman, Richard Boyatzis, and Annie McKee.[25] *Primal Leadership* was written for the purpose of articulating and advancing a new concept of leadership. The authors suggest that the "fundamental task of leaders . . . is to prime good feeling in those they lead," because "the primal job of leadership is emotional."[26]

This is a very provocative study for continuing theological education (and, indeed, for all of theological education generally), because it challenges the paradigm of leadership development inherent in most continuing education programs and curricula. In order to discuss the authors' educational proposals, some summary of their research is necessary. "The glue that holds people together in a team, and that commits people to an organization, is the emotional resonance they feel with and for each other."[27]

"The key . . . to making primal leadership work to everyone's advantage lies in the leadership competencies of *emotional intelligence*."[28] These competencies can be learned and are "(1) Personal Competence: (*a*) Self-Awareness and (*b*) Self-Management; (2) Social Competence: (*a*) Social Awareness and (*b*) Relationship Management."[29]

To discover the personal capabilities that were key to outstanding leadership, the authors analyzed nearly five hundred competence models in government, business, and not-for-profit organizations (including a religious institution).[30] They were interested in the role three categories of capabilities played in good leadership: technical skills, cognitive abilities, and emotional intelligence.

What they discovered is stunning: "Our rule of thumb holds that EI [emotional intelligence] contributes 80 to 90 percent of the competencies that distinguish outstanding from average leaders

—and sometimes more."[31] My guess is that most professional continuing education programs and theological schools assume just the reverse of this.

The good news in this well-documented study is that the competencies that distinguish outstanding leaders can be learned. However, the learning must happen in ways that are different from what traditional schools usually employ. Emotional intelligence, according to the study, "involves circuitry that runs between the brain's executive centers in the prefrontal lobes and the brain's limbic system, which governs feeling, impulses, and drives. Skills based in the limbic areas, research shows, are best learned through motivation, extended practice, and feedback."[32]

Although the neocortex, that part of our brains that makes us uniquely human, is a quick learner and capable of learning from reading, computer programs, hearing lectures, and so forth, the limbic brain "is a much slower learner—particularly when the challenge is to relearn deeply ingrained habits. This difference matters immensely when trying to improve leadership skills . . . habits learned early in life. . . . Reeducating the emotional brain for leadership learning, therefore, requires a different model from what works for the thinking brain: It needs lots of practice and repetition."[33]

The educational research conducted by Goleman and colleagues concludes that the competencies most important for effective leadership are best learned through what they term *self-directed learning.*[34] What they mean by self-directed or self-motivated learning looks a lot like what United Methodists for many years called Laboratory Training and what Malcolm Knowles called andragogy.[35]

According to the Goleman research, self-directed learning involves five movements. The first is answering the question, who do I want to be? The second involves assessment of who and where I am now and comparing that to the answer to the first question. The third movement is establishment of learning objectives that address the gap between where I am and where I want to be. The fourth movement is the action of practicing new behaviors to the point of mastery. The fifth movement must be simultaneous with the first four and involves developing a community of support and challenge where honest assessment feedback makes change possible.[36]

The research reported in *Primal Leadership* is coherent with perspectives in the thinking of Cervero, Goleman, Senge, Knowles, CPE, and theological field education. All the approaches to adult education and learning reviewed so far have several common characteristics:

1. People are most motivated and energized to learn when they are working at finding answers to internal questions and at discovering more adequate ways of thinking and working (Piaget, Senge, Knowles, King and Kitchener).

2. Adult learners need a climate of openness (Knowles), a community of truth (Palmer), a supportive and challenging team for learning (Cervero, Goleman, and Senge), and a facilitator to hold the process (Senge and Heifetz, as well as experience from CPE and theological field education).

3. Great energy is released for learning when adults are involved in determining together in community what they want to learn, in planning learning activities, and in evaluation as a process of deciding what to learn next (Knowles, the Methodist Laboratory Schools, laboratory method, Cervero, and Goleman).

Following is a model of professional continuing education that demonstrates these characteristics.

A Model of Peer Group Learning: Methodist Educational Leave Society (MELS)

In 1985 the Dixon Foundation in Birmingham, Alabama, began experimenting with the creation of clergy peer groups aimed at improving preaching in the North Alabama Conference of the

United Methodist Church. Edwin M. Dixon started the project after finding a peer group program for business leaders extremely helpful to him personally. Dixon, a long-time and loyal United Methodist layperson, recruited a United Methodist pastor, Burrell B. Hughes, to help establish a peer group program, the first of its type. The Dixon Foundation had been doing work in clergy continuing education prior to the peer group experiment in which individual pastors would be funded for a leave, hence the name, the Methodist Educational Leave Society (MELS). Eventually the peer group program replaced the funding of individual study leaves because of the perception that what happened in peer groups was far more powerful. Early in 1996, the FCP faculty (Facilitator/Convener/Process Person) of the Methodist Educational Leave Society asked Robert E. Reber to design an evaluation process for MELS to determine whether the program had been effective over ten years and to develop recommendations for the future. Bob Reber subsequently invited me to help with the evaluation.

By the spring of 1996, approximately 130 pastors had participated in MELS over the ten years of its existence (not all of whom were in peer groups). We sent all of them surveys and 97 were returned, 67 from peer group participants. In addition, we interviewed 114 people individually or in groups ranging in size from three to ten. The groups were representative: four MELS peer groups; eight pastor-parish relations committees; four spouse groups; judicatory officials; a peer group of "Spirit Women" (a group of women pastors); and the MELS Board. In addition, we read the annual reports of six peer groups and reviewed two partial histories and a DMin thesis on MELS.

The usual MELS pattern was for peer groups to gather themselves together (they were self-selecting) into groups of six to eight pastors. Peer groups were assigned a facilitator who would assist the group in deciding what they wanted to learn, developing plans for the learning, creating and submitting a proposal to the MELS Board, executing the plans, making applications of learnings in individual ministry practice, and evaluating at every step. Most of the groups ranged from three to six years in duration and met between ten and fifteen days per year, so they experienced a planned and sustained search for appropriate resources, experimentation in practice, and accountability in a lively community of conversation. The facilitator's role was an important aspect of the program; FCPs were responsible for holding the process (observing group dynamics and making interventions to help the group meet its goals), for managing conflict, and for asking critical questions at every point.

From what we heard in the interviews and read in the surveys, there is little doubt that the peer group process improved preaching in general as well as helped create new energy in pastoral leadership. One spouse said of her husband, "When he got involved [in MELS] it was like someone built a fire under him!"[37] A participant summed up many other perspectives saying, "I believe that MELS has been the most transformative educational experience of my life. Through my MELS experience, I have been forced to reexamine the foundations of myself, my ministry, and my future." Some of the judicatory level leaders were convinced that MELS had improved the preaching in the whole North Alabama Conference, and one person reported that lay committees were now making participation in MELS one of the criteria in reviewing possible pastoral appointments to their churches.

The basis for this kind of transformational learning may lie in the nature of adult learning surveyed earlier. When we asked MELS participants what had been most effective for their learning, we received two primary responses. First we heard, "My favorite and best instructors were the other folks in my group. We taught each other by interaction, honesty, critique, and love. They were by far my best teachers, the true experts."[38] Second, participants mentioned about six resource people in preaching who were considered to be excellent teachers primarily because of their style of teaching: "collegial, interactive, challenging, enthusiastic, upbeat, and passionate."[39] In his best-selling book, *Principle-Centered Leadership*, Stephen R. Covey says that learning can create tremendous energy when it includes the following elements: (1) determine what learning is needed, (2) expand on what has been learned, adding your own ideas, (3) find, review, and capture the essence of relevant material, (4) teach the material, sharing what has been learned, (4) apply the learnings in the context as an experiment, and (5) evaluate the results for further learning.[40]

The MELS peer group process not only embodied all of Covey's elements and did, indeed, create energy in both the participants and in the congregations they served, but it also embodied all of the characteristics noted in the material reviewed from adult education and the models cited above.[41] A facilitator helped create a *community of truth* in which pastors were invited to identify what learning was needed. The peer groups became, in effect, learning teams, which explored *mental models* with each other, supported experiments in the practice of ministry, and helped each other evaluate what was learned. The results of people working together in such learning communities were high energy and motivation that led to willingness to risk innovations and explorations—exactly the kind of leadership needed for the church in our time.

Notes

1. Loren B. Mead, *Transforming Congregations for the Future* (Herndon, VA: Alban Institute, 1994), ix.

2. Ibid., 119.

3. Edwin Friedman, *A Failure of Nerve: Leadership in the Age of the Quick Fix* (Bethesda, MD: The Edwin Friedman Estate/Trust, 1999), 38.

4. Ronald M. Cervero, "Professional Practice, Learning, and Continuing Education: An Integrated Perspective," *International Journal of Lifelong Education* 11, no. 2 (April–June 1992): 92–98.

5. Ibid., 98–99.

6. See Jean Piaget, *The Construction of Reality in the Child*, trans. Margaret Cook (New York: Basic Books, 1954), 354; and *Six Psychological Studies*, trans. Anita Tenzer (New York: Vintage Books, 1967), 103.

7. Peter M. Senge and others, *The Fifth Discipline Fieldbook* (New York: Doubleday Currency, 1994), 235.

8. Jean Piaget, *Science of Education and the Psychology of the Child*, trans. Derek Coltman (New York: Viking Press, 1970), 12.

9. Mary A. S. Pulaski, *Understanding Piaget: An Introduction to Children's Cognitive Development* (New York: Harper & Row, 1974), 200.

10. No attempt is made here to be inclusive of all theoretical sources that substantiate Piaget's approach to adult learning. Only a few have been selected that seem particularly relevant to peer learning research.

11. Patricia M. King and Karen Strohm Kitchener, *Developing Reflective Judgment* (San Francisco: Jossey-Bass, 1994), 15.

12. Parker Palmer, *The Courage to Teach: Exploring the Inner Landscape of a Teacher's Life* (San Francisco: Jossey-Bass, 1998), 95.

13. Ibid., 104.

14. Ibid., 103.

15. Malcolm Knowles, *The Modern Practice of Adult Education: Andragogy versus Pedagogy* (New York: Association Press, 1970).

16. Malcolm S. Knowles, *The Modern Practice of Adult Education: From Pedagogy to Andragogy*, rev. ed. (Chicago: Association Press, 1980), 59.

17. Leland P. Bradford, Jack R. Gibb, and Kenneth R. Benne, eds., *T-Group Theory and Laboratory Method: Innovation in Re-education* (New York: John Wiley & Sons, 1964), 18, 19.

18. Ronald M. Cervero, *Effective Continuing Education for Professionals* (San Francisco: Jossey-Bass, 1988), 56.

19. Peter M. Senge, *The Fifth Discipline: The Art and Practice of the Learning Organization* (New York: Doubleday Currency, 1990), 10.

20. Ibid., 237ff.

21. Ronald A. Heifetz and Marty Linsky, *Leadership on the Line: Staying Alive through the Dangers of Leading* (Boston: Harvard Business School Press, 2002), 13.

22. Ibid.

23. Senge, *Fifth Discipline*, 243.

24. Ibid., 246.

25. I first published this summary of Goleman, Boyatzis, and McKee's research regarding primal leadership in my article, "How Can Continuing Theological Education Serve the Church?" *Quarterly Review* 24, no. 2 (Summer 2004): 122–24.

26. Daniel Goleman, Richard Boyatzis, and Annie McKee, *Primal Leadership: Realizing the Power of Emotional Intelligence* (Boston: Harvard Business School Press, 2002), ix.

27. Ibid., 20.

28. Ibid., 6.

29. Ibid., 39, 253ff.

30. Ibid., 249.

31. Ibid., 251.

32. Ibid., 102.

33. Ibid., 103.

34. Ibid., 109.

35. Knowles, *Modern Practice of Adult Education: Andragogy versus Pedagogy*, 37–49.

36. Goleman, Boyatzis, and McKee, *Primal Leadership*, 111–12.

37. Robert E. Reber and D. Bruce Roberts, "Study of The Methodist Educational Leave Society" (Birmingham, AL: The Dixon Foundation, 1996), 31.

38. Ibid., 29.

39. Ibid., 30.

40. Stephen R. Covey, *Principle-Centered Leadership* (New York: Simon & Schuster, 1991), 71.

41. For more recent and corroborating peer learning studies and models, see other chapters in this volume: my chapter 8, "Energizing, Supporting, and Sustaining Religious Leaders through Peer Learning Groups," chapter 9, "Making Sense of Ministry: A Clergy Cluster Project" by Tim Dolan, and chapter 6, "Peer Groups Matter: The Impact of Leadership, Composition, and Cost" by Penny Long Marler.

Peer Groups Matter: The Impact of Leadership, Composition, and Cost

Penny Long Marler

Pastoral leaders gather for many reasons: for fellowship, denominational business, interfaith collaboration, community-based service and action, and continuing education, often in the form of
workshops, seminars, and conferences. Sometimes, however, clergy make longer-term commitments in smaller groups for more
intensive experiences of learning. Peer groups as a particularly
potent context and process for theological education have been
of special interest in the last several decades. Based on a survey
of more than two thousand pastoral leaders in such groups, this
chapter provides the first comprehensive look at their impact.
Peer group matters such as the role and function of leadership,
the extent of member diversity or curricular autonomy, and the
effects of cost are all examined. With some confidence, continuing educators in theological education can say that peer groups *do*
matter and, more, what types and in what way.

What We Already Know

Previous research on the effects of clergy peer group participation has been limited. A review of literature reveals fewer than

a dozen on the topic.[1] The number of groups studied has been small—ranging from one to fifteen. The most significant in terms of impact and attention to evaluation has been the work of Bruce Roberts and Tim Dolan, both discussed in this volume. Roberts's "Energizing, Supporting, and Sustaining Religious Leaders through Peer Learning Groups" (chapter 8) describes fifteen clergy peer learning groups in Indiana, and Dolan's "Making Sense of Ministry: A Clergy Cluster Project" (chapter 9) details the results of three clergy clusters in Spokane, Washington. Their findings are quite similar despite the fact that the Indiana group experience spanned three years, rather than four months; the Spokane clusters required financial resources of about five hundred dollars, rather than more than fifty thousand dollars; and the Indiana groups were self-selected and what they did was self-determined, rather than being assigned and sponsor delivered. Diversity was an important feature of both group experiences, particularly in that it created an environment of safety and accountability.

In 2007 a study of 25 clergy peer groups was initiated by the College of Pastoral Leaders (CPL) of Austin Presbyterian Theological Seminary, supported by the Lilly Endowment's Sustaining Pastoral Excellence (SPE) initiative. Focus groups were conducted, and then a survey created, to explore the characteristics of participation. Of 91 respondents, 62 percent were male, 85 percent were married, 67 percent were theologically liberal Protestant, and the average age was 50. The groups met about eight times a year for four hours per meeting. Up to twenty thousand dollars was made available for each group to support learning activities. As with the Indiana project, groups were self-selected and self-directed. Different from the Indiana and the Spokane experience, the CPL did not provide trained facilitators and diversity within the groups was not an intentional goal. In fact, the majority tended to be denominationally and racially homogeneous. Like Roberts and Dolan, the researchers found that clergy peer groups provided significant, positive impact on the spiritual life and day-to-day work of ministers.[2]

The results of the studies of clergy peer groups reported in this volume and the Austin study raise questions about the effects of diverse models for peer learning. *What difference does the type of group leadership make for members and their ministries? In particular, what is the impact of a trained facilitator? What are the effects if members determine who belongs to the group and what it does? What is the impact of diversity on groups and their members? What about costs to participants and their congregations? Does money make a difference?* This chapter explores the results of a survey of more than two thousand pastoral leaders involved in peer groups initiated by the SPE among thirty-two seminaries, judicatories, colleges or universities, counseling or retreat centers, and other church-related nonprofits. This large-scale study of clergy peer groups sheds light on these important questions.

Do Peer Groups Matter?

Funded by the Lilly Endowment, Austin Presbyterian Seminary's College of Pastoral Leaders initiated a national study of SPE peer groups in 2007.[3] SPE-funded organizations with ongoing small groups of pastoral leaders were identified. Project directors contributed contact information for participants, and Research Services, Presbyterian Church (USA) in Louisville, Kentucky, was contracted to disseminate the surveys in the spring of 2008. Surveys were developed based on (a) focus groups with SPE project directors who oversee peer group programs and (b) other national surveys of pastoral leaders, including the Faith Communities Today (FACT) and the U.S. Congregational Life Survey (USCLS).[4] The SPE Ministers and Other Pastoral Leaders Peer Group Study was comprehensive and included sections on peer group experience; work in ministry; ministry roles and expectations; beliefs, attitudes, and approach to faith; health and well-being; faith and ministry background; and personal background.[5] A total of 2,101 completed surveys were received from participants in SPE-related peer group programs; the response rate was 48 percent.

Characteristics of SPE Sponsoring Organizations

Thirty-two SPE sponsoring organizations with pastoral peer group programs were identified and 96 percent completed a survey on program structure, content, and administration.[6] The majority of sponsoring organizations are seminaries or divinity schools, judicatories, colleges or universities, or partnerships between judicatories and seminaries or colleges. The remainder are divided between conference or retreat centers, pastoral counseling agencies, and inter- or nondenominational agencies.

The denominational affiliation of sponsoring organizations is predominantly Protestant. The majority (32 percent) are from theologically moderate Protestant denominations including the American Baptist Convention, Cooperative Baptist Fellowship, United Methodist Church, Church of the Brethren, Reformed Church in America, and the Cumberland Presbyterian Church. Sixteen percent identify with more conservative theological traditions including Southern Baptist; Missionary Baptist; Church of God, Anderson; Church of God, Cleveland; and the Christian Reformed Church in North America. More theologically liberal Protestant organizations such as the Presbyterian Church (U.S.A.), the United Church of Christ, and the Christian Church (Disciples of Christ) make up 19 percent of sponsoring groups. A similar percentage of sponsor organizations are explicitly inter- or nondenominational. Thirteen percent of organizations sponsoring pastoral leader groups are Roman Catholic. From 2003 to 2008, these diverse sponsors reported starting 1,390 pastoral leader groups with more than 4,000 identified participants.

Sponsoring organizations primarily use a peer learning model that emphasizes group-directed approaches. Other models employed included group spiritual direction (10 percent said this approach best described their process) and pastoral education using a sponsor-delivered curriculum (13 percent selected this as their favored approach). Most organizations had been sponsoring peer group projects for five years, and they started about 25 groups

Figure 6.1. SPE Sponsoring Organization Types

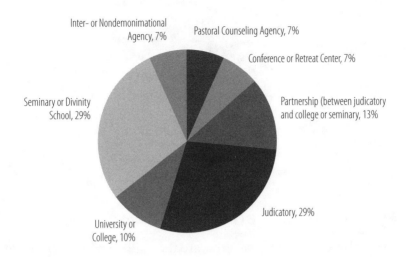

during that period. The median cost for the program in 2007 was $248,000; most sponsors reported two full-time employees, one program and one support staff person. Eighty-eight percent of program costs are covered by grants, including the generous Lilly-funded SPE initiative. More than half of the sponsoring organizations, however, report that their programs are "very likely" or "certain" to continue beyond the Endowment grant period.[7]

The great majority of SPE peer groups have designated leaders or facilitators, and two-thirds of sponsoring organizations provide training for them. Most offer twelve hours of initial training followed by ten hours of ongoing training and supervision per year. Indeed, when asked what ingredients are necessary for effective clergy peer groups, nearly half of sponsoring organizations listed "trained leaders or coaches" first, followed closely by the development of "trust and vulnerability" within groups. These qualities, in fact, are the principal reasons sponsors consider peer groups important for ongoing education in ministry. In fact, SPE project directors are nearly unanimous in their conviction that these groups make a positive impact on members, their congregations, and even the sponsoring organizations themselves.

Figure 6.2. Theological Orientation of SPE Group Participants

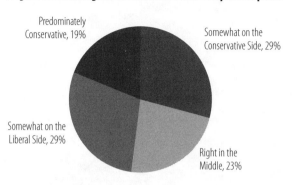

Characteristics of SPE Group Participants

What about participants? Who are they and what is their experience of SPE groups? Among the study sample, the majority are male (71 percent), white (87 percent), married (88 percent), and well educated (82 percent holding a master's degree or higher). They are predominantly middle-aged: 61 percent are aged 40–59, 29 percent are over 60, and only 10 percent are 20–39. A majority is Protestant (96 percent) and the remainder includes Roman Catholic, Eastern Orthodox, Jewish, and Baha'i, among others.

The Protestants in the study are denominationally diverse with the largest proportional representation from American Baptist Churches (14 percent), Presbyterian Church (U.S.A.) (11 percent), Christian Reformed Church in North America (11 percent), United Methodist Church (8 percent), Reformed Church in America (8 percent), United Church of Christ (6 percent), Church of God, Cleveland (5 percent), Cooperative Baptist Fellowship (4 percent), and Church of the Brethren (4 percent). The theological positions of study participants roughly reflect that of their denominations but with some nuance, given the divisions that have occurred within denominations since the 1950s.

The faith and ministry backgrounds of SPE participants reveal something about their formation and vocational journeys. While growing up, significantly more belonged to conservative Protestant churches, particularly smaller sects and the Southern Baptist Convention, and more were Roman Catholic.[8] Participants report that they were very active in church during their teenage years; 86 percent say that they attended church weekly, 62 percent say they were involved in youth activities regularly, and 65 percent say they had a leadership role. A majority of the congregations that nurtured them both "encouraged a call to ministry" and "invited serious questions." Only a third of those churches "confronted issues of justice" or "included others who were different." The most significant sources of influence in their vocational discernment process were "a clear sign or message from God," "positive experiences with church leadership," and "counsel from your pastor or other minister."

Two-thirds of SPE group participants are senior or solo pastors, priests, or ministers; the remainder is mostly made up of associate ministers, pastoral counselors or chaplains, and judicatory-related clergy. Two percent are lay ministers or pastoral leaders. A great majority report that they have taken part in continuing education events at least once in the past year and nearly half have done so three or more times. More than 80 percent say their congregation or ministry organization provides financial support for their continuing education, and a little over a third reports that their congregation or judicatory requires it. One-quarter of participants say that they have taken a sabbatical leave in the past ten years, and the median length of leaves is ten weeks.

According to SPE participants, most of their groups have met nine times a year for three hours per meeting over the course of two years. Their attendance has been very strong: 60 percent say they have attended "all meetings" and 37 percent a "majority of meetings." In addition, about half report they have participated in e-mail discussions or conference calls as a part of the group process. Eighty-seven percent say their groups had a designated leader or facilitator, and more than half of these report that the leader was their "reason to stay" in the group. Two-thirds of participants also say that their group had a formal covenant or written group guidelines.

The most prevalent SPE group practices balance the needs of ministers for a place where (and peers with whom) personal

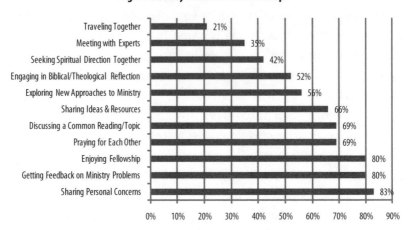

Figure 6.3. Key Practices of SPE Groups

concerns are shared, feedback about ministry challenges is exchanged, and fellowship enjoyed. Other group practices reported frequently include praying for each other, discussing a common reading or topic, and sharing ideas and resources for more effective ministry. About half of participants are involved in group practices that focus on innovation and deeper reflection such as exploring an interesting subject or a new approach to ministry together or engaging in intentional biblical or theological reflection. Forty-two percent of participants report "seeking spiritual direction together" as a key group activity. Finally, about a third of group participants say that meeting with experts in common fields of interest is important and a quarter cite traveling together as a key practice.

In response to a series of items about group dynamics over time, two-thirds or more say that the following characteristics were present throughout their group experience: they got the feeling that they were really being heard, the facilitator or other leader was a good fit for the group, constructive criticism was welcome, and they could say anything without fear of harsh judgment. Twenty percent, however, did report that "constructive criticism" and "saying anything without fear of harsh judgment" developed only later in their group process. Not surprising, "people put on their best face" at the start of many groups (45 percent), and the groups tended to gel later (34 percent). Reflecting both the hectic schedules of clergy and their commitment to these groups, 27 percent report that "some group members showed up late or left early" throughout the life of the group.

What the majority agreed were *not* characteristics of their group *at any time* included that "people talk to the leader rather than to each other," "there is significant conflict," and "there is competition for leadership." Twenty-one percent admitted that "one or two strong personalities dominated" at the beginning of the group. All of which are a tribute to the quality of facilitators and leaders in this sample and consistent with the feedback from sponsoring organizations.

Most participants in peer groups report good to excellent health, and more than half report that they have felt "calm and peaceful," "had a lot of energy," and "been happy" most or all of the time. About 80 percent say they are "satisfied" or "very satisfied" with their overall effectiveness as a pastoral leader, their spiritual life, their family life, and their relationships with work colleagues. The majority report that people in their congregation or ministry organization have made them feel loved and cared for, told them they prayed for them, and publicly praised some aspect of their ministry in the past three years. More than half say they have never doubted that they were called by God to the ministry or thought of leaving pastoral ministry in the past year. In spite of this emotional strength, work satisfaction, and congregational support, the majority admit that they experience stress because of the challenges they face in their current position, experience stress as a result of dealing with people who are critical of their work, and have felt lonely or isolated in their work.

Overall, participants expressed a high level of satisfaction with their SPE group in the last year that it met. The majority report that their congregations, work colleagues, and family have been "somewhat" or "very positively" affected by their involvement. In fact, when participants were asked to compare their SPE experience with that of other peer groups they have participated in during the past ten years, more than half rated the SPE group as "better"

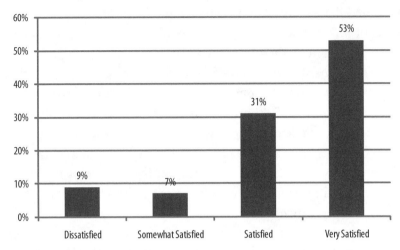

Figure 6.4. Level of Satisfaction in the Last Year Group Met

or "much better" in terms of positive ministry impact, spiritual growth, creativity, intellectual challenge, personal guidance and support, and group leadership.

As in previous studies, therefore, the majority of SPE participants report that their pastoral leader groups provide safety and accountability and renew their commitment to ministry. They also report high levels of satisfaction that increased over the course of their group life and positive impact on their congregations and families. Beyond previous studies, this research provides additional information about clergy backgrounds, health and emotional well-being, group dynamics, and comparison between SPE groups and others. Most important, however, the survey reveals the extent of variation in structure, content, and practice among clergy peer groups.

What about Peer Groups Matters?

The data from the SPE peer group survey provide a new and unique opportunity to examine differential effects related to group leadership, composition, and cost. What the researchers explored, first, were characteristics related to (a) peer groups led by trained facilitators, (b) peer groups that choose their members and decide what they do, (c) denominational and racial and ethnic diversity among peer group members, and (d) participant and congregation contributions toward peer group cost.[9] Second, we examined those factors that matter most, in other words, those factors that directly affect involvement in these types of peer groups. Third, and finally, we explored whether peer group leadership, composition, or cost matter more (or less) for positive ministry impact.

What Difference Does a Trained Facilitator Make?

More than 80 percent of SPE participants say that their group had a designated leader or facilitator. The figure below displays their responses to descriptions that best fit their group leader's preparation and role. The majority report that their leader is a "minister peer" with special training for group leadership; about a third, that their leader is a "trained group facilitator"; and close to a quarter that the leader is a member selected by the group. Less frequent are denominational ministers with responsibility for group leadership or credentialed professionals such as a pastoral counselor or spiritual director. A number of respondents indicate that more than one of these descriptions best fit their leader. Analysis of the data shows that peer group rhythms, types, satisfaction, and impact vary depending upon whether group leaders are trained facilitators.[10]

SPE participants in groups with trained facilitators are more likely to be theologically conservative and are less well educated than those in groups with no designated leader or a member leader who is not a trained facilitator. Participants in peer groups without trained facilitators tend to be theologically liberal; most hold a master's degree and many have earned doctorates. Those without trained facilitators also tend to be significantly younger, and they are more likely to report high levels of church involvement during their teenage years in a congregation that "invites serious questions."

Pastoral leaders in SPE groups with trained facilitators are more likely to report that they joined the group because of denominational encouragement, they are impressed by the leader, they trust the sponsoring organization, and they need an account-ability group. On the other hand, those in groups without trained facilitators are more likely to join because a close friend encouraged them. Those without trained facilitators are more likely to join because they need "a break from their day-to-day routine" and because "travel opportunities are appealing."

Participants in peer groups with trained facilitators report that they meet less often and for shorter periods. Those without trained facilitators are more likely to say that their groups are smaller; also, conference calls or e-mail discussions are a part of their group process. Those with trained facilitators are more likely to report that their meetings are "structured and predictable," a "sponsoring organization provides curriculum," the group is composed of "people who are very different from each other," and there is a "clearly recognized leader in the group." Those in groups without trained facilitators, on the other hand, say that their meetings are spontaneous, they are "made up of people who are very similar to each other," and "leadership is shared." The key practices that differentiate them from trained facilitator groups are enjoying fellowship (including eating, drinking, laughing, and talking casually) and traveling together.

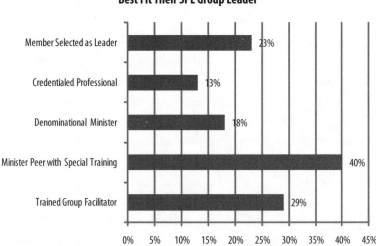

Figure 6.5. Percent of Participants Reporting the Role(s) that Best Fit Their SPE Group Leader

SPE participants in groups led by trained facilitators are more likely to report engaging in spiritual disciplines, action and reflection, and "sharing ideas and resources for more effective ministry."[11] The range of activity focused specifically on ministry action and enrichment is reflected in the fact that participants report that their group involvement has made a positive impact on their congregations, families, and friends.[12] Focus on spiritual practices also is reflected in greater satisfaction with members' spiritual lives.

Participants in groups with trained facilitators are significantly more likely to report that their group provides safety, accountability, spiritual refreshment, and greater creativity and empathy.[13] Pastoral leaders in groups with trained facilitators have longer tenures in their congregations. They also report that their churches provide more intense, intimate experiences with God as well as hold and teach strong beliefs and moral values. They are more likely to spend time in recruitment and evangelism, and their churches tend to emphasize Bible study, evangelism, and spiritual development. They also are more likely to say that people at their church have "taken notice or affirmed their participation in an SPE clergy peer group."

By contrast, pastoral leaders in groups without trained facilitators are significantly more likely to say that their group has "a lot of fun." Tenures in their current pastoral role are shorter. Their congregations have significantly more staff support, they are more likely to take a day off every week, and their congregations are more likely to provide funds for continuing education. Nevertheless, they report "stress experienced because of the challenges of their position" during the past year with greater frequency. Indeed, clergy in peer groups without trained facilitators are significantly less likely than participants from trained facilitator groups to have taken a sabbatical in the past ten years. Finally, they are more likely to report that in the past year they have "doubt[ed] they have been called by God to the ministry."

Participants in groups with trained facilitators, however, were not more likely to have congregations that were growing or to experience less overall congregational conflict. Neither type of group is more or less likely to report better physical or emotional health and well-being. Neither type of group is more or less likely to report satisfaction with their peer group experience. Participants in trained facilitator groups, however, are more likely to say that their satisfaction increased over time whereas those without trained facilitators are more likely to say their satisfaction decreased. Differences in leadership appear to reflect more instrumental versus relational needs among participants. Members in peer groups with trained facilitators are interested in leadership, content, and practices specifically structured to help them in their day-to-day ministry. Those who participate in groups without trained facilitators are more interested in collegiality, conversation, good humor, and a break in the routine of ministry, whether through regular group meetings or traveling together.

Among the range of characteristics and effects explored here, which ones directly affect participation in a trained facilitator peer group?[14] The results of multivariate analysis reveal that the theological orientation and education level of the group members don't matter very much. These are, instead, indirect effects mediated by other factors—so while the relationships may be present, at least in our model, they are not causative. Bottom line, pastoral leaders join an SPE peer group with a trained facilitator because it provides *accountability* and *not intellectual challenge*. They also are attracted because the *quality of the leadership* impressed them. Other group factors that are required for involvement in this kind of peer group include: that a *sponsor organization provides a curriculum, meetings are structured,* and the group has *a recognized leader.* Practices that are determinative include *sharing ministry concerns, ideas, and resources* and *engaging in action and reflection.* Of interest is that SPE groups led by trained facilitators focus learning and action close to home rather than traveling together. That *participants' congregations are older* and *don't provide funds for continuing education* also determine participation. Finally, *satisfaction with one's spiritual life* is required for ongoing participation in a SPE peer group with a trained facilitator.

What Difference Does Self-Determination Make?

SPE participants were asked whether "members make decisions about who belongs" to the group and whether "members make decisions about what the group does." More than 60 percent of participants report that members are selected by the group itself; however, 90 percent say that members make decisions about what the group does. Nearly a third of participants participated in groups whose members were recruited or assigned but who nevertheless made decisions about group content and process. To make the sharpest possible contrast, we measured the impact of groups who, like those in the Indiana and Austin studies, are self-determined both in membership and activities.[15]

Participants in self-determined peer groups are significantly more likely than those in groups assigned by a sponsor to be theologically liberal and better educated. Participants in self-determined peer groups are principally motivated to join because a close friend influenced them and they need an accountability group. Participants in sponsor-directed groups, on the other hand, more likely join because they know and trust the sponsoring organization and they were impressed by the leader. Participants in self-determined peer groups are also less likely to say that they joined because "the travel opportunities were appealing," although they are more likely to say that "traveling together" was a key practice.

Pastoral leaders in self-determined peer groups participate longer and meet more often, yet for significantly less time per meeting. They report that their peer groups are smaller. They knew more of the members before the group and they socialize with more members outside the group. They also are more likely to report that group members are "similar," the group feels "like a family," and "leadership is shared." Like peer groups without trained facilitators, group composition is more homogeneous. It follows, then, that participants in self-determined peer groups are more likely to say that key practices include "enjoying fellowship." They are significantly less likely to report engaging in spiritual disciplines than are those in sponsor-directed groups.

SPE participants in self-determined groups do not differ significantly from those in sponsor-directed groups in terms of the length of tenure in their congregations, staff size, congregational support for continuing education, and overall church conflict. Participants in self-determined groups are, however, significantly more likely to be in declining congregations and less likely to have taken a sabbatical in the past ten years. One wonders if the collegial support of a circle of friends with shared struggles in their congregations is a kind of proxy. Indeed, participants are much more likely to report that their peer group is a model of what community should be and that it is a place where members can say anything, criticism is welcome, egos are "checked at the door," and people are "really being heard."

Pastoral leaders in self-determined groups are no more or less likely than those in sponsor-directed groups to report positive ministry impact. Nevertheless, those in self-determined peer groups say that people in their congregations express significantly fewer concerns about "new directions or changes." Further, participants in self-determined groups say they are more satisfied with their salaries and benefits, and they are more likely to report that peer group participation renews their commitment to ministry. Finally, they are significantly more likely to report that their group "allows for frank disagreement," is "safe" and "a lot of fun," and is "something [they will] need for years to come."

Among these characteristics, what matters most for participation in the self-determined peer group?[16] Based on multivariate analysis, particular reasons for joining don't appear to matter either way and neither does the theological orientation nor the educational background of the member. What matters is the structure and activity of the group itself. Involvement in an SPE peer group that chooses its members and curriculum is primarily determined by (1) *group longevity* and *meeting brevity* (a longer group life and shorter group meetings), (2) *intimacy* and *familiarity* (smaller groups with members who knew each other before), (3) *shared leadership* and *curricular autonomy*, and (4) *travel together*. Another characteristic that significantly predicts involvement in a self-determined peer group is the fact that participants *haven't had a sabbatical* in the past ten years. One gets a picture of a clergyperson with fewer instrumental concerns related to his or her ministry position and greater relational needs. Absent more formal breaks from routines like a sabbatical, there is the temporary refuge of the self-determined peer group.

What Difference Does Diversity Make?

SPE participants report variations in the denominational and racial and ethnic composition of their peer groups. Close to a quarter say that their peer group includes both people of different denominations and people of different races or ethnicities. A similar percentage reports that their SPE peer group is made up of people from the same denomination, although the group has racial or ethnic diversity. The smallest proportion (15 percent) of participants reports that their peer group is composed of one race or ethnicity, although the group is denominationally diverse. Finally, the largest percentage is SPE participants who report neither denominational nor racial and ethnic diversity: 40 percent of groups are homogeneous. We were, again, interested in the sharpest contrast and we therefore created a scale that measures peer

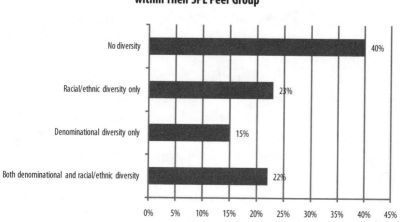

Figure 6.6. Percent of Participants Reporting Diversity within Their SPE Peer Group

group diversity from no diversity to denominational and racial and ethnic diversity.[17]

SPE participants in groups with greater diversity are more likely to be older and female. In many U.S. denominations, gender is experienced as an important kind of diversity. So it is not surprising that female clergy are significantly more likely to participate in peer groups that are also diverse in other ways. On the other hand, theology and education do not differentiate participants on the basis of the reported diversity in their SPE peer groups.

Of interest is that participants in peer groups with less diversity tended to be more active in church as a teenager; on the other hand, participants in peer groups with more diversity say they were significantly less active. This, of course, raises a question about the relationship between the intensity of early religious socialization, a particular kind of culture of similarity, and the continued impact on a minister's experience with, opportunities for, and openness to others who are different.

Denominational encouragement to join tends to discourage would-be participants in more diverse peer groups. SPE participants in more diverse groups, however, are significantly more likely to say they joined because "a close friend influenced me," they "felt stuck in their ministry," the "subject matter was important" to them, and they desired an "intellectual challenge." They also are more likely than those in groups with little or no diversity to say they joined because they were impressed by the leader.

Participants in peer groups with more diversity have been meeting together longer, their meetings last longer, and conference calls and e-mails are a part of their group process. Theirs is high-contact involvement. They also are significantly more likely to report that a "sponsor organization provides curriculum" and that "there is a clearly recognized leader." The diverse peer group also is larger, has retained more of its original members, and includes more members that did not know each other before. The key practices that significantly differentiate participants in more diverse groups from those that are less diverse include practicing spiritual disciplines and engaging in action and reflection.

SPE participants in peer groups that are more diverse have been in their current congregations or ministry organizations longer. They also spend significantly more of their time in evangelism and recruitment than participants in less diverse groups. Not surprising is that their congregations are more likely to be growing. Their significantly younger congregations are less likely to provide funds for continuing education. In addition, those in peer groups that are diverse are more likely to report that their congregations are "engaged and energized by serious study of Scripture and theology" and "hold and teach strong beliefs and moral values." Diversity here is not related to relativistic values and beliefs—just the opposite.

SPE participants in groups with greater diversity are more likely to say that their involvement has a positive impact on their congregations, families, and friends. They also are more likely to say that participation in their peer group "allows for frank disagreement," "is a lot of fun," and is "something I will need for years to come." They say that their group provides safety, accountability, and spiritual refreshment.

As compared to less diverse SPE groups, these participants report greater creativity and empathy. Involvement in more diverse peer groups also is associated with better health and greater satisfaction with one's spiritual life. On the other hand, SPE participants in diverse peer groups tend to be less satisfied with their salaries and benefits and the support they receive from their denomination.

But what matters most for involvement in a SPE peer group composed of people who are diverse denominationally, racially, and ethnically?[18] Interesting to note is that the results of multivariate analysis show that neither gender nor theology matter. That there is *little denominational pressure to join*, however, is paramount, as is *anonymity*. What also directly affects participation in a peer group with greater diversity are *a recognized leader* and a *sponsor-delivered curriculum*. What members share are the subject matter and leadership, perhaps including the leadership of the Spirit, rather than denominational, racial, or ethnic cultures. Indeed, determinative group practices are focused on *spiritual disciplines.* Participation in more diverse SPE peer groups also is associated with ministering in a *younger congregation* that may be less encumbered by a particular denominational and subcultural identity. Finally, involvement is directly affected by the *extent to which peer group participation is perceived as contributing to a member's commitment to and energy for ministry.*

What Difference Does Money Make?

Participants were asked to record their own personal annual average contribution toward SPE peer group involvement as well as that of their congregation or ministry organization. About half of participants and congregations made no contributions toward this activity. About a third of participants and congregations contributed up to five hundred dollars, and close to a tenth of participants contributed more. However, nearly a quarter of participants' congregations or ministry organizations contributions exceeded five hundred dollars, with 13 percent contributing more than one thousand dollars annually. Correlations between those who contribute more to the cost of their peer group and those who contribute less, examined below, combine both the personal contributions and the congregational contributions for SPE participants.

Participants and congregations that contribute more to the cost of SPE peer group involvement did not differ significantly in theology, age, or gender from those who contribute less. Those who contribute more, however, tend to be better educated. Further, those who contribute more tend to report that they joined the group because "a close friend influenced me," the "travel opportunities were appealing," and "I felt stuck in my ministry." SPE participants who contribute less, on the other hand, tend to say they joined because of denominational encouragement.

SPE participants that contribute more did not differ significantly from those that contributed less in terms of the length of the group's life or the number of times that it met. However, those

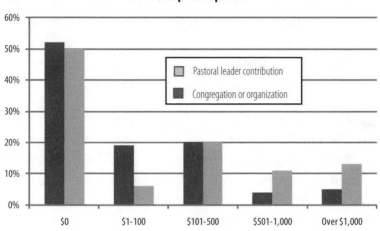

Figure 6.7 Annual Average Contributions toward SPE Group Participation

who contributed more did report that their meetings are longer and conference calls and e-mails are part of their group process. A more bang-for-the-buck effect? In addition, participants who contribute to the cost are significantly more likely to report a higher degree of diversity within their group. Participants that contribute more, however, did not differ significantly from those who contributed less on characteristics of group leadership.

SPE participants that contributed more to the cost have larger peer groups, increasing the total funds available for group activities and decreasing the per capita expenditures. They are significantly more likely than participants who contributed less to practice spiritual disciplines and travel together. Those that contribute more also are more likely to practice action and reflection. Finally, participants that contribute more tend to report that their congregations "take notice and affirm their participation in an SPE peer group."

Significant is that participants who contribute more to the cost said that their SPE peer group involvement had a stronger positive impact on their churches, families, and friends. They also report more satisfaction with their peer group over time. Participants who contributed more say that their peer group provided spiritual refreshment and helped them to feel closer to God. Compared to those who contributed less, they say that peer group involvement increased their creativity and empathy.

The Effects of Leadership, Composition, and Cost

Perhaps the best way to measure what really matters in relation to types of groups and what congregations and participants are willing to contribute is to predict an anticipated outcome of SPE peer group involvement. For example, to ask what characteristics affect the extent to which group involvement positively influences participants' relationships with those they minister to (and work with) on a day-to-day basis, their spouses, intimate friends, and children. Further, to gauge the effects of peer group leadership, composition, and cost on this important outcome, it is necessary to include types of groups and total contributions in the analysis.[19]

What matters most for participants who report that their SPE peer group involvement resulted in positive impact? The results of our analysis are clear. Motivations for joining a peer group don't matter. Neither the rhythm of peer group life nor its size matters. The particular characteristics of participants' congregations don't matter. What matters most is (1) *diversity among peer group members*, (2) *contribution toward group costs*, (3) *satisfaction with their spiritual lives*, and (4) *conviction that peer group participation renews their commitment to and energy for ministry* and *provides spiritual refreshment*.

Participation in SPE peer groups with trained facilitators or in groups that were self-determined did not predict positive ministry impact. This is not very surprising for self-determined groups; no significant relationship was found between this type of group and positive impact. Recall from the analysis above, however, that positive ministry impact was significantly associated with participation in peer groups led by trained facilitators although not

Figure 6.8. Characteristics that Matter Most by Group Type

Peer Groups with Trained Facilitators	Self-Determined Peer Groups	Peer Groups Composed of Diverse Members
Members desire accountability (not intellectual challenge)	Members desire intimacy & familiarity (focus on relational needs)	Members desire anonymity (denominational encouragement is a negative)
There is a recognized leader of high quality	Leadership is shared	There is a recognized leader
A sponsor organization provides curriculum & meetings are structured	There is curricular autonomy	A sponsor organization provides curriculum
Practices are diverse & focused on instrumental needs	A key practice is traveling together	Practices focus on spiritual disciplines
Members are satisfied with their spiritual lives	Members need a sabbath break	Group involvement renews members' commitment to and energy for ministry

predictive. To the extent that trained facilitator groups are related to positive impact, this effect is indirect and likely mediated by other characteristics such as peer group diversity or participants' satisfaction with their spiritual lives. The same is true of other participant, group, and congregational characteristics that are related but not causal: they reflect patterns of association between characteristics but do not indicate whether those effects are direct or indirect.

Conclusions

The results of surveys of SPE project directors and pastoral leaders involved in peer groups reveal a strong, positive picture of group practice, member commitment, and ministry outcomes. The comprehensive nature of the survey in addition to the size of the sample, moreover, provides an unprecedented opportunity to explore the differential effects of peer group leadership, composition, structure, and outcomes. The results are summarized in the figure above.

Participants in peer groups with trained facilitators are primarily interested in an accountability group. Group participation is positively influenced by denominational encouragement and trust in the sponsor organization. Involvement in such groups is motivated by instrumental more than relational needs. Members are involved in group practices focused on ministry-related learning with highly skilled and trusted leaders. A sponsor-delivered curriculum is important as well as a dependable meeting structure. Participants in such groups tend to serve in older, well-established congregations without particularly strong traditions of (or policies for) promoting clergy development. Involvement in a peer group with a trained facilitator also requires, allows for, and reinforces satisfaction in the member's own spiritual life.

Participants in self-determined clergy peer groups desire the intimacy and familiarity of a smaller circle of known friends. These groups tend to be denominationally, racially, and ethnically homogeneous. Different from the trained facilitator group, those involved in self-determined groups appear interested in the group more for its own sake rather than for the practical wisdom that it can deliver. Enjoying fellowship and traveling together are key practices. The group's life tends to be longer, curricular autonomy is especially valued, and shared leadership is required. Lacking time, support, or opportunities for more formal breaks in their routine such as sabbath or study leaves, these pastoral leaders repair to their clergy peer group.

Different from participants in self-determined groups, those involved in peer groups with greater diversity are attracted by its relative anonymity. Similar to trained facilitator groups, those composed of diverse members prefer a recognized leader and a sponsor-delivered curriculum, although for sociological reasons rather than instrumental ones. Their social glue is a well-defined structure, process, or novel content rather than a common denominational, racial, or ethnic subculture. The kinds of structured process and leveling content that group spiritual direction provides, in fact, may be just the ticket. Those involved in peer groups with diverse members also tend to serve younger, growing congregations. Thus, content focused on new ministry knowledge and skills may seem less urgent. What is clear, however, is that spiritual depth leverages ministry strength. A strong effect of participation in a diverse peer group is a renewed sense of commitment to and energy for ministry. Further, as demonstrated above, involvement in heterogeneous peer groups directly and positively affect members' congregations, families, and friends.

Finally, the contributions of participants and congregations toward peer group cost are a potentially powerful double investment. They appear to increase member commitment and congregational impact across model types. Along with peer group diversity, in fact, the contributions of participants and congregations strongly predict positive impact. This reflects a truism in program delivery; namely, that contributing to the cost both reflects and shapes other forms of investment, including time, energy, and attention.

The typology is helpful for understanding a particular kind of peer group. But it may be especially useful for interpreting mixed types. For not all self-determined SPE groups lack trained facilitators, and not all sponsor-directed SPE groups have trained facilitators. In a similar way, not all diverse or heterogeneous groups have trained facilitators and not all self-determined groups are homogeneous. As in the Indiana study, when a peer group is led by a trained facilitator and also is self-determined, the probability is that participants will express and experience characteristics associated with both models. When the trained facilitator group is self-determined and also heterogeneous, an especially powerful combination of effects is possible. Nevertheless, trained facilitator-led groups with a prescribed process that includes self-determination may have difficulty meeting the requirement of anonymity. This might explain the fact that diversity is hard to achieve in such groups.

The Spokane clergy clusters delivered effects very similar to the Indiana groups, although with fewer meetings over a shorter period of time. The fact that these groups represent rather pure trained-facilitator types with the added features of intentional diversity and relatively high contributions toward cost, however, makes their success more understandable.

The Austin peer groups were self-determined and had few designated leaders. Self-selection, as expected, led to primarily homogeneous groups. In one of a few exceptional cases, a self-determined peer group was composed of male clergy in one small Texas community. Their denominational diversity provided some degree of freedom outside their denominational silos; the glue for the group was (in their words) the difficulty of working with townspeople traditionally considered to be "mean." For this peer group, the advantages of diversity plus self-determination resulted in powerful outcomes. To fellowship, friendship, and travel were added leveling spiritual experiences such as a group communion by the Aegean Sea led by two erstwhile "strangers," a Church of Christ and a Pentecostal minister. The result was not only renewal of members' ministries but also renewal in a Texas community.

In conclusion, this analysis provides diagnostic and prescriptive characteristics that are useful for both forming new clergy groups and reinvigorating existing ones. What the surveys of SPE project directors and participants in pastoral leader groups do not provide are answers to whether and how clergy in peer groups differ from clergy who are not. As described above, the SPE Clergy Peer Study includes participation in two national pastoral leader surveys. The results of that research will be of inestimable worth in evaluating the importance of peer learning for continuing education in ministry. The current findings are clear: over two thousand participants report that peer groups do matter and our analysis shows how and why. Those concerned with lifelong education in ministry will do well to consider the value of creating and sustaining peer group endeavors within their institutions.

Notes

1. E. W. Mills, *Peer Groups and Professional Development: Evaluation Report of the Young Pastors' Pilot Project* (Nashville: Division of the Ordained Ministry, United Methodist Board of Higher Education and Ministry, 1973); J. P. Phillipi, "Use of Peer Support Groups to Enhance Clergy Self-Esteem" (DMin thesis, Lancaster Theological Seminary, 1985); M. Weidner, "Sabbath Living for Sabbath Leaders: Clergy Renewal by Peer Groups" (DMin thesis, United Theological Seminary, 1995); W. E. Kelly, "Developing a Peer Self-Help Group Focusing on the Role-Related Stress among Clergy of the Jersey City District, New Jersey Annual Conference, African Methodist Episcopal Zion Church" (unpublished doctor of ministry thesis, Hebrew Union College, 1997); D. Bruce Roberts, "Motivated Learning and Practice: A Peer Group Model," in *A Lifelong Call to Learn: Approaches to Continuing Education for Church Leaders*, eds. Robert Reber and D. Bruce Roberts (Nashville: Abingdon, 2000), 105–119; R. Bott, "Collegial Caring: The Effect of Peer Supervision Groups on the Stress of Ministry Personnel in the United Church of Canada" (DMin thesis, Ashland Theological Seminary, 2003); T. C. Young, "A Multi-Case Study of the Learning Cluster as Holding Environment for Clergy Leaders" (PhD diss., Gonzaga University, 2004); T. Dolan, "A Multi-Case Study of the Experience of Pastors in a Leadership Learning Cluster" (PhD diss., Gonzaga University, 2004); C. A. Sowle, "From Experience to Learning: Using Peer Groups and Theological Reflection as a Model for Providing Support to Ministers" (master's thesis, Saint Mary-of-the-Woods College, 2006); D. Bruce Roberts and Robert Reber, "Indiana Clergy Peer Group Study Program: Final Report and Evaluation" (report, Christian Theological Seminary, 2007).

2. "Theological Depth, Creativity, and Ministry Impact among Clergy Peer Group Participants," *Review of Religious Research* 49, no. 4 (2006).

3. Janet Maykus of Austin Presbyterian Theological Seminary and Penny Long Marler of Samford University are the coprincipal investigators of the SPE Clergy Peer Study. Robert Reber and D. Bruce Roberts serve as study consultants.

4. Surveys were distributed twice from late January through early May 2008 with at least two postcard or e-mail reminders to nonrespondents; participants also had the opportunity to complete the survey online if they so chose.

5. The Sustaining Pastoral Excellence (SPE) Initiative Survey of Participants in Groups for Ministers and Other Pastoral Leaders is available online at www.austinseminary.edu/cpl. The survey instrument was developed by Penny Marler, Janet Maykus, Bruce Roberts, and Robert Reber and analyzed by the principal researcher Penny Marler.

6. The Sustaining Pastoral Excellence (SPE) Initiative Survey of Participant Project Directors is available online at www.austinseminary.edu/cpl.

7. The survey responses quoted in this chapter are taken from "The Sustaining Pastoral Excellence Survey of Ministers and Other Pastoral Leaders Peer Group Study."

8. This reflects a pattern of religious upward mobility typical in the twentieth century that in more recent years has diminished due to rising access to and higher levels of education and the increasing visibility and political clout of more conservative religious groups. The predominantly middle-aged to older sample in this study echoes earlier trends.

9. The relationships (Pearson's correlation) between trained facilitator groups, self-determined groups, heterogeneous groups, and group cost and a variety of participant, congregation, and peer group characteristics discussed in this chapter are all statistically significant (p<.05). Tables are available from the author.

10. "Trained Facilitator" was measured by means of a scale computed so that 0 = no designated leader or member leader only; 1 = other kind of leaders *except* member leader only or trained facilitator in any kind of array; 2 = trained facilitator only or in combination with other types.

11. Practices were measured by computing two additive scales. The Spiritual Disciplines scale includes "praying for each other," "seeking spiritual direction together," and "participating in silence or meditation" (Alpha = .515) and the Action/Reflection scale includes "expressing spirituality through art, music, literature, or drama," "engaging in community service or mission activities," "utilizing case studies to improve pastoral skills," and "meeting with experts in fields of common interest" (Alpha = .590).

12. "Positive Impact" was measured by adding responses to the question, "To what extent have the following persons or groups been affected by your involvement in an SPE group?" Responses included "your work colleagues or staff," "your intimate friends," "those you minister to on a day-to-day basis," "if you are married, your spouse," and "if you are a parent, your children" (Alpha = .826).

13. "Creativity and Empathy" was measured by a scale that computes the responses to "To what extent do you agree or disagree that your SPE group . . . ?" Responses included "helps you to see the world differently," "exposes you to fresh ideas," "stretches you," "fosters openness and empathy toward people who are different," and "makes you a better listener" (Alpha = .760).

14. A least-squares regression model was created and conducted that included variables expected to predict participation in peer groups led by trained facilitators (R^2 = .335). The model included control variables (gender, education, age, and theological orientation); motivation variables (reasons for joining, including a close friend, accountability, and denominational encouragement among others); group characteristics (group tenure, meetings per year, hours per meeting, number in group, and so forth); group structure and practice (group identity items and group practice scales); congregation or min-

istry organization characteristics (age of congregation, financial support for continuing education, sabbatical leaves, congregational identity items, and so forth); and outcome variables (physical and emotional health measures, congregational growth, congregational conflict, and scales related to group-related outcomes both personal and ministry related). Table is available from the author.

15. "Self-Determined" groups were measured by means of a scale computed so that 0 = no self-determination (members neither decide who belongs nor what the group does); 1 = some self-determination (members either decide who belongs or what the group does); and 2 = pure self-determination (members both decide who belongs and what the group does).

16. A least-squares regression model was created and conducted that included variables expected to predict participation in self-determined peer groups (R^2 = .355). For model characteristics, see note 13 above. Table is available from the author.

17. "Denominationally, racially, and ethnically diverse" groups were measured by means of a scale computed so that 0 = no diversity (group neither includes people of different denominations nor different races or ethnicities); 1 = some diversity (group either includes people of different denominations or different races or ethnicities); and 2 = pure diversity (group includes people of different denominations and different races or ethnicities).

18. A least-squares regression model was created and conducted that included variables expected to predict participation in more diverse peer groups (R^2 = .206). For model characteristics, see note 14 above. Table is available from the author.

19. A least-squares regression model was created and conducted that included variables expected to predict positive impact (R^2 = .374). Table is available from the author. See Positive Impact scale description above, note 12. For model characteristics, see note 14 above. *Note: the model for this analysis substitutes the trained facilitator, self-determined, diversity, and cost measures for items in the group structure step that measured leadership, heterogeneity, cohesion, and structure, which served as proxies for hypothesized dynamics of the peer group types in the earlier regressions.*

CHAPTER 7

What Constitutes Effective Teaching with Adults?

D. Bruce Roberts

> So they took him and brought him before the Court of Areopagus [or
> to the middle of Mars Hill] and said, "May we know what this new
> doctrine is that you propound? You are introducing ideas that sound
> strange to us, and we should like to know what they mean."
>
> —*Acts 17:19–20, New English Bible*

Standing on Mars Hill with the Parthenon-crowned Acropolis
towering on the right and the ruins of the ancient Athenian market place below, one can imagine the wonderful setting for the
powerful teaching moment Paul enjoyed, described in this passage from Acts. The actions of Paul leading up to this dramatic
moment help define teaching. Teaching is not only what happens
on Mars Hill, teaching is also the activity that develops a climate of
inquiry and curiosity in which people want to learn and in which
they ask, "What are these ideas? We want to know."[1]

This dictionary definition of *teaching* informs the discussion: "Teach; teaching . . . 1a: to cause to know a subject, b: to
cause to know how . . . 2: to guide the studies of, 3: to impart
the knowledge of."[2] The definition most associated with our subject is the third definition concerned with imparting knowledge;
this is certainly an important aspect of the practice. However, the

first meaning suggested is the intriguing notion that teaching is "to cause to know." In this definition, teaching is helping a person know something, the process of helping another learn. In a 2008 audio recording "The Power of Presence," Peter Senge, the founding chairperson of Society for Organizational Learning and a senior lecturer at the Massachusetts Institute of Technology, suggests that "learning is a defining aspect of being human." He goes on to say that learning is always active, involving cycles of thinking and doing that are lifelong. Learning, for Senge, is about a transforming awareness; we "change through learning not through schooling."[3] One of the primary questions of a teacher, therefore, is, What are the effective alternatives for assisting other human beings to learn, for exercising this defining aspect of being human?

In seeking an answer to the question of how to help others learn, the elements of Paul's activity preceding his Mars Hill appearance are suggestive. First, Paul was waiting in Athens and became aware of a problem or issue he wanted to address (v. 16). We are told that he went to the synagogue and city square and argued with people and "passers-by" (vv. 17–18). So the second movement is to engage in a conversation that raises questions and challenges perspectives relative to a communally observed experience. We can assume that Paul did that in an engaging way, creating curiosity and a desire for further inquiry, because he was invited to speak further (vv. 18–19). The third movement was to engage the questions more formally on Mars Hill: "People of Athens, I see that in everything that concerns religion you are uncommonly scrupulous. For as I was going round looking at the objects of your worship, I noticed among other things an altar bearing the inscription 'To an Unknown God.' What you worship but do not know—this is what I proclaim" (vv. 22–23).

The third movement involves an attempt to engage people from the perspective of their own experience. To teach, then, is to enter a relationship with people in a way that helps engage them in learning. Richard Osmer, professor of Christian education at Princeton Theological Seminary, puts it this way: "Teaching focuses on an increase in the student's ability to comprehend and grasp the meaning of what is being learned. The subject matter must interact with the patterns of knowing that the student already possesses, being assimilated into them and expanding them. At the deepest level, teaching is based on respect for the student, respect that takes seriously his or her personal appropriation of the subject matter being taught."[4] Teaching is a relational activity that helps identify questions for exploration, suggests resources for alternative answers, encourages experimentation, challenges by raising questions for further learning, and supports work as a peer in lifelong learning.

This interpretation of Paul's teaching in Athens is consistent with his theology. God loves all of humankind. We know this by the life and teaching of Jesus Christ and by God's affirmation of Jesus Christ in the resurrection. Everything we do must be done in and with love (1 Cor. 13), and teaching in a way that invites people into a larger and deeper conversation is a way of loving.

The task of teachers, therefore, is to create relationships in which teaching as deep caring is possible. What are some ways to create a learning relationship? Let me suggest for conversation two elements for helping adults learn that I think are consistent with the Pauline model of Mars Hill: (1) shared control and (2) provision for and support of critical and constructive thinking efforts.

Shared Control

Malcolm Knowles identified four assumptions about adult learners in his work on adult education.[5] The first of the assumptions is that adults understand themselves to be independent and self-directing. Any educational enterprise aimed at adults must take into account the notion that adults will want to be respected as peers in the learning process.

The second assumption that affects the teaching of mature people is that adults bring to any learning activity or setting a reservoir of experience and knowledge. New learning is understood and organized in relation to this accumulation, even if the new ideas mean a drastic change in the way the person understands a given problem. Involving adults in learning activities will be most powerful if it finds a way for them to relate new ideas to their own experience.

Third, people who experience themselves to be more self-directing will be ready to learn when a question or problem arises in their own life. This assumption was corroborated by a study done by Carol B. Aslanian and Henry M. Brickell who sought to find out why adults undertook any learning activity. They found that "eighty-three percent of the adults interviewed said that they were learning in order to cope with a life change."[6] Teachers of adults will need to find a way to tap into this strong source of motivation.

Finally, Knowles suggested that adults orient their learning toward here-and-now tasks and problems they want to address. More mature people are strongly interested in applying new ideas and information to their life tasks and roles and will need opportunities to make individual use of material. Refusal to allow for this idiosyncratic employment of new learning can lead to rebellion or to dropping out, depending upon the circumstance. Teaching people with this orientation means finding ways for them to act directly upon the material and to make it their own.

Do these assumptions fit with your experience as an adult learner? They do with mine. A friend of mine observing me in an adult education course for beginning guitarists once asked, "Are you going to let the instructor teach this course?" At that moment I realized that my frustration level was high because the course was not covering my expectations. My response was to keep asking questions—this eventually frustrated others who wanted to hear from the instructor. What was happening was that I wanted to be more independent and self-directing than the setting allowed, and I became frustrated. I think that I often observe this self-directing dynamic in continuing education programs and in the courses I teach.

In looking over the four assumptions that Knowles and others make about the nature of adult learners and the implications for teaching, it seems that they could be summarized under the heading "control." In other words, all four of the assumptions purport that adults learn best when they are invited at least to help control the learning setting and activities. The power of control to motivate and facilitate performance is wonderfully captured in a story told by Thomas Peters and Robert Waterman in their study of leadership in the business world:

> Adult subjects were given some complex puzzles to solve and a proof-reading chore. In the background was a loud, randomly occurring distracting noise . . . producing a composite, non-distinguishable roar. The subjects were split into two groups. Individuals in one set were just told to work at the task. Individuals in the other were provided with a button to push to turn off the noise, "a modern analog of control—the off switch." The group with the off switch solved five times the number of puzzles as their cohorts and made but a tiny fraction of the number of proofreading errors. Now for the kicker: ". . . none of the subjects in the off switch group ever used the switch." The mere knowledge that one can exert control made the difference.[7]

A similar dynamic was observed by Warren Bennis and Burt Nanus in their study of leadership in American companies. They observed that when people are given some control over their work and empowered to learn and create, they "seem to get so immersed in their game of work that they forget basic needs for long periods of time!"[8]

The first hunch about teaching adults is, therefore, that the issue of control is central. When teachers share control (learners do not even want total control, they simply want some way to influence the direction) of learning tasks and environments, most adults will be empowered to work on their most pressing agenda, and a result is that incredible energy for learning is released. Two of Cyril Houle's nine assumptions for adult education support this hunch. Houle's first assumption is that "any episode of learning occurs in a specific situation and is profoundly influenced by that fact."⁹ His fourth assumption is that educational activity is always cooperative in two senses.

> In education the term *cooperative* is used in two major senses. In its profoundest meaning, it signifies action by both learner and educator in accordance with the dictates of nature. Learners must work in terms of their innate individualism as well as in terms of the social stimulation supplied by any learning group of which they are a part. . . . In its second sense, the term *cooperative* implies voluntary interaction among individuals during learning.¹⁰

Effective teaching will involve learners in ways that tap into the specific situations that give rise to their motivations for learning and will invite cooperation that is deeply voluntary.

Space does not allow for a discussion of the many ways learners can be invited to help control the direction of learning, but a few can be mentioned:

- Collaborative planning processes such as the Nominal Group Technique (see http://www.joe.org/joe/1984march/iw2.php),
- Opportunities for learners to work on specific interests within the focus of the program or course,
- Flexible ways for learners or participants to give evidence of learning that invite application of personal experience to new information,
- Evaluation procedures that invite the creation of new direction based upon the application of new learning,
- Opportunities to experiment.¹¹

Important to note here is that the climate for learning should be one based upon the norms of openness and experimentation. Some of the most important learning comes from trying something that does not work; there must be a climate that invites people to risk a failure and be evaluated not on the outcome but upon the process and the learning derived from it. This idea of emphasizing learning processes leads to the next section of this chapter dealing with critical thinking.

Supporting Critical Thinking

The second hunch about teaching adults is that effective teaching has to do with helping learners internalize a way of learning that can be applied to almost any situation. Many adults continue to believe that learning is a matter of memorizing what experts have written on a given subject. They have not yet relativized authority and come to the conclusion that they are also authorities who participate in the process of determining what is true through reflective experience and thought. Utilizing an open systems approach to learning and research is a complicated and complex process. The assumption is that no single factor can be used in determining what is true, a number of considerations must be taken into account, and context is a very real component in determining what is fact.

Stephen Brookfield, a professor and researcher in adult learning, teaching, and critical thinking, calls this complex process of arbitrating between truth claims and constructing working hypotheses "critical thinking." For Brookfield, critical thinking is a primary task of adulthood:

> When we become critical thinkers we develop an awareness of the assumptions under which we, and others, think and act. We learn to pay attention to the context in which our actions and ideas are generated. We become skeptical of quick-fix solutions, of single answers to problems, and of claims to universal truth. We also become open to alternative ways of looking at, and behaving in, the world.
>
> When we think critically, we come to our judgments, choices, and decisions for ourselves, instead of letting others do this on our behalf. We refuse to relinquish the responsibility for making the choices that determine our individual and collective futures to those who presume

to know what is in our own best interests. We become actively engaged in creating our personal and social worlds.[12]

For Mary Field Belenky and colleagues, who examined women's ways of knowing, learning "to see that all knowledge is a construction and that truth is a matter of the context in which it is embedded" is also a task of adulthood and a way of thinking critically.[13]

> Once knowers assume the general relativity of knowledge, that their frame of reference matters, and that they can construct and reconstruct frames of reference, they feel responsible for examining, questioning, and developing the systems that they will use for constructing knowledge. Question posing and problem solving become prominent methods of inquiry. . . . They [tend to rely] on examining basic assumptions and the conditions in which a problem is cast.[14]

Learning to become critical thinkers may be a difficult task for many people. The shift from dependence on an external authority to participation in constructing knowledge may be quite wrenching and bring with it a sense of loss. Sharon Daloz Parks, director of the Leadership for the New Commons initiative of the Whidbey Institute, Clinton, Washington, calls the loss of truth and of established authority "the shipwreck of self, world, and 'God.' The truth of life itself betrayed."[15] Such a sense of loss presents many young adults with a very real crisis that requires strong support and pastoral care. William Perry, in his classic study of young adult intellectual development, describes the sense of loss in the first person:

> Soon I may begin to miss those tablets in the sky. If [relativism] defines the truth for term papers, how about people? Principalities? Powers? How about the Deity . . . ? And if this can be true of my image of the Deity, who then will cleanse my soul? And my enemies? Are they not wholly in the wrong?

> I apprehend all too poignantly now that in the most fateful decisions of my life I will be the only person with a first-hand view of the really relevant data, and only part of it at that. Who will save me then from that "wrong decision" I have been told not to make lest I "regret-it-all-my-life"? Will no one tell me if I am right? Can I never be sure? Am I alone?[16]

Helping learners become critical thinkers, therefore, involves not only familiarity with a subject matter or area of inquiry but also strong human relations skills, powers of empathy, and the inclination to see pastoral work as part of the teaching task. Indeed, Stephen Brookfield lists ten strategies for facilitating critical thinking, and of the ten, eight are dependent upon human relations and communications skills:

- Affirm self-worth.
- Listen attentively.
- Support critical thinking efforts.
- Reflect and mirror efforts and actions.
- Regularly evaluate progress [provide feedback].
- Help learners create networks for support.[17]

Laurent A. Daloz, in his work on teaching and mentoring, also emphasizes the importance of the teacher-learner relationship in suggesting that good teachers "do three fairly distinct types of things. They *support,* they *challenge,* and they *provide vision.*"[18] He goes on to suggest that support and challenge must be in balance. Support for Daloz comprises "those acts through which the mentor affirms the validity of the student's present experience"[19] and builds trust. The important role of challenge "is to open a gap between student and environment, a gap that creates a tension in the student, calling out for closure."[20] High support and low challenge may produce a stasis; conversely, a high challenge and low support may yield a retreat by the learner. A balance is needed between challenge and support. By vision, Daloz means the dialectical process of reexamining current ways of perceiving the world. Mentors help provide vision over time with learners in order to facilitate construction of more comprehensive understandings that are modeled by a teacher rather than directly taught.[21]

Brookfield, Perry, and Belenky and colleagues all suggest that critical thinking must be publicly modeled by teachers: "Students need opportunities to watch women professors solve (and fail to solve) problems and male professors fail to solve (and succeed in solving) problems. They need models of thinking as a human, imperfect, and attainable activity."[22]

Perhaps the most important notion relative to critical thinking and its facilitation is that it is a "never-ending search for truth, which is coordinate with a never-ending quest for learning."[23] Brookfield suggests that "critical thinking is a continuous process composed of alternating phases of (1) reflecting on a problem or theme; (2) testing new solutions, strategies, or methods on the basis of that reflection; (3) reflecting on the success of these actions in particular contexts; and (4) further honing, refining, and adapting these actions according to alternative contexts.[24]

This understanding of critical thinking has important parallels in some of the literature on practical theology. A survey of these works suggests several common steps in practical theological methodology. They are: (1) describing an issue, problem, or event; (2) attending to or contextualizing issues or problems relative to cultural information, Christian tradition, and Scripture; (3) critical analysis and comparison of various alternative answers or solutions; (4) construction of alternative interpretations and responses; and (5) deciding on a strategy for action.[25]

The point of this is that critical thinking methodologies are remarkably similar. They involve the inseparable movements of reflection and action that test the results of reflection in action and then move back to reflection, revision of theory, and identification of further alternatives for action to be tested. Other thinkers could be added to the list of those whose method has much in common with this basic outline of critical thinking.[26] I dare say that for all serious thinkers, the method used for the pursuit of truth is at once a way of lifelong learning.

The teaching of critical thinking, therefore, involves a number of elements. Supporting students in their first steps in relativizing authority, welcoming them into the conversation of a community of inquiry in which all are participants by virtue of being human beings, strengthening and encouraging students in the internalization of a critical thinking methodology, and reinforcing the fact that the epistemology inherent in the method of critical or constructive thinking assumes that we are all lifelong learners.

In the early 1980s, Sara Little, lecturer and teacher in the field of Christian education, developed five basic approaches to teaching that may help define the kinds of teaching activity that support critical and constructive methodology in students: information processing, group interaction, indirect communication, personal development, and action-reflection.[27] Of these approaches, only the last one seems out of place. Indeed, in the introduction to the chapter dealing with action-reflection, Little admits that this particular way of teaching does not fit with the others.[28] The reason it does not fit is that the action-reflection way of teaching she describes is at once the epistemology assumed in the above descriptions of critical thinking and undergirds all other methodologies for teaching and thinking. Action-reflection, as she describes it, is both an epistemology and a way of learning. Little's chapter on action-reflection describes the way people learn by exercising some control on subject matter; the other four approaches to teaching then become alternative ways of facilitating the process of critical thinking, constructed knowing, or lifelong learning.

There is no one right way to teach critical thinking or anything else. Jean Piaget once suggested that the way to teach teachers is to have them do continuous experiments on teaching.[29] True to the epistemology assumed in this paper let me suggest that teaching critical thinking demands experiments that involve students in activities that they help to control and in which they are asked to take some kind of relevant action on the subject matter under inquiry. There may be literally hundreds of ways to do this, most of which could be understood under four of Sarah Little's approaches: information processing, group interaction, indirect communication, and personal development.

Effective Teaching with Adults

Paul's activity in Athens, preceding and including the Mars Hill speech, provides a challenging model for teaching that is affirmed by some of the modern work on adult education. Good teaching is a relational and caring activity that (1) begins by establishing a conversation in which the learner's questions and curiosities are brought to awareness, (2) challenges learners to explore resources and perspectives for alternative answers to their questions, (3) lets learners see how the teacher struggles with the same questions, and (4) challenges learners to relate new perspectives to their own experience in constructive and critical ways.[30]

Good teaching is a process that introduces learners to the questions of authority and truth and invites them to join the teacher in a lifelong quest, a quest involving the construction of contingent and unfinished affirmations of what is true and what is appropriate to do in a given context. It is a process of constant experimentation in a community of exchange, a process that involves learning to share control and to think critically with others. As the authors of *Common Fire* put it, "Learning is most powerful when students are given experiential opportunities to integrate new information about the world into their existing frameworks in ways that lead to fresh insights and new habits of mind."[31]

Approaching the teaching task with adults from the position of one who shares control of learning experiences and as one who invites learners into a community of conversation and inquiry is to tap into the internal motivation of people. In *Women's Ways of Knowing*, the authors refer to the excitement and motivation for learning reminiscent of the Peters and Waterman study and the observations of Bennis and Nanus: "When truth is seen as a process of construction in which the knower participates, a passion for learning is unleashed."[32]

Since teaching is relational and more art than science, those of us who want to teach effectively must be willing to be lifelong learners about teaching, modeling a reflective practice method in our profession. That means taking an experimental approach to our teaching activity, always searching for more effective ways to facilitate learning. In addition, the selection and education of teachers will require attention to human relations skills as well as competencies in subject areas, teaching, and action-reflection research methodologies. Finally, those of us who not only teach but also recruit others to teach must surely keep before us the qualities and skills of effective teaching if our institutions and programs of lifelong learning are to flourish and be centers where teaching is an interdisciplinary and rigorous endeavor aimed at what Peter Senge calls the defining aspect of being human: learning.

Notes

1. An earlier version of this article was published in *Encounter* 59 (Winter/ Spring 1998) and with permission in *A Lifelong Call to Learn*, eds. Robert E. Reber and D. Bruce Roberts. (Nashville: Abingdon, 2000), 67.

2. *Webster's New Collegiate Dictionary* (1981), s.v. "Teach," "Teaching."

3. Peter Senge, "The Power of Presence," audio recording (Boulder, CO: Sounds True, 2008), compact disc.

4. Richard R. Osmer, *A Teachable Spirit: Recovering the Teaching Office in the Church* (Louisville, KY: Westminster/John Knox, 1990), 21.

5. Malcolm S. Knowles, *The Modern Practice of Adult Education: From Pedagogy to Andragogy* (Chicago: Association Press, 1980), 43–62.

6. Carol B. Aslanian and Henry M. Brickell, *Americans in Transition: Life Changes as Reasons for Adult Learning* (New York: College Entrance Examination Board, 1980), 51.

7. Thomas J. Peters and Robert H. Waterman Jr., *In Search of Excellence: Lessons from America's Best-Run Companies* (New York: Harper & Row, 1982), xxiii.

8. Warren Bennis and Burt Nanus, *Leaders: The Strategies for Taking Charge* (New York: Harper & Row, 1985), 84.

9. Cyril Houle, *The Design of Education*, 2nd ed. (San Francisco: Jossey-Bass, 1996), 41ff.

10. Ibid., 45.

11. See also Ronald M. Cervero and Arthur L. Wilson, *Planning Responsibly for Adult Education* (San Francisco: Jossey-Bass, 1994), and Cyril O. Houle, *Design of Education*, 2nd ed.

12. Stephen D. Brookfield, *Developing Critical Thinkers* (San Francisco: Jossey-Bass, 1987), ix–x.

13. Mary Field Belenky and others, *Women's Ways of Knowing* (New York: Basic Books, 1986), 139.

14. Ibid.

15. Sharon Parks, *Big Questions, Worthy Dreams: Mentoring Young Adults* (San Francisco: Jossey-Bass, 2000), 58.

16. William G. Perry Jr., *Forms of Ethical and Intellectual Development in the College Years* (New York: Holt, Rinehart, and Winston, 1970), 33.

17. Brookfield, *Developing Critical Thinkers*, 72–85.

18. Laurent A. Daloz, *Mentor: Guiding the Journey of Adult Learners* (San Francisco: Jossey-Bass, 1999), 206.

19. Ibid.

20. Ibid.

21. Ibid., 223.

22. Belenky and others, *Women's Ways of Knowing*, 215.

23. Ibid., 140.

24. Brookfield, *Developing Critical Thinkers*, 230.

25. See Don S. Browning, *Religious Ethics and Pastoral Care* (Philadelphia: Fortress Press, 1983); James W. Fowler, *Faith Development and Pastoral Care* (Philadelphia: Fortress Press, 1987); Thomas H. Groome, *Sharing Faith: A Comprehensive Approach to Religious Education and Pastoral Ministry* (San Francisco: Harper & Row, 1991); James N. Poling and Donald E. Miller, *Foundations for a Practical Theology of Ministry* (Nashville: Abingdon, 1985); and James D. and Evelyn E. Whitehead, *Method in Ministry*, rev. ed. (Kansas City, MO: Sheed and Ward, 1995).

26. A partial list would include Jean Piaget, Alfred North Whitehead, David Tracy, Edgar S. Brightman, Gordon D. Kaufman, Charles M. Wood, and Edward Farley.

27. Sara Little, *To Set One's Heart: Belief and Teaching in the Church* (Atlanta: John Knox, 1983).

28. Ibid., 76.

29. Jean Piaget, *Science of Education and the Psychology of the Child*, trans. Derek Coltman (New York: Viking Press, 1970).

30. For an informative discussion on teaching for critical thinking, see Mary E. Hess and Stephen D. Brookfield, eds., *Teaching Reflectively in Theological Contexts* (Malabar, FL: Krieger, 2008), particularly chapters 1 and 4; and Patricia M. King and Karen Strohm Kitchener, *Developing Reflective Judgment* (San Francisco: Jossey-Bass, 1994).

31. Laurent A. Parks Daloz and others, *Common Fire: Leading Lives of Commitment in a Complex World* (Boston: Beacon Press, 1996), 221.

32. Belenky and others, *Women's Ways of Knowing*, 140. For corroborative data about educational processes that unleash and release passion and energy for learning, see the chapters in this volume dealing with clergy peer learning, chapters 5, 6, 8, and 9.

PART III

Innovations in Continuing
Theological Education

Energizing, Supporting, and Sustaining Religious Leaders through Peer Learning Groups

D. Bruce Roberts

"Is there any evidence that the practice of ministry in real congregations is positively affected or influenced by continuing education events for laity and clergy?" You can imagine my surprise and shock when, as a recently hired director of continuing theological education, I heard experienced directors asking this question of each other at an annual meeting of the Society for the Advancement of Continuing Education for Ministry (SACEM). Over the next twenty-six years I became increasingly thankful for that honest question, because it helped frame the discussions among continuing educators as we examined our work.

In one of the first books on continuing education for ministry, *Competent Ministry*, Mark Rouch suggests that the "primary aim of continuing education is to produce growing competence."[1] In accepting this as a key purpose for continuing education for ministry, continuing theological educators have two central evaluative questions to ask: (1) To what extent does continuing education for ministry produce increased competence in church leadership? (2) Does continuing education develop positive change in leadership for congregations and in congregational life?

Most of the past research on continuing education for ministry has been concerned with who did and who did not do it, and for what reasons, and what effect, if any, did it have on clergy. It did not focus on the question of increased competence or congregational development. I often had the suspicion that what was happening in my programs was more a kind of professional entertainment for congregational leaders than transformative education bringing real change to participants or to their congregations. Continuing educators were left with only scanty anecdotal evidence indicating that traditional approaches had much, if any, effect on the actual practice of ministry.

Now, however, growing evidence indicates that new approaches are yielding positive answers to the questions. Over the past dozen years ongoing experiments in continuing theological education show positive results worthy of further work and creative elaboration. One is the movement to facilitate peer learning groups that meet over time and are funded by participants and outside sources. Another is coaching processes used to assist congregational leaders in becoming aware of specific areas for leadership improvement and in finding resources for learning and enhanced practices. This chapter is one of three that address peer learning processes (coaching is elaborated in another chapter).

Description of Indiana Clergy Peer Group Study Program

In January 1999 and 2002, Christian Theological Seminary in Indianapolis received grants from the Lilly Endowment for the Indiana Clergy Peer Group Study Program (PGSP).[2] The proposal was developed and submitted by Robert Reber and me. The purpose of PGSP was to provide leadership education, consultation, and resources for local congregations by forming clergy peer groups. Peer groups of eight pastors (or other full-time congregational leaders) were assigned a group facilitator and developed three-year learning plans with a focus on leadership in ministry. The range of topics selected for study, reflection, and action included areas such as congregational life, worship, preaching, teaching and education, spirituality, self-care, evangelism, global and local mission, and the ministry of the laity in their workplaces and communities.

PGSP is based upon an evaluation research assessment of the Methodist Educational Leave Society (MELS) of the Dixon Foundation in Birmingham, Alabama, conducted by Robert Reber and me.[3] The MELS study and PGSP have been formative for other peer projects as well: "In 1998 the MELS model served as the basis for a pilot project at the Christian Theological Seminary (CTS) in Indianapolis, and this year it helped shape Lilly Endowment's national Sustaining Pastoral Excellence initiative."[4]

PGSP participants developed learning plans for a three-year period that involved the creation of learning objectives (identified by the group), study, experimentation in congregations, assessment of results, and creation of new objectives from the experience of learning in practice. Peer groups met regularly for worship, planning, study, reporting on congregational experiments, and identification of new learnings and directions in ministry. Meetings involved pastors in theological reflection, communal planning processes, shared leadership, travel, and peer reflection.

The grant from Lilly Endowment allowed each group to have access to $2,200 per person per year or $17,600 per year for a group of eight. In addition, both pastors and churches were asked to contribute $400 each ($800 per year), bringing the total to $3,000 per participant per year. When pastors and churches all met their share, each group had access to $72,000 total for the three-year period. More is said about funding levels and outcomes later in this chapter.

The PGSP model utilized specially selected and trained Learning Consultant/Facilitators (LCFs) who were responsible for helping peer groups identify learning needs, develop learning objectives, discover and utilize resources appropriate to the identified learning objectives, carry out learning activities in an attitude of experimentation and anticipation of new learning, engage in theological reflection, and gather feedback for evaluating results. Each evaluation was expected to lead to new and more engaging learning objectives for the participants. The peer groups monitored each member's experiments in ministry so that members experienced both direct learning and learning by association with others. The LCFs and the group were responsible for attending to learning—not on whether a particular idea or initiative worked. The groups had a "no failure" norm; that is, the emphasis was upon what can be learned, not on whether a particular idea or initiative failed or succeeded. A no-failure atmosphere sponsors creativity and experimentation by fostering what Parker Palmer calls open space: "creating space in which the community of truth can be practiced."[5]

In addition to generous financial support, three key components of the peer groups in both MELS and PGSP contributed greatly to high motivation for learning. The first was that each group was made up of people who chose to work with each other. That is, each group was self-selecting within suggested criteria for diversity: denominational, ethnic, and gender. The second important component was that the groups themselves decided what they wanted to learn over a three-year period. No one told them what they ought to or must learn. Each peer group decided its own direction. The staff learned that freedom to select peer group members and to determine learning objectives produced energy and motivation in the groups and that the energy from the participants spills over to congregations. The third key aspect of the project was assigning Learning Consultant Facilitators (LCFs) to each group to help groups in selecting resources and in designing learning activities. LCFs were carefully selected for knowledge and skills in working with groups in nondidactic ways as process consultants. They were given initial training and were formed into a peer group that met during the three-year period and consulted with each other in the work of process consultation.

PGSP developed fifteen peer groups in Indiana (three in the Evansville area, two in Lafayette, one in Fort Wayne, one in South Bend, one in Columbus, and seven in the Indianapolis area). The Columbus peer group disbanded during the first year.

Not counting the Columbus group of ten, 115 participants applied and began with a peer group. A total of seventeen others dropped out. Fifteen individuals dropped for different reasons not related to the project (one subsequently joined another peer group after one year), and two left when they were given an ultimatum by their peer group to adhere to policies of PGSP. Of the fifteen individuals who dropped for various reasons, three were for family or personal illnesses, three moved out of state, two got divorced, two took new jobs, two left active parish ministry, one got married, one cited church problems, and one decided the peer group direction was not for him.

Ninety-eight participants finished the three-year study process.

There were 125 Indiana congregations involved in PGSP. However, twenty congregations experienced clergy moves and did not have a full three years to experience their pastor in PGSP.

Denominational Participation

Participants represented 16 church bodies as follows:

39	United Methodist (43 including LCFs)
14	Christian Church (DOC) (19 including LCFs)
10	Episcopalian
10	New Life Apostolic Church
9	Baptist (different traditions) (10 including an LCF)
8	Lutheran (ELCA) (9 including an LCF)
8	United Church of Christ
5	Presbyterian (U.S.A.) (7 including LCFs)
5	Independent
3	Unitarian Universalist

2   Independent Christian

2   Church of the Brethren

2   Assemblies of God

1   Church of God

1   African Methodist Episcopal (2 including an LCF)

1   Seventh Day Adventist

Total = 120

The reason there are five more applicants than congregations represented is that in two cases two participants were from the same congregation, and one participant was a United Methodist district superintendent who did not have a congregation.

Ethnic Participation

20   African American (including two LCFs)

10   Hispanic (including an LCF)

2   Asian (including an LCF)

Gender

44   women (including 6 LCFs)

81   men (including 8 LCFs)

The next section outlines some findings from the evaluation research using the words of participants as much as possible.

PGSP: Findings from Evaluation Research

An evaluation process was carefully designed in consultation with two evaluation coordinators for the Lilly Endowment Religion Division, Kathleen A. Cahalan and Elizabeth Lynn. The design included both formative and summative evaluation procedures.

The formative evaluation tools were an Every Meeting Feedback form (which had to be submitted in order to receive further funding) and an LCF Critical Incident report (required from LCFs for LCF Committee meetings). These evaluation tools were very helpful in the early stages of the project and accounted for a number of adjustments as the LCFs and PGSP staff were developing the project.

The summative evaluation instruments included a Participant Survey, a Last Meeting Reflective Questions Interview, a Congregational Representative Interview, and an LCF Ending Interview.

Data for the following evaluation research findings came from the application of these tools and instruments.

An Energized, Empowered Clergy

In both the MELS and the PGSP evaluations, participants reported being energized and motivated to explore new ideas and new practices of ministry by the peer learning process.[6] In all the PGSP groups, the participants agreed that their peer learning group "was the best continuing education [they] ever had."[7]

- "I'm thinking how can the other kinds of continuing education experience I've had ever be anywhere near as valuable as this? . . . I usually take a little notebook with me to these continuing education events that I go to. I have all of these wonderful notes and wonderful ideas and I bring them home and I set them somewhere on my desk. And sometimes, frankly, I never look at them ever again. [In the peer group,] I've probably integrated more of what I [learned and] experienced here into the life of the church than any other continuing education that I went to."

- In response to a question about change participants had experienced, the most frequent response was that they developed trust and felt more connected and less isolated: "It was a safe place to vent concerns . . . and know that it would remain in the group." Second, they reported growing more confident and willing to take risks and try new things in ministry. Some participants reported "reconsidering their own theology in light of the theological diversity in the group."

From these data and many more from the evaluation interviews, a reliable conclusion is that participants were energized and empowered by work in peer learning groups.

Participants Grew in Knowledge, Understanding, and Commitment to Leadership

Responses from participants indicated that pastors felt they did achieve their learning objectives slowly and over time and that the objectives were not once and for all but "would always be with us as a challenge."

One group suggested that the interplay between the group and the determination of what to learn were important: "I think that the way we set the goals was important. And just the group process—I think the intentionality of reflection in a group, to me . . . is the whole purpose of being in a group. It makes us think about [applying our learning] in this situation and to have people to be accountable to about that is one of the reasons why the goals work. . . . It is an interplay between those things [group process and accountability]."

Other groups named the whole process as assisting their learning: "I think a big carrot in the beginning of the process is the ability to travel. The big trip! I've got to say that after it's all said and done that was just one piece. I really enjoyed it, but . . . I wouldn't say it was the major learning. . . . Just the whole thing was so powerful to me. [Travel] was a carrot that got people interested in doing something, [but it] was, as I said, a carrot. Ultimately it was the other stuff that we did and all of the learning events that really [brought it] all . . . together. And again, the people, the process, it works."

Some participants thought the supportive nature of the peer group was as important as the professional learning: "I . . . was going through a . . . difficult time, personally and professionally. I don't think I would have come through that period . . . , if it had not been for this group."

A pastor in another group credited the group with helping avoid burnout: "My environment, [has] been so . . . stressed—I think I would have withered up and died if it wasn't for these experiences. I don't even know if I would have made it."

Yet another group had as an original objective "to gain an understanding of family systems, . . . leadership in congregations," and "to learn ways of maintaining self-differentiation as a leader." In answering the question of whether they had met their learning objectives, one member mused, "I wanted to be a stronger leader and I think I am. . . . I think it was also a group objective to be in an environment where we could all become stronger leaders. And I think leadership is one of those things that you can't really just put . . . in somebody's mind, or you don't get it from a lecture. You get it from who you are and then what your experience is and then what you've learned and a combination of all those. I think being in a group setting where we trusted one another and being together for a number of years made it easier to do that integration of those three things."

A safe conclusion from the evaluation interviews is that participants were involved in learning about and commitment to growth in leadership for ministry.

Participant-Directed, Self-Selected, and Accountable Peer Learning Yields Change in Ministry Leadership and Practices

The key elements in peer learning that our research identified are (1) participation in selecting other group members, (2) group identification of resources and directions for learning, (3) sustained work together over time with accountability to each other, and (4) enough resources to support the learning activity.

- "I was just sitting here thinking what a better three years could we ever have? Being able to design our own continuing education events, you know—that's priceless! . . . I think a lot of times we don't attend continuing events because they just don't relate or they're not that important, that personal. Being able to design your own events—to me that was the highlight of this whole program!"

- "We got to design our own study program. Now that is a level of professionalism that goes beyond almost anything else I have experienced. . . . We got to decide what it is we wanted to study and set our own objectives—create the solution to [our] problem. . . . It's unique in my experience."
- "I think it was extremely effective, because we were able to come up with the goals."

A number of responses indicated that the changes in the pastors and in the church might not even be recognizable by most church members. Some participants, for example, reported that their willingness to remain at the church as pastor was a direct result of being in a peer group: "I probably wouldn't still be in my congregation if I wasn't able to come here and vent, and also rediscover that I'm not always crazy—that I can rediscover . . . the courage to go with my insight and use my gifts even though they weren't always well received by everybody."

Others noted the way the group helped them grow personally and professionally as pastors:

- "The group helped me become a better me, more willing to take some risks and explore new territory and use my gifts in new ways. I probably wouldn't have had the stamina to keep doing that year after year."
- The group "helped me stay sane . . . just because I had a chance to come and say, 'I hate being a minister!' or 'I don't like the church!' and it was okay to say it [in the group]."
- "Probably what the congregations could not articulate . . . they had not seen. What I know is that this group has kept me sane on many occasions with my congregation and so they see me as a much more gracious person because I've got this group."

Evidence from evaluation instruments used in PGSP (as well as in MELS and the Institute for Clergy Excellence) indicates that peer group procedures that include self-selecting groups, participant-directed learning, and accountability over time yield change and growth in ministry practices.

Congregational Support for Clergy Peer Learning

The evaluation found strong evidence that congregations supported their congregational leaders participating in peer learning groups. Sixty-one percent of participants felt "strongly" supported by their congregations and another 34 percent felt "somewhat supported" by congregations.[8] Congregational representative interviews corroborated the perception of participants. Though lay representatives were often vague about specific changes or improvements in the congregations, they were nearly unanimous in reporting that peer learning had benefited their congregation, often citing the biggest change as being in the participant him- or herself. Lay support was illustrated most clearly by the large majority of congregations who indicated that they would gladly financially support future participation in peer learning by the same level or even more. As some of them said, "We got our money's worth!"

Less evident is that congregations themselves experienced systemic change or that the lay constituency understood what their pastors and leaders were attempting to learn and do. If we had opportunity to do this again, we would make some changes in the lay component of the project. First, we would not require any lay participation or formation of lay components until after the peer learning group had time to develop and form into a cohesive unit. Groups needed time to form and become comfortable with each other before inviting laypeople into the dynamic. Second, objectives for the lay component would be set with lay leaders so that new directions or programs would be owned by everyone.

The Role of LCF Was Important to Group Life

More than 90 percent of participants reported that their LCF had done an effective job in assisting the group in meeting its learning objectives and carrying out life together. Comments included, "Our LCF has been outstanding!" "of enormous help!" "excellent!" "a wonderful leader, facilitator, and friend." Only seven were not happy with the LCF from their group—and with ninety-eight participants who completed three years with a group, that is not an unexpected result.

We learned that the most important part of having effective process consultation in the groups was ongoing training and support. While LCFs were engaged with their groups, there were LCF meetings every two months. An important training tool was use of critical incident reports required of each LCF at least once in six months. The LCF committee became a consultation group for each committee member, helping determine alternative interventions or courses of action in particular situations such as conflicts, planning process issues, consideration of various resources, and policy difficulties.

In working with the LCFs in the PGSP project and in several other projects that utilized facilitators with peer learning groups, Robert E. Reber and I compiled a list of roles and responsibilities of peer group facilitators. The list has been drawn from conversations with more than forty people serving as facilitators or process consultants in Alabama, New Jersey, Ohio, and Indiana, and then refined by feedback from all of them. Here is the latest list, which reflects an evolving perspective:

Roles and Responsibilities of Peer Group Facilitators

Facilitators should

1. State clearly and succinctly to your peer group what you understand your roles and responsibilities to be and contract with the group about your roles.
2. Uphold the goals, purposes, and policies of the peer group program.

3. Encourage your peer group to be creative and risky in developing proposals.

4. Help the peer group develop its particular program of learning and practice by helping them to understand and use forms provided for doing this.

5. Call attention to peer group members' responsibilities in budgeting and funding.

6. Develop and use a repertoire of interventions that focus on group process and content, offer behavioral data and describe behaviors, listen to your intuition.

7. Facilitate the development of trust, accountability, and openness in the peer group by suggesting procedures and roles (agenda, steps, and guidelines, for example).

8. Encourage shared leadership in the peer group and building agendas for each meeting.

9. Suggest a broad and in-depth consideration of leadership, places, and resources in putting proposals together for any given year.

10. Give attention to your skills for addressing or processing conflict in the group in a way that gives the group skills for doing this in an ongoing way.

11. Participate in all peer group meetings.

12. Encourage evaluation of peer group meetings and activities on a regular basis.

13. Raise questions about learning in terms of what, why, how, where, and when.

14. Spend time with all members of the group.

15. Stay in a single room when on trips.

16. Insist that all should minimize use of e-mails for peer group decision making.

17. Always be on time for peer group meetings.

18. Encourage critical thinking and theological reflection.

19. Participate in learning activities or exercises when appropriate and if the available "air time" for peer group members is limited, negotiate in advance how the time will be managed.

20. Insist upon collaboration and group decision making.
21. Give attention to having a good balance of learning, activities, rest, fun, and worship in peer group life.
22. Call attention to particular resources for planning study and travel both inside and outside the United States.
23. Work yourself out of a job so that group members may take responsibility for their own learning, facilitation, and consultation.

Facilitators should not
1. Convene, chair, or lead meetings.
2. Hesitate to describe the roles of the facilitator and the travel costs that must be covered by the peer group.
3. Vote in peer-group decision making.
4. Act as treasurer or secretary for the peer group.
5. Make follow-up calls to group members before or after meeting.
6. Plan events, activities, or trips.
7. Write proposals or budgets.
8. Serve as a therapist or spiritual guide for the peer group.
9. Play favorites or make alliances.
10. Talk about people behind their backs or engage in triangulation.
11. Take on the role of being the diversity representative in the group.
12. Recruit members for their peer groups.
13. Direct, lead, defend, take sides, or assume anything.
14. Do for the group what the group can do for itself.

Diversity in Peer Groups Assists and Provokes Learning

We had intended to have several kinds of diversity in each group: ethnic, denominational, and gender. Despite our efforts to achieve ethnic diversity, only five of the fifteen groups that formed were ethnically diverse. Since we had listed the diversity criteria for formation, groups really worked at it.

One group in particular spent months and were not successful in gaining ethnic diversity, though they did end up with two
women in the group: "We worked at it. We honestly tried to invite
people of color to participate with us and we were just unsuccess-
ful. . . . It wasn't that we didn't want it. . . . I want to say that I think
it's important. . . . It changed things from what they would have
been if we had been just eight white guy United Methodists. So
I'm grateful for that diversity. I'm probably the least likely person
around this table to say something like that." Two women in the
group responded, "I'm just thankful that they were asked to be
diverse. I think we probably wouldn't have been included, and I
wouldn't have missed this for the world." The response from the
men was, "We would have missed a lot if you weren't there."

Most groups witnessed to the importance of diversity:

- "I learned more from the members of the group than the
  teachers or speakers or consultants. . . . Maybe it's because
  of the diversity."
- "I think the diversity . . . made us a little more alert about
  our language and our assumptions when we use terms and
  phrases and attitudes."
- "Both the ethnic background diversity and the denominational background has been very enriching and important
  to this group. There have been times where we sat down and
  we would listen to each other about our faith or our experiences or about ethnic experiences that I would not have
  experienced anywhere else."
- "We probably ought to suggest that CTS [Christian Theological Seminary] make sure . . . [peer groups are] as diverse
  as possible."

Our conclusion is that the peer groups that were diverse worked
better. Groups of all one denomination had to intentionally resist
slipping into gossip mode, and the diversity kept everyone honestly seeking differing perspectives. Although some groups experienced problems with cultural differences around priorities of
starting time and attendance, all but one group was able to work

through those differences. The one that did not work through the cultural differences still stayed together for the whole time and reported positive results.

At the point of addressing some of the ethnic differences in the life of a group, the role of the LCF was critical. One group had a major conflict between white and African American participants. After a heated confrontation over the issue, the group came together and bonded in a remarkable way; they remained a group even after the project ended. A possible factor in the successful resolution of that conflict may be the fact that the facilitator was African American.

Is Funding Necessary and What Are Alternative Funding Sources?

It is evident that some funding is necessary for effective peer groups. Many participants told us that funding, with opportunity for travel and for engaging well-known leadership resources, was a key early motivator to their enrollment in PGSP. As their peer groups ended the three-year study, many participants were clear that funding was not the primary factor in their learning. Primary factors in their learning were several: (1) freedom to identify and pursue their own learning goals, (2) opportunity to help select the group, (3) developing trust and accountability in the group, (4) and a facilitator who helped with group process issues. Funding for carrying out learning objectives was perceived as important, but not as critical as participants first believed. It is not clear, however, that such a program could happen without some subsidy.

So the question is, how much money does it take to get the same results? A variety of models have been tested in the Sustaining Pastoral Excellence (SPE) grants provided by Lilly Endowment over the past seven years.[9] In the Indiana project, groups had access to $72,000 over three years. In the SPE Alabama Institute for Clergy Excellence program, each group had up to $100,000 over three years, and there is some evidence that the peer groups in the program are struggling to spend it all in the three-year period because of limitations of time for planning, meeting, and travel.

These have been models with access to funding provided by outside sources, and the evaluation research indicates that they have been very effective in creating energy and creativity in participants. An example of a project with far less funding is one executed by Tim Dolan in a PhD study of clergy cluster groups in eastern Washington. Dolan got results similar to PGSP by charging clergy $450 each and shortening the time groups met together.[10]

These models are the two extremes financially. What is needed are carefully constructed and evaluated experiments to determine effective funding levels for maximum peer learning. It is clear that there is a wide range of experience from which to develop further projects and experimentation.

Given information from MELS, PGSP, and the results from the Dolan study, it is important for further research on peer learning to establish pilot projects to determine ideal funding levels. New research will require projects started with varying amounts of funding, for example, with $20,000, $15,000, $10,000, and even smaller amounts that include contributions from pastors, congregations, and other sources such as denominations, continuing education centers, and seminaries. These efforts would need careful evaluation in order to determine at what level similar results are gained and what level of support is sustainable in the long run.

Implications of the PGSP Project

From the beginning of the PGSP grant application and then through eight years of administration, Robert Reber and I have been interested in identifying implications from the PGSP data that apply to continuing theological education and to basic seminary education. We are also interested in directions for further research inherent in the evaluation research data. What follows are intended as suggestions for further conversation and exploration.

Continuing Theological Education

There is evidence that continuing theological education "was being offered by significant numbers of ecclesiastical organizations at least by the decade of the 1950s."[11] Most of it was short term, lasting one or two days, and involved a well-known leader or expert. Although the reasons are varied as to why these kinds of events have a place in the life and mission of a seminary, judicatory, or conference center, it is also true that there is little or no evidence that these traditional continuing education activities have led to change in local congregations. The "Lone Ranger" and "cafeteria" models for continuing theological education have very limited value when viewed from the perspective of changes in the practice of ministry or in congregational life.

What, then, is needed? To some degree, the answer may go back to the way seminaries are organized and the way they teach. The Master of Divinity is the primary focus of seminary education and usually involves taking a specified number of courses for graduation. Professors organize courses using a detailed syllabus with the expectation that students follow the requirements for the course and receive a grade for their work. Students, therefore, have limited experience in learning how to learn, in learning how to establish their own learning objectives, in carrying out learning activities, and in developing evaluation criteria and processes for judging the adequacy of what they have done. Although some of this is changing as professors learn how to engage students in more effective learning, for the most part seminary education has produced dependent learners. Most have had no experience of developing a syllabus or course for a semester, let alone a learning plan for one to three years!

Indeed, in the PGSP project, we learned that groups of pastors had difficulty in imagining the learning directions they needed, in constructing learning objectives, and in creating and discovering learning activities focused specifically on what they wanted or needed to learn. We had to assign facilitators to groups earlier in the process than we had originally planned in order to help pastors develop three-year learning plans. Once they were challenged to assess their pastoral experience for learning directions, the groups quickly stopped proposing canned events offered by experts and began creating learning activities focused on what they wanted to learn. Sometimes this involved working with "experts," but the experts came as consultants working with the groups on the agenda created by the groups themselves. This process produced high motivation and application of learning in ministry contexts.

Seminary Education

The PGSP project and other peer learning programs around the country have demonstrated the opportunity peer learning groups provide to self-select into groups, to identify learning goals and objectives, to set up or create learning activities to meet the goals, and to evaluate new learning through application in ministry practice is one way to generate excitement, motivation, and energy for learning. One of the questions to ask, therefore, is how seminaries might utilize some of these findings in preparing congregational leaders.

Increasingly, seminary students are not in residence at seminaries. Students are often commuting from some distance for two or three days a week or juggling full-time jobs, families, church responsibilities, and studies from permanent residences—which have mortgages and maintenance requirements. Therefore, learning from living and studying together over three years at a seminary is lacking.

One way to address the formation issue in theological education is to have students self-select into peer groups according to specific diversity criteria and then to develop learning directions related to the practice of ministry and the application of material from the seminary curriculum to congregational leadership. A question for such peer groups might be what it means to be an excellent pastor and how to sustain that excellence over time through face-to-face and online opportunities. Field education at many seminaries already is done with peer groups reflecting with each other and with a supervisor on what is happening in the student's placement congregation. We recommend that the groups be self-selecting, help each other develop plans for learning in their individual settings, and consult with each other over time on their progress.

Seminaries and judicatories need to be preparing students to be lifelong learners and to value processes for continued learning. Creating peer groups would make clear the assumption that learning for the practice of ministry is never finished and lasts throughout a career. It may begin in seminary, but it is important for it to continue. Developing habits of describing a ministry incident, receiving peer perspectives and theological reflection on the incident, and getting peer consultation in developing alternative ways of proceeding are important ways to demonstrate the need for continued learning.

For the most part, PGSP has involved seminary graduates, not the growing numbers of both full-time and part-time "local pastors" or "licensed pastors" who have not attended seminary. Denominations face a huge educational challenge in this area, and, from the evaluations of PGSP, it seems that peer learning groups could be of enormous benefit to these nonseminary graduates.

It may also be important for individual seminary faculty to understand how motivation and energy for learning are created when students are invited to participate in developing learning objectives within a course structure. Students do not want or need to be completely responsible for what is learned in a course, and faculty certainly should be responsible for course parameters. However, motivation is multiplied when students are invited to help determine the direction of a course and participate in identifying evaluation criteria. In my experience working with students to help set course directions, students have responded with far more work than I would have dared to require! This motivational dynamic has also shown up in peer learning groups and is reflected in their characterization of the instructors and teaching styles they favored: "dialogical, participatory/interactive, knowledgeable, personable, open, and flexible . . . practical, passionate, collegial, creative, humorous, and caring."[12]

Finally, the literature on leadership and how it is learned is growing. Seminaries, whether they admit it or not, are schools for ecclesiastical leadership development, and they would do well to consult books such as *Primal Leadership* by Daniel Goleman and colleagues.[13] They make the case that "leaders are made not born." In research to discover the personal capabilities that were key to outstanding leadership, the authors analyzed nearly five hundred competency models in government, business, and not-for-profit organizations (including a religious institution). From their work they have concluded that leadership is learned primarily through the limbic part of the brain, which is much slower than the neocortex, and that learning leadership, therefore, requires opportunities for personal reflection, practice, and feedback in communities of trust. It is the personal work within the communal support and challenge that facilitates change in leadership behavior.

Another resource seminary educators would find helpful is Sharon Daloz Parks's book *Leadership Can Be Taught*.[14] Parks studied the teaching methods of Ronald A. Heifetz, director of the Center for Public Leadership at the John F. Kennedy School of Government, Harvard University. Heifetz uses what he calls "case-in-point" learning that turns the classroom into a rigorous laboratory for leadership in which his own and the student's leadership efforts are available for dissection, analysis, and learning. The book is very provocative and presents a particular challenge for theological faculty charged with creating leaders for the church.

Both the Goleman and the Parks studies suggest that a combination of personal openness, systems thinking, and reflection on leadership practices, along with a supportive and challenging community of peers, creates possibilities for learning and change in leadership. Peer learning groups, when facilitated in a rigorous way, create safe space for such learning to take place.

Principal Learnings

To summarize what has been learned from PGSP and the MELS evaluations, the primary characteristics of peer learning that produced high energy, motivation, and application of learning to ministry practices are: (1) freedom to participate in selecting other members of a peer learning group; (2) participants creating learning directions and foci from an examination of issues in ministry practices; (3) peer groups working together with a facilitator (process consultant) over time so that safety, friendship, shared leadership, and accountability have time to develop in the groups; and (4) availability of some funding to support the learning activities. These learnings indicate positive answers to the two questions asked at the beginning of the paper. First, peer learning groups have produced an increase in competence in church leadership, and, second, there is ample evidence that peer learning has developed positive change in leadership in participants, even if the evidence for congregational change is not as strong. Finally, peer learning, as a direction for continuing theological education, is pregnant with possibilities for further work and innovation.

Notes

1. Mark Rouch, *Competent Ministry: A Guide to Effective Continuing Education* (Nashville: Abingdon, 1974), 33.

2. For the full report, see D. Bruce Roberts and Robert E. Reber, "Indiana Clergy Peer Group Study Program: Final Report and Evaluation," Christian Theological Seminary, February 28, 2007, http://www.cts.edu/Documents/PGSPAnnualReport2006Final.pdf. Hereafter referred to as PGSP: Final Report.

3. Robert E. Reber, D. Bruce Roberts, *Study of The Methodist Educational Leave Society, December 1996* (Birmingham, AL: The Dixon Foundation, 1996). For underlying educational theory and a brief sketch of MELS, see my article: "Motivated Learning and Practice: A Peer Group Model" in *A Lifelong Call to Learn*, ed. Robert E. Reber and D. Bruce Roberts (Nashville: Abingdon Press, 2000), 105–19, and chapter 5 in this volume.

4. Lilly Endowment Annual Report 2002 (Indianapolis: Lilly Endowment, 2003), 49.

5. Parker Palmer, *The Courage to Teach: Exploring the Inner Landscape of a Teacher's Life* (San Francisco: Jossey-Bass, 1998), 132.

6. For an account of the formative and summative evaluation instruments used in this study, see Roberts and Reber, PGSP: Final Report.

7. This quotation and all those from peer group participants quoted in this chapter are taken from Roberts and Reber, PGSP: Final Report.

8. Roberts and Reber, PGSP: Final Report, 18, 50.

9. For a report on a comparative study of SPE projects with peer learning components, see chapter 6 in this volume by Penny Long Marler, "Peer Groups Matter."

10. See chapter 9 in this volume by Tim Dolan, "Making Sense of Ministry: A Clergy Cluster Project."

11. D. Bruce Roberts, "How Can Continuing Theological Education Serve the Church?" *Quarterly Review* 24, no. 2 (Summer 2004): 117–29.

12. Roberts and Reber, PGSP: Final Report, 17.

13. Daniel Goleman, Richard Boyatzis, and Annie McKee, *Primal Leadership: Realizing the Power of Emotional Intelligence* (Boston: Harvard Business School Press, 2002).

14. Sharon Daloz Parks, *Leadership Can Be Taught: A Bold Approach for a Complex World* (Boston: Harvard Business School Press, 2005).

CHAPTER 9

Making Sense of Ministry:
A Clergy Cluster Project

Tim Dolan

Most observers of contemporary society agree that we are living in a time of increasingly rapid change. Social scientists and others who study congregations today believe that this unprecedented rate of change, and the turmoil and uncertainty that goes with it, is having a disproportionately negative effect on churches and church leaders. A growing consensus, based on denominational statistics, indicates that the institutional church—especially mainline churches (Presbyterian, Episcopalian, Methodist, Lutheran, and Congregational)—will not only continue to struggle in the midst of these rapid changes but by the middle of the twenty-first century will also be increasingly sidelined and radically altered. James Wind and Gilbert Rendle of the Alban Institute, in their landmark study on the leadership situation facing American congregations, report that "we are in a time of great crisis and American religion still has not faced up to the depths of its predicament despite mountains of statistics about decline and countless stories of institutional pain."[1] One major challenge facing the church that Wind and Rendle highlight in their study is a perceived decline in the quality of pastoral leadership.

A number of reasons have been identified as to why pastors seem to be less prepared for the continuing challenges of ministry today. Some blame is directed towards traditional models of theological education, including continuing education, that are outdated and inadequate for the realities of church life at the beginning of the twenty-first century. Wind and Rendle argue that "the recruiting, training, and support of new leaders require major changes in our assumptions, behaviors, and the systems in which we live."[2]

Clergy Clusters

One model for doing continuing education that I believe has great potential for helping pastors thrive in a rapidly changing world is clergy clusters. For my doctoral dissertation I organized and studied three clergy clusters. A main purpose of the study was to explore the usefulness of the clergy cluster model as a way of doing continuing education for church leaders.

Twenty-three ordained and lay pastors participated in the clusters. Half of the participants had a Master of Divinity degree and half did not. One cluster had six participants, one had seven, and the third had ten. The participants in the clusters came from eight different denominations. They were recruited through general e-mail announcements, brochures, and personal invitation. As much as possible, care was given to make sure each cluster was composed of male and female pastors who represented ethnic diversity, various sized churches, and both evangelical and mainline theological traditions.

To cover expenses and insure personal commitment to the cluster program, each participant was asked to contribute $495. The fee covered refreshments, printed materials, and honoraria for the facilitators and content presenters. Many participants came from smaller congregations with limited budgets. Because of this, several participants asked for and received significant financial scholarships.

The three clusters met at a central downtown church from 9:00 AM to 1:00 PM twice a month over a four-month period (for a total of eight sessions). All three clusters were led by a skilled facilitator and content presenter. All three group facilitators had pastoral experience and were trained as process consultants through the Center for Organizational Reform (COR). COR was founded in 1993 as a not-for-profit service organization in Spokane, Washington, that provides training and consultation services to individuals and organizations, including congregations, struggling with issues related to change. The content presenters were also associated with COR and in some cases the facilitators doubled as presenters.

Each cluster meeting generally consisted of prayer, a time to check in, personal sharing, and peer mentoring and support. In addition, the clusters included a major learning component focused on leadership and organizational topics that have been identified in the literature as being critical for pastors to understand and practice in ministry. The topics included transformational and adaptive leadership, dealing with resistance to change, understanding congregational culture and the significance of church size and founding influences, managing conflict, power and politics in congregations, and understanding congregations as systems. As part of the group process, participants were invited to give input about additional topics they wanted the content presenters to focus on.

At the end of each cluster meeting, participants were encouraged to put into practice what they learned and then come back and reflect on their experiences two weeks later. Confidentiality was highly valued and maintained throughout the entire process.

At the conclusion of the study, several participants indicated a desire to continue meeting in some form of "advanced" cluster experience. Because of budget constraints and the unavailability of the facilitators and content presenters, we were not able to offer these additional cluster opportunities.

Findings

For the data gathering, I took extensive field notes on each cluster and personally interviewed each cluster participant before, during, and after the cluster experience. The following seven findings summarize my conclusions.

Overall Positive Experience

All participants described their clergy clusters as a positive experience. For some participants, the clusters were literally life changing. The clusters provided them not only helpful information and support but also courage to stay the course regarding their future ministry. Participants made several suggestions as to how the clusters could be even more effective, including

- more emphasis on practical application of the content (through role playing, case studies, videos),
- more opportunities for processing the content,
- more time spent on each topic, and
- a more regular meeting schedule.

Participants also indicated that follow-up clusters or ongoing clusters would further enhance the learning begun with the initial clusters.

Skilled Facilitators and Presenters

Skilled facilitators and content presenters played a key role in the success of the clusters. Not only were the presenters very knowledgeable about their topic areas and the issues facing pastoral leaders, but they also presented their material in a way that seemed to connect with the cluster participants. The facilitators were trained and experienced in group process and they facilitated their clusters with skill and sensitivity. The facilitators were also able to be role models for the participants regarding how to facilitate a group effectively.

Valuable Content

Virtually all cluster participants described the organizational leadership content as being a valuable part of the cluster experience. For some participants, the content had a significant impact on their understanding and practice of ministry and future career decisions. The content was basically new to almost all of the participants; few had any training, either formal or informal, in understanding congregations as organizations. Several participants could not point to any one topic as being most significant; instead, most indicated that the total experience of the cluster made the most impact on them.

Holding Environment

For the majority of participants, the clusters provided a safe setting, a holding environment, for them to share their personal struggles and challenges in ministry. The clusters provided a secure base for participants to process their ministry experiences and make sense of the issues they were facing.

Interdenominational Makeup of the Clusters

The single most significant factor in creating a safe place to share was the interdenominational makeup of the clusters. All cluster participants indicated that the interdenominational makeup made the clusters safe and easier for them to share at a deep level. Because of competition and fear of reprisals or sanctions, participants found it more difficult to share in this way in their own denominational settings and among peers in their own denominations.

Greater Personal and Professional Growth

All participants indicated that the clusters helped them grow personally and professionally. The areas of personal growth that were most often mentioned included

- better understanding of personal strengths and weaknesses,
- a less anxious attitude,
- greater self-confidence, and
- encouragement in one's devotional life.

Areas of professional growth most often mentioned included
- greater creativity in ministry,
- greater ability to relate more effectively with other church leaders, and
- ideas for future continuing education.

A significant side benefit of the clusters was helping participants better understand and relate to pastors from denominations and theological traditions other than their own.

Significant Impact on Ministry Practice

For several participants, the clergy cluster experience had a significant impact on their practice of ministry. Being involved in a cluster literally kept some participants in pastoral ministry at a time when they were going through difficult situations in their churches or trying to make decisions about future ministry. The areas of ministry impact most frequently mentioned included
- greater clarity regarding present and future ministry,
- greater understanding of congregational dynamics,
- more tools for pastoral ministry,
- greater insight on how to deal with church members, and
- more clarity regarding future continuing education.

Many participants commented that they took what they learned in their clusters and used it with their church leadership boards, church staffs, or other local church settings.

Implications

The overall effectiveness and positive response of the participants to the clergy cluster experience raises a number of significant issues regarding how pastoral leaders are traditionally trained and supported in ministry. All of the research on pastoral ministry today suggests that the climate for ministry has changed dramatically. Generally speaking, North American culture no longer supports congregations and pastors in the way it once did. As with all institutions, congregations are facing enormous changes.

Lyle Schaller, a prolific writer about Protestant congregations, wrote that "the challenge to be an effective parish pastor is far more demanding and difficult today than it was 40 years ago."[3] A number of reasons are usually cited as to why ministry is more demanding, including the "graying" of many congregations, increasingly limited human and financial resources, unreal expectations, resistance to change, general mistrust of institutions (including congregations), and the loss of denominational loyalty.

A pastor in one clergy cluster summed up the feeling of many pastors regarding the current ministry climate: "My dad was a minister and my grandpa was a minister. I determined early on that I was never going to be a minister. I thought, 'Good Lord, why would anybody?' But in conversations that I had with my dad before he passed away, and in conversations I even had with my grandpa, was how different ministry is today than it was a generation ago. . . . I can remember having a conversation with my dad after he had retired. We were talking about ministry and . . . challenges that I was facing . . . as compared to the challenges he faced. It's just a different world. It is absolutely a different world. A lot of the stuff that is just blatant in our faces today was beneath the surface or never talked about or not addressed in public settings or even in private settings. And I guess that's just being confirmed. It was really confirmed for me through the clusters that twenty-first century ministry is challenging. And it's overwhelming, and a lot of hard work."

Henry Klopp, church consultant and president of International Graduate School of Ministry in Edmonds, Washington, describes the changes as "unparalleled in the history of the world." Klopp comments that "everyone is trying to figure out how to deal with this new and changing environment. Old systems and methodologies no longer work. New methods of thinking are required to cope with our new environment."[4]

Making Sense of Ministry

Against this backdrop of chaotic and discontinuous change, many pastoral leaders are struggling to make sense of what it means to be a pastoral leader in the contemporary church. Although it was not specifically mentioned in so many words by the participants in this study, one major benefit of the clergy cluster was helping these pastors make sense of their lives and ministries in an increasingly complex and chaotic world. So many pastors *do* ministry, but so often have little opportunity to step back and reflect on—and make sense of—what it is they are doing.

In a similar study of clergy clusters, Terry Young in his doctoral research at Gonzaga University discovered that "sense making"— helping pastoral leaders "bring clarity to the ambiguous world of church ministry"[5]—was one of the most significant, and usually unplanned and unintended, outcomes of the cluster experience.

> The sense making . . . was consistent across cases as one of the most dominant gains resulting from the learning cluster experience. Frequent references were made to the gaining of perspective; making sense of issues, challenges, conflicts, or expectations; finding help with the tunnel vision problem; and "seeing the forest instead of just the trees."[6]

Although participants in my study did not specifically label it as such, it is clear that one primary benefit of the clusters was the opportunity to struggle with making sense of a rapidly changing world and the increasing ambiguities and complexities of pastoral ministry. Many comments made by cluster participants indicate that the experience was helpful in giving them perspective on their congregations and greater understanding of the leadership and organizational challenges they face every day. The following comments are typical of the sense-making responses I received from many pastors in the clusters:

"A lot of what happened in the cluster is that it just literally gave a language to lots of things you deal with that you didn't know how to categorize; you didn't know where to put it. You knew it was there, you knew you were dealing with it, but you didn't have any handles or terminology or language. And just that has been helpful in being able to say, 'Okay, now I know what that is.' So just getting somebody saying to me, 'This is what that is,' was like—wow!"

"The particular paradigms, lenses, and so forth that we were given and understanding the church as an organization, and as a culture, and from the point of view of family systems—all of those things were one of those serendipitous kinds of experiences where, in a sense, you can never view things the same again. This cluster made me see something I've never seen before, and I can never unsee it. It will always change the way I view the church, and therefore the way I go about ministry and the way I respond to it."

Safe Setting for Sharing

These and similar comments made by other cluster participants provide evidence that pastors are longing for opportunities to engage in meaningful reflection and dialogue regarding their vocation and their experiences in ministry. But for this sharing to happen, pastors need to feel they are in a safe and confidential setting.

Young discovered that this kind of deep, intentional sharing most naturally occurs when pastors feel they are in a relatively safe holding environment. The term *holding environment* was originally developed by psychologists to describe the process by which mothers *hold* their children as they move from dependence to independence. Later, this concept was expanded to refer to a therapist's ability to provide a safe space for clients to explore deeply ingrained personal issues. Eventually, the term was applied to organizational settings and the need for individuals to have safe places in which to share.[7]

Holding environments support, sustain, and develop individuals as they deal with the complexities of their lives and their work. Ronald Heifetz, professor at the Kennedy School of Government at Harvard University, defines a holding environment as "any relationship in which one party has the power to hold the attention of another party."[8] Such relationships put appropriate boundaries on people's anxiety and help regulate the distress people feel when they are being stretched to make challenging adjustments in their lives.

Holding environments are helpful because they contain and channel the problems, stresses, and pain that come from growth and development. They are safe places for leaders to express their fear and pain while at the same time help guide them to deal with adaptive challenges they need to face. Young refers to these environments as a "secure base" and suggests that they refer to "any positive context for healthy development."[9]

All pastors who participated in the clergy clusters commented that they felt the clusters provided a relatively safe and secure holding environment in which to process their lives and their ministries. This feeling is reflected in the following comments:

"I would feel very safe to bring confidential information into this group. If I had something that was applicable that I could discuss . . . it's a safe place to be able to bring that. I would feel safe that it wouldn't go anywhere, and I'd be able to discuss the issue and get some others' ideas."

"I was surprised at how openly some of the people shared. And that's not something that I do real easily. Particularly if it's a difficult area. So I was surprised, and I was also impressed that they felt that much trust and were able to speak about even the hard things that they were facing in the work that they were doing. So I felt that there was a lot of openness."

Interdenominational Makeup

One of the most significant findings of this study was how important the interdenominational makeup of the clusters was to creating a safe place for pastors to share. All participants indicated that they would not have been able to share at the same level, and with the same openness, if the clusters had been made up entirely of pastors from their denomination. For a variety of reasons, many pastors find it difficult to share at a deep level with these peers. The following comments made by two pastors typify participants' feelings about sharing in their own denominational groupings:

"I never once felt like I had to be guarded in the cluster. And to be honest with you, I could probably be more honest and transparent in the cluster setting than I could with my denominational brothers. One of the other cluster participants is also part of my denomination and we talked about this. I said, 'I'm not sure I could have said what I shared in the cluster at our denominational meeting or at the pastors' conference or the workshops.' You know the politics of the church, and the whole bit, and you hate to think that's a part of it, but there's times where you're just a little bit cautious, a little bit guarded about what you say in the presence of denominational peers. I never sensed that in this cluster group; it was so diverse. The cluster folks not only were not connected to my network through my denomination but when we left that place, that stuff that we shared was sacred. And it was protected. And I never went away feeling like, 'I wish I could have said this or that.'"

"There are two other pastors' settings that I meet with, one is the local ministerial association, and the other is the area conference for my denomination. In that setting, that last one, I always weigh my words with caution because our denominational

executive is present, and he's my husband's boss. He has responsibility for placement for us, and in that kind of a setting, you
wouldn't spill your guts out necessarily. Whereas, if you're in a
setting like the cluster . . . I just feel like it's been an okay place . . .
a little bit safer . . . a safe place."

This finding has important implications for denominational
leaders who are responsible for the care and support of pastors.
They need to realize that most pastors need a secure base in which
to process the many challenging demands of ministry. Unfortu-
nately, many pastors do not feel their denominational groupings
offer a safe place to do this. This reluctance is due, in part, to a
feeling of competition with other pastors, high expectations of
pastoral performance by denominational leaders, or both.

One pastor in my study commented that he often feels like a
failure when he attends denominational gatherings because of the
expectations placed upon him to make his church grow. Another
pastor commented that he no longer reports at denominational
gatherings how much his church has grown because admitting
that it has not grown at all is too painful and embarrassing. In
addition, pastors often fear reprisal, sanctions, or criticism if denominational leaders discover they have a problem or an issue
they cannot handle.

In their study of the spiritual development needs of midcareer
clergy, William Lord and George Brown also discovered that many
clergy prefer learning opportunities outside their denominations:
"Beyond a few close colleagues, most pastors need a space that is
open, safe, and trusted, where they can engage themselves and others on significant issues, without feeling already judged or needing
to protect themselves by playing a role or putting up a false front."[10]

Lord and Brown offer some reasons as to why clergy seek
learning outside their denominations: a perceived lack of competence on the part of judicatory staff to put on quality educational
events and, more significant, "a desire for anonymity that under-
lies avoidance of learning opportunities sponsored or provided by
clergy of their own denomination."[11]

The feeling of being judged or cut off from denominational support systems often leads to loneliness and isolation, especially among pastors who do not have other sources of support or who serve in isolated areas. These feelings were vividly described by one cluster participant:

"How isolated I am as an individual. I have no friends, spouse, or individual support system. It is a small town. I easily get triggered into that old insecurity. Part of me is saying, 'What about me?' I stay connected, but there is a level of friendship in which I cannot enter in. I have friends in a neighboring community, but it's hard. I'm disgusted with the system. I called my denominational executive to let her know what's going on—that I might not make it through the year. She was about to give me fifteen minutes of her time on the phone, but she has not called back. That's all the support I get from the system. I told her I'm dealing with this nasty situation in my congregation. She said, 'It sounds like you have other support through the cluster so we have none to give you.' When I mentioned this cluster group as a resource for other pastors, she was not interested. My isolation is systemic. The system leaves its clergy isolated. The message is: 'We are too busy. We need you not to need us. We need clergy to take care of themselves, but we will not help you.' This is the system I am in and dealing with."

Although this particular pastor's relationship to her denominational leadership is not necessarily typical of all the pastors in the clusters, it does illustrate the loneliness many pastors face and the unresponsiveness many of them perceive from denominational leaders and support systems. Klopp confirms this observation when he comments that "most pastors of denominational churches indicated they get very little in the way of assistance or support from their denominational office."[12]

My research indicates that one of the best ways to provide this support is to encourage pastors to be involved in small peer groups made up of participants from a number of different denominations. Interdenominational clergy clusters have the potential to provide much-needed support and encouragement to pastors who are facing loneliness, burnout, or difficult ministry situations.

Lifelong Learning in Community

Most educators and business leaders understand that education today needs to be in-service, continuous, and lifelong. For church leaders, three years of seminary training is no longer adequate preparation for pastoral ministry. Three (or four) years can provide a necessary and important foundation to build upon. But for pastoral leaders to navigate successfully today's "white water" of change,[13] they need continual training and support in a safe and confidential environment.

Jay Conger, professor of leadership studies at Claremont Mc-Kenna College, and Beth Benjamin, director of the Center for Leadership Development and Research at Stanford Graduate School of Business, argue that adults learn best when they are involved in educational models that combine time, relationships, and a process that honors how adults learn. Their research indicates that "information learned [by adults] under distributed periods of training is generally retained longer than in a one-time program."[14] According to Conger and Benjamin, learning tends to be most effective for adults when it is spread out over time, is conducted in groups (rather than by lone individuals), and is oriented towards "action."[15] Adults, generally, are motivated to learn things they perceive are practical and have immediate relevance to their lives. Reggie McNeal, consultant with Leadership Network of Dallas, Texas, describes the learning that Conger and Benjamin advocate as "intentional learning in community."[16]

My study confirmed that training and support for clergy can be very effective when it is regular, ongoing, and includes opportunities for group interaction, peer mentoring, and self-directed learning. Although the pastors strongly resonated with the content presented to them in the clusters, they especially appreciated opportunities to put some "shoe leather" on their learning through role plays, case studies, and group dialogue. Most participants indicated a desire for even more opportunities to flesh out, in practical ways, what they were learning.

When pastors in the clusters were asked what they found most helpful about the clergy cluster model, they often mentioned the opportunity to process the content with others who were "in the same boat" as being an important part of the learning process. The following comment was a typical response:

"I need the connection with folks out there who are doing what I'm doing, who are struggling in the areas that I'm struggling, who are having some successes, and I can say 'Well, talk to me about that.' It helped me to know that there are other guys out there who are in the same boat I'm in, and I can pick up the phone. I'm smart enough to know I'm not smart enough. The more help I can get, the more input I can get, the more resource people that are out there that I know, I can just . . . knock on their door or pick up the phone or shoot them an e-mail. It breaks me out of the isolation thing. Just to be able to talk to somebody who is out there . . . doing it and wrestling with it. That helps me so much.

McNeal suggests that for leaders to be successful in the future, they will need to be lifelong learners. He argues that learning in the past was "linear, didactic, privatized, and parochial." But for learning to be effective in the twenty-first century, it will need to be "nonlinear, layered, experiential . . . and also just in time."[17] Effective learning will include coaching, peer mentoring, and reflecting and processing with others in community. McNeal suggests that mentoring groups, intentional learning communities, and clergy clusters are some of the most effective ways to make this happen.

A critical intellectual capacity for twenty-first century leadership success will be the ability to build knowledge together with other colleagues. The rate of information growth coupled with the collapse of the Christendom paradigm make it no longer possible to prepare for ministry challenges through traditional preparation processes. Academic, conferential, and self-guided learning must be supplemented through a peer-mentoring process in which life and ministry experiences are debriefed.[18]

Recommendations for Future Research

The problems that pastors in the clusters seemed to be struggling with were primarily organizational or relational in nature. These included problem parishioners, congregations stuck in the past, resistance to change, unrealistic expectations from church boards or denominational officials, loneliness and isolation, limited resources, conflicts with church members or staff, lack of energy and vision, and stagnating congregations or congregations in decline. Yet, in almost every instance, these leaders had little or no formal or informal training in how to deal with these challenges. Further research should be done as to how well seminaries and theological training programs are preparing future church leaders in these important areas and how they can improve what it is they do offer.

The finding that pastors often feel inadequate support from denominational systems raises questions as to how denominational systems function and how they could be adjusted and improved to be more responsive to the clergy in their organization. Further research into the extent of this problem and ways that denominations could provide better support and a holding environment would be beneficial.

A Journey Traveled Together

My research and observations have convinced me that the most effective and transformational learning usually occurs when it happens in an ongoing, safe community with others. Pastoral leaders can benefit from being involved in small, ongoing cluster communities in a number of ways; not only can they learn valuable new leadership and ministry skills, but they also can learn them in a safe and supportive environment. Clusters can also provide opportunities for pastors to discuss and reflect on their learning and also practice what they have learned through case studies, role playing, and other means.

The skills pastors develop, and the support they receive through clergy clusters, helps them to be healthier leaders, build stronger congregations, and deal more effectively with the predictable crises that characterize all organizations, including congregations. Involvement in a clergy cluster also helps prevent discouragement, burnout, and that gnawing sense of isolation and loneliness that many pastoral leaders experience.

One of the most valuable side benefits of clusters, which I frequently heard expressed, is that the clusters are a tangible reminder that pastors are not alone. This pastoral leadership journey that each one is on is a journey all travel together.

"I think the cluster has really been good for me. Because it's very easy to focus on challenges or difficulties in the work you're doing and feel like you're facing them alone. So to be in a group and to talk about it and to find out that other people face similar challenges—is a real supportive thing."

Notes

1. James Wind and Gilbert Rendle, "The Leadership Situation Facing American Congregations, An Alban Institute Special Report" (Herndon, VA: Alban Institute, 2001), 3.

2. Wind and Rendle, "Leadership Situation," 20.

3. Lyle E. Schaller, *Discontinuity and Hope: Radical Change and the Path to the Future* (Nashville: Abingdon Press, 1999), 15.

4. Henry Klopp, *The Ministry Playbook: Strategic Planning for Effective Churches* (Grand Rapids: Baker Books, 2002), 24.

5. Terry C. Young, "A Multi-Case Study of the Learning Cluster as a Holding Environment for Clergy Leaders" (PhD diss., Gonzaga University, Spokane, Washington, 2004), 198.

6. Ibid., 273.

7. Ibid.

8. Ronald A. Heifetz, *Leadership Without Easy Answers* (Cambridge, MA: Belknap/Harvard University Press, 1994), 104, 105.

9. Young, "Multi-Case Study of the Learning Cluster," 23, 17.

10. William Lord and George Brown, "Where and How Religious Leaders Learn," in *A Lifelong Call to Learn: Approaches to Continuing Education for Church Leaders*, ed. Robert E. Reber and D. Bruce Roberts (Nashville: Abingdon Press, 2000), 92.

11. Ibid.

12. Klopp, *Ministry Playbook*, 69.

13. Peter B. Vaill, *Learning as a Way of Being: Strategies for Survival in a World of Permanent White Water* (San Francisco: Jossey-Bass, 1996).

14. Jay A. Conger and Beth Benjamin, *Building Leaders: How Successful Companies Develop the Next Generation* (San Francisco: Jossey-Bass, 1999), 52.

15. Conger and Benjamin, *Building Leaders*, 19.

16. Reggie McNeal, *A Work of Heart: Understanding How God Shapes Spiritual Leaders* (San Francisco: Jossey-Bass, 2002), 130.

17. McNeal, *Work of Heart*, 132.

18. Ibid., 131.

CHAPTER 10

Coaching as Continuing Education: The Auburn Seminary Experience

Laurie J. Ferguson and Frederick W. Weidmann

Since 2002, leaders from across a spectrum of church backgrounds and ministry locations have experienced coaching through programs developed and directed by Auburn Theological Seminary in New York City. At first these included continuing education classes and seminars at Auburn Seminary as well as an intensive coaching component within the New York Sabbatical Institute, a program for accomplished clergy who for one or more reasons were considered at risk. The programs were funded by Lilly Endowment in conjunction with its Sustaining Pastoral Excellence Initiative and administered by Auburn in partnership with Union and New York theological seminaries. In 2006, with the support of a Lilly Endowment sustainability grant as well as support from a foundation wishing to remain anonymous, Auburn established the Auburn Coaching Institute (ACI) to provide a program for clergy and church leaders that would include residential components as well as ongoing coaching in "real time." The ACI quickly expanded into a series of programs to meet the requests of different constituencies, including partnerships with denominational and other church and parachurch organizations that wished to offer a coaching component within other programs, one-on-one coaching, and expanded classes in coaching and leadership skills.

Stories of Coaching

Richard came into the room and sat down across from Jim, his coach, for their first session.[1] "I don't know where to begin," he said. "I've been in my current church for about four years. I know there's something more that I can do there, but I'm not sure what it is. I want to work on my leadership skills, and I want this congregation to be more active, but I don't know how to motivate them to do more." As his coach listened, he could hear not only Richard's frustration but also his hope. He also heard that Richard had energy for his work, along with some uncertainty about how to proceed. Jim asked him to identify some goals for their work together over the next six months. "That's hard," Richard responded. "I don't usually think of goals. I find myself reacting to whatever comes in the door and don't have time for much more. But when you ask me, sure there are some things I want to accomplish, but who's got the time."

"What kinds of things?" Jim wanted to know.

"Well, this sounds silly, because they're little things, but organizing a training day for lay leaders. I never seem to get around to it. I'd also like to outline sermon topics for a few months in advance so I could develop my thinking, but I find I preach from week to week and I'm worried that my sermons are a bit shallow."

At this point Jim realized they had some short-term concrete actions they could use for focus, but he wanted more from his first meeting with Richard. In terms of Auburn's coaching method, he saw that they could easily establish some *horizontal* goals. These are plans or action steps that can be tracked and completed. When pastors develop a sense of *finishing* and accomplishment, it can shift their sense of how effective they are at ministry. So much of the work of ministry is ongoing and never done. Setting benchmarks and goals helps a pastor track what has been achieved over time. But for coaching to be deeply effective, it must also move on a *vertical* plane to help connect pastoral leaders with their sense of purpose and calling and their connection with God's presence in their lives and work. In Auburn's model for coaching, the work moves back and forth between an emphasis on the goals and action strategies, which are the horizontal level of work, and the vertical dimension of connection with God and a sense of call and purpose.[2]

Jim began to move the conversation in a more personal direction. "Where do you feel most alive in the work you are doing now?" he inquired. Richard had to pause and think for a bit. When he gave his answer, he and Jim began exploring deeper issues about who he was as a leader and a person in his ministry setting. They were creating an environment where Richard could feel comfortable reflecting on himself in his role and in his work, and in that safe space he would also begin to identify places where he wanted to grow and challenge himself. He might be able to be vulnerable about his worries, his doubts, and his hopes; in that open space, growth and new possibilities can occur.

A coaching conversation, as part of a coaching relationship, is a cocreated space where the pastor and the coach can move between accountability for some daily and weekly tasks to a perspective that looks to where the pastor can be in a year or more and who the pastor can be as a leader and as a person. The minister crafts a personal agenda for the work that can include some big, bold challenging dreams along with more immediately effective, achievable goals. The coaching conversation provides a place to try some things out, to dream big, and to break challenges and opportunities into smaller doable pieces. Coaching encourages the minister to begin, to take first steps, rather than give up because something seems too overwhelming to do.

That was the situation that Karen brought to coaching. Her personal life mirrored her ministry. Things weren't getting done, and she felt frustrated and angry. She sought coaching not to learn how to improve on some skills, like Richard, but as a place for sorting herself, and her personal and professional interests, out. In her first meeting with Sue, her coach, she asked about the difference between coaching and therapy. "We aren't going to focus on your past or look for insight," Sue said. "Our work in coaching will be to remind you of your strengths and to identify where you most want to grow and develop. We'll look at your congregation and what you imagine you want your ministry to be like. We'll listen for where the Spirit is nudging you."

Over the eight months of their work, Karen identified some small projects she could go back to and finish. That increased her energy, and she began to tackle the largest issue in the church's life, the failing building. Sue encouraged her to do some research and to connect with colleagues and denominational support. Together they created a step-by-step plan to deal with the problems in a systematic way. The other less measurable aspect of the coaching was for Karen to find some nourishment for her soul. Karen needed some development on the vertical dimension of her life.

Before she became a solo pastor and "no longer had enough time," Karen had always made some kind of art. Sue challenged her to find the time to do what was important, and Karen located some studio space and resumed painting. This had a significant and immediate impact on her preaching and more broadly on the sense of commitment, energy, and creativity she brought to her ministry.

These are just two snapshots of how coaching works to increase learning. Often the word *learning* connotes head knowledge when, in fact, it includes understanding, skills, attitudes, and values. When a pastor works with a coach, he or she may well develop cognitively, but the main gains are greater self-knowledge, greater awareness of the organizations and systems of which one is part (congregation or other ministry, denomination or other governing bodies, wider community), and increasing confidence as a leader and professional. This is usually coupled with skill development that supports a pastor's personal and professional goals. One participant said that before coaching she tended to react to situations. Since working with a coach, she has learned to respond; she has also become more proactive in developing and setting agenda in concert with others.

Growth comes to each pastor in a different way. Individuals bring to the coaching experience lives and ministries that are varied and complex. Coaching is tailored to fit the specific needs of the pastor at a specific time and to work on real challenges and opportunities in real time. The pastor sets the agenda. The coach comes alongside to guide, listen, prod, and encourage. Coaching creates a learning environment; it is a flexible and agile way to support leaders at various points in their careers and with different needs, who want to learn on their own terms and in their own way.

Coaching on vertical and horizontal planes (as indicated above) is a key element in Auburn's coaching methodology. The third emphasis is coaching to develop *hardiness* or *resilience*.[3] According to its own founding documents, Auburn Seminary was established to develop church leaders hardy enough for ministry on the frontier. Today's professional church leaders are faced with new frontiers of religious change, not to mention a host of economic, social, and other cultural shifts, often of seismic proportions. *Hardiness* is defined as an ability to thrive even in times of stress and change. It is an attitude, or an inner resource, that can be developed, the essential element of which is a sense of commitment, control, and challenge. Auburn's method of coaching helps leaders identify and strengthen these qualities in their lives and ministry.

Development of Auburn's Coaching Method: The New York Sabbatical Institute

As mentioned above, Auburn partnered with two seminaries in 2002 to create a Lilly-funded project known as the New York Sabbatical Institute (NYSI). This project was a two-year investment for clergy who had been chosen on the basis of two criteria: (1) their work was recognized by colleagues or other mentors as excellent, and (2) they were—statistically speaking—at risk of burnout given one or more demographic identifiers (women clergy, young clergy, traditionally underrepresented) or circumstantial identifiers (they or their congregation were immediately affected by the events of 9/11). However ambiguous the term or concept *excellent* may be, coupled with each participant's commitment to the whole (two-year) program, excellence set an important consistency to the project: NYSI was about the individual as leader and about excellence in ministry. These two factors combined, excellence and commitment, undergirded the coaching component of the program and, more broadly, undergirds any effective coaching relationship.

Professional coaching had originally been planned as a six-month offering within the two-year program. Universally recognized by the NYSI fellows to be an effective activity, coaching was extended by popular demand and became the major method used to cultivate hardiness and sustain pastoral excellence. Fellows reported that coaching succeeded because it was convenient, private, constant, reliable, and centered on supporting the pastor's goals. That is, it provided a *place* for nourishment, checking in, and growth to which they could, and did, return. Further, it required accountability and goal setting and offered a place for safe reflection, planning, identifying needs or gaps, spinning out ideas, and developing and practicing skills. Coaching was safe, and it called them to account; it opened them up to that which nourishes them and their ministries.

Fellows indicated that the coach served as an objective presence genuinely interested in their whole development, personal and professional, and not just their persona within the congregation (as is often the perceived case regarding denominational executives or peers). That concern for the whole didn't take away from, but enhanced, the positive effect of coaching on the minister and for the ministry site.

In sum, coaching proved effective because it required goal setting and accountability and offered a safe and supportive context for reflection on, and response to, issues and challenges raised at each fellow's ministry site. Further, the coaching component was developed by and for church leaders, including a director and coaches familiar with, experienced within, and dedicated to the church's life and its people and mission.

These basic criteria—working with and for real challenges and opportunities at each participant's ministry site; (re)establishing the pastoral leaders' sense of call as well as their particular goals and objectives; and providing coaches well versed and experienced with the theory and practice of coaching and dedicated to and experienced with the life of churches—have continued to be at the foundation of ACI's work.

The Auburn Coaching Institute

The Auburn Coaching Institute (ACI) was formally launched in the fall of 2006. As indicated above, the seminary had secured the continuing support of Lilly Endowment through a sustainability grant and a development grant from an anonymous foundation. A planning team of stakeholders was established, including senior staff of the seminary, members of the seminary's board of directors, and the advisory board of the Center for Church Life (the place within the seminary structure where the coaching institute was to be established and housed), and consultants trained in and experienced with coaching, theological education, and church life. The seminary spread a relatively broad net in identifying potential coaches, many of whom have remained directly involved in various aspects of ACI programming.

Building on findings from the coaching experience within NYSI as indicated above, three criteria for the ACI coaching team were set: (1) training and experience in professional coaching; (2) experience in coaching or consulting or both, with individual church leaders, congregations, or denominational structures; (3) some formal training in and experience with psychological theory and methods. Another criterion, less closely held, emerged:

Because several ACI coaches are also trained in and practice it, spiritual direction emerged as a fourth, though less closely held, criterion. The reasons for establishing the first two criteria are likely self-evident, though an added word about the first is called for. "Professional coaching" as used here indicates that the coaching work is set within the context of, and is primarily regarding, the individual's professional position(s) and career; personal matters and concerns can and do emerge, and as has already been shown in the examples above, are engaged. Professional coaching is distinguished from "life coaching" that can and does often include consideration of profession and career, but has broader and less professionally focused applications. The value of the third and fourth criteria may be less obvious: though these disciplines may indeed influence some of what happens in a coaching relationship, it is more so the depth of wisdom they bring in distinguishing what coaching is and is not that stands out foremost in the coaching situation. For coaching to be effective—and for a coaching program to model coaching for church leaders—it must be distinguished from other engagements such as mentoring, spiritual direction, and various psychological therapies that are valuable and legitimate in their own right, and are called for by particular circumstances and by particular individuals at particular times, but that are not coaching.

Pilot Program

The model on which the planning team settled, and with which ACI was founded, was a year-long program, including two three-day residential conferences with facilitators, coaches, and peers, and extensive one-on-one work with a professional coach. The residential conferences were held at the beginning and middle of the program (October and April). One-on-one coaching occurred in person within each residential conference as well as twice monthly via telephone outside each conference, November through September.

The pilot program included thirty-one participants (all of whom completed the full program) and nine coaches. The basic pattern was four participants per coach, with some exceptions due to personal schedules and the fit of participant to coach. Each participant had responded to an advertisement in denominational magazines or professional journals, to information sent to judicatory offices, or to invitations made and information passed via word of mouth. A fee of $750 (roughly the sum that many—by no means all—clergy have available in continuing education funding per year) was set; the program as outlined above (twenty-six coaching sessions; two three-day conferences, including programming, room, and board) is easily reckoned as providing five to six thousand dollars worth of goods and services. Each participant was asked to complete an information form about themselves, their ministry site, and their experience with and expectations of coaching.

Though the presumption—and, as it turned out, reality—was that most of the participants would be congregation-based pastors, the parameters for those the program would target was purposely set broadly: solo, associate, and senior pastors as well as nonordained "church leaders" serving in a professional capacity at a given "ministry site." Such language, and such openness, yielded several health care chaplains and other noncongregation ministers, including one who was not ordained.

The work—and play—of the residential conferences was conceived and planned to provide the opportunity to establish some theoretical scaffolding and practical methodology of coaching, introduce models for considering and reflecting on oneself and one's work within wider institutional and cultural systems, engage in formal and informal assessment of gifts and challenges, provide some training and practice in the use of coaching skills in one's ministry and in support of oneself and one's peers, and provide time for worship, recreation, and sharing among peers and facilitators. Both structured and unstructured times allowed for developing peer relationships. Though developing group identity and support was not an overt focus of the residential conferences, ACI staff did suggest informal use of coaching skills and methodology as one way by which participants might support and challenge each other in their ongoing work and development.

Practical considerations ranged from scheduling (midweek, breaking in time for colleagues to return to their ministry sites for weekend and Sunday programs and activities) to physical and creature comforts (single room, suggesting and allowing for down time and reflection, including minimal but important writing assignments and assessments), good food, and space (both physical and temporal) for recreative activities such as hiking, meditation, and arts and crafts. Though ACI leaders were tempted to ask and invite colleagues to be involved in worship planning and leadership, the former was strictly avoided and the latter kept to a minimum precisely because this was to be a recreative time away that suggests and allows for stepping outside of familiar patterns: worship (planned by seminary staff, coaches, and facilitators) and meditation, yes; worship planning and preparation by participants, no!

One-on-one work with an Auburn coach was conceived of as being the heart of the program. This included initial, and extended, in-person sessions at the residential conferences and was sustained with twice monthly sessions via telephone, fifty to sixty minutes in length. Initial work established the relationship and confirmed the commitment of both participant and coach. A preliminary schedule and a first phone session were set before departure from the first residential conference.

Experiences and Findings

There is much that can be reported based on both formal and informal feedback from participants and coaches received from the pilot program described above, as well as from its continuation as the Comprehensive Coaching Program. Simply put, the results of coaching have been positive and in many cases transforming for individuals and ministries.

Since this chapter focuses on the pilot program that, even considering its continuation in the Comprehensive Coaching Program, includes a limited participant base to date, standard case studies or composite portraits have been avoided. This is to guarantee the confidentiality that Auburn promises and also asks of participants as they engage in one-on-one work with their coaches, plenary sessions, facilitated discussions, and workshops with other participants. In what follows, we report on and highlight representative challenges and opportunities that church leaders in different positions have worked on with their coaches and within the program more broadly.

Before proceeding, a word about the matter of *fit*. The planning team determined that due to practical considerations, the director, in consultation with the director of coaching, would assign participants to a coach. Practical considerations included: (1) a body of participants from various locales around the country, (2) limited and tightly scheduled time at the residential conferences (including a limited amount of free, recreational time, which ACI leaders were keen to honor), and (3) the cost-effectiveness of maximizing the ratio of participants to coaches (which, as noted above, was set at 4:1). With the aid of the information form each participant had submitted prior to the first residential conference (providing information about educational background, professional setting, perceived challenges and opportunities, interests, goals and hopes for coaching, and so forth), this method proved effective. Of forty-eight participants over the first two years of the program, only two have requested reassignment.

For many solo pastors, a recurring or ongoing challenge is that of balance. Simply put, this involves the balancing of personal and professional life, the establishing of appropriate boundaries between the two, and using and planning professional time effectively and with *purpose*, a word often overused and even abused in some popular parlance. Via Auburn coaching, many have come to a renewed and deepened sense of call as well as greater boundary-setting and time-management skills; indeed the one, a renewed sense of call, often directly feeds and focuses the others—boundary setting and effective use of time. Relationships are considered: on the professional side, those with congregational leadership, staff and volunteers, and with the congregation more widely; on the personal side, those with family and friends, with oneself, and, hardly last, with God.

Different colleagues treat their relationship with their coach differently, especially as it influences and allows for reassessment regarding various other relationships. Regarding their ministry site, for many participants a process or pattern along this line develops with their coach: (1) developing ideas for meeting goals; (2) presenting those ideas and receiving feedback from lay leadership and, in turn, assessing that feedback with the coach; (3) implementing the ideas. In the overwhelming majority of cases, attention to call (one's own and the congregation's), to relationships, and to the development and implementation of goals results in positive change to and for individuals, systems, and, in many cases, the overall culture of the congregation.

Particular sorts of challenges face those in particular pastoral positions other than solo pastor, including, for example, senior pastors, associates, and interims. ACI is blessed with participants from all the above within the pilot and comprehensive programs and, as indicated above, that is not by chance. ACI leaders purposely established a broad participant base of clergy and professional church leaders. Interim ministers, by design and intention, regularly move from one ministry site to another. Impact is in some ways easier, and in other ways more difficult, to gauge as interim ministers work with individuals, ministry teams, and whole congregations for a limited amount of time before moving on. Personal and professional goals and aspirations need to be clear, and assessable, as interim ministers establish and reestablish their leadership (style, goals, systems) in one site after another and maintain a wider and somewhat more flexible network of colleagues throughout their ministries. Associates are dealing with some of the standard challenges of middle management, not least being those of "managing up"—in this case to a senior minister and directly or indirectly to a governing committee (or a series of committees)—and often "managing out" to other members on a ministry team. Further, many associates contend with the expectation (often presumed, by themselves and others) that they will be moving on to another more senior position elsewhere. Managing expectations, relationships, and short-term and long-term goals are among the broad and specific challenges and opportunities that these colleagues bring to Auburn coaching programs. Those, and any number of particulars at their ministry site, account for the work accomplished.

Senior pastors, as indicated by the attendant title that at least one denomination regularly attributes to them, are heads of staff. That responsibility alone—including supervision, development, and direction of individual staff and staff teams, especially in many larger congregations—can keep a responsible leader's time and energies occupied. Beyond that, senior ministers variously work on setting vision and strategy, leading cultural change, planning transitions (of programming, leadership, partnerships, or other systems) that benefit the congregation, not to mention preaching and other pastoral duties.

The matter of role looms large for all in pastoral leadership including, of course, senior ministers. For some or even many members of a given congregation with a multiclergy staff, the senior minister is the pastor. How can senior ministers fulfill that role or, even, should they? How can senior ministers empower others—including lay leaders and congregation members—to exercise their authority and leadership in healthy, creative, and constructive ways? Beyond that, how and when should positions or programs be added, and how and when should the congregation embark on capital campaigns and the like, can be vital questions for a senior minister. Work around clarity of call and purpose, and awareness and development of leadership style, purpose, and role are recurring areas of challenge and opportunity for senior ministers.

As has already been noted, central to the work of all colleagues is relationship: with oneself, with one's role, with God, with one's sense of call, and with others—professional colleagues, lay leadership and nonprofessional colleagues, the congregation (or in the case of noncongregation-based leaders, the employing organization and larger constituencies), denominational heads. Another commonality among pastoral leaders who are drawn to coaching is the matter of change. They all live with and within it, and their areas of ministry and ministry sites are all affected by it. Effective leaders want and work to become agents of change for those individuals and institutions with whom and for which they work.

Two other broad categories from which pastoral leaders come to coaching at Auburn are judicatory or denominational leadership and special ministries such as health care and other community-based institutions. Many of these leaders have what might be called administrative roles, but many are involved directly in pastoral ministry in one way or another; and many are involved in nurturing and enhancing the ministry of others, both individuals and communities. The stories of reorganization in and among denominational structures and in and among health care and other service-delivery organizations are many and varied, often painful, and occasionally uplifting. The needs of individuals and communities served by these structures and organizations are many and varied and, often as not, central to ministry. Such leaders' engagement of coaching often involves working with change—effectively working with and within larger structures and movements to become agents of positive change and, in turn, support others in doing so.

Leading in a way that encourages and allows others to take up their authority, variously defined, is no easy task. It can be, and often is, crucial to developing healthy ministries and healthy leaders, whether professional, volunteer, ordained, or lay who are equipped to forward particular mission(s) and forward the work of churches broadly. For many colleagues, that larger and more crucial challenge—leading in a way that encourages and allows others to take up their authority—serves as the center of their work within the coaching program.

Meeting the Needs and Challenges of a New Religious Frontier

Beyond the direct, practical, and practicable results for and among individual leaders are other goals and outcomes. Auburn's coaching initiative was launched with the express purpose of promoting excellence in religious leaders and developing hardiness for the challenges faced on the new frontier of religious life in the twenty-first century. Many old models for learning no longer fit. Clergy come from vastly diverse backgrounds and life experiences. The expectations of clergy are also vast and varied. Pastors need to be all or some combination of the following (and much else could be added to the list!): community organizers, fund raisers, grief counselors, building contractors, administrators, and visionaries to degrees never before experienced, along with the more traditional roles of preacher, teacher and theologian-in-residence, and pastoral care provider. Communities experience an unprecedented rate of change; clergy need to lead and act, and not merely react to the different world in which we all live. Coaching encourages pastors to learn by meeting challenges and identifying opportunities, assessing and taking risks, and developing and trying different approaches. This real-time learning and practice increases leaders' confidence and positively affects the individuals and institutions engaged by it.

One pastor experienced discussion and dissension on her board as threatening. Her old habit was to quash too much controversial material in a meeting in order to preserve a feeling of peace. But if the church was going to address some serious needs in their community by opening their building for new uses, they had to have some difficult conversations. She needed to learn to be less threatened by arguments and disagreements and to moderate with a centered authority. With her coach, she described and analyzed what this new skill set would look like. At the next board meeting she tried it out, practiced, and then came back to the coach to analyze what worked and what didn't. Practice, analysis, feedback—all these promote learning that addresses both thorny old patterns and new challenges. Developing and practicing a repertoire of responses creates a well of resources for a leader and increases confidence for handling critical situations.

To be effective leaders, pastors must be learning and changing with their congregations. They often have a difficult message to communicate, and in order to do their work with wisdom and intelligence they have to step back to reflect and evaluate. Coaching provides the pastor a sacred container or space to discern and test the Spirit's leading with someone who can ask hard questions and give thoughtful encouragement. The coaching conversation is a time for pastors to assess their role as leaders, examine their practice of ministry, deepen their vision, and develop strategies for the challenges and opportunities of twenty-first-century church leadership.

Another observation from work with almost two hundred pastors is that each person has distinctive gifts and a unique and particular call. One hazard of ministry is that clergy (and educators) sometimes adopt an unconscious assumption that there is a right way to do ministry. Pastors sometimes begin to lop off aspects of themselves to fit a role or carry on a tradition. Auburn bases its coaching program on the theology of 1 Corinthians 12 where Paul makes the strong statement about varieties of gifts, and how valuable and necessary that diversity is for the body of Christ to be whole. We at ACI know that every church and every pastor is different, with varying strengths, weaknesses, needs, challenges, calls, and opportunities for ministry. Coaching is suited to support the growth and learning of clergy as they claim their specific call and their particular work; indeed it promotes self-awareness, self-assessment, self-care, responsibility, and proactive engagement. As each leader is more true to the reason God called them, each ministry site and, by extension, the church universal, is strengthened and becomes more vibrant and resilient.

A Variety of Programs and Engagements

Auburn's coaching method assumes that a leader is coached for a time-limited engagement. Leaders come and learn what is needed for a specific time, use the coaching, and then move on. Some clergy have returned for different learning when they make a transition to a new setting with new requirements. Situations like changing calls, retiring, considering transitions to different kinds of ministry, or reinventing what is present all benefit from learnings gleaned through a coaching engagement. The provision of just-in-time learning is the teachable moment and especially effective for situations like ministry, where the demands evolve and shift with little warning. One pastor found after three years of ministry that the funding for supporting his work had dried up. With the assistance of his coach, he designed three separate strategies for what might come next: securing monies, changing what his job description required, or moving to another call. Nurturing that flexibility of mind and spirit enabled him to stay calm and trusting as the Spirit worked to open the door that was right for his next step. Then he had the courage to do something risky but fruitful as his subsequent call emerged.

The ACI now encompasses several programs. The pilot project described above is now called the Comprehensive Coaching Program and retains the hallmarks of the pilot, though it no longer includes any training in coaching skills; ACI staff found that for candidates for the program and, to some degree, for participants themselves, inclusion of skills training was grounds for confusion: Were we training coaches? No, we were and are providing professional coaches for supporting and sustaining pastoral excellence.

Other programs include customized, contracted coaching for individuals or teams interested in working with an Auburn coach.

Alumni of the pilot program and others have engaged Auburn coaches through this program. Much exciting work has been done, on a contracted basis, with individuals and ministry teams in local church, denominational, and other settings around matters of goal setting, transition, understanding and defining roles, and so forth. ACI also provides classes and seminars at Auburn dealing with conflict, developing emotional intelligence, and use of coaching skills in and for ministry. The latter provide the opportunity for those who so choose to develop further knowledge of coaching theory and skills for application in their own ministries. The coaching training is also movable and able to be customized: that is, ACI has worked onsite with ministry teams in both local and regional (judicatory) settings to learn and develop coaching skills.

Beyond engagements that occur under the umbrellas of customized coaching and onsite training, ACI has also worked directly with denominational offices and faith-based groups to provide coaching for participants in specific programs. One church body approached Auburn to provide a modified version of the Comprehensive Coaching Program for a targeted group of its own clergy. The results have been analogous to those within the pilot and comprehensive programs, with the added benefit of greater support and more efficient meetings among the area's denominational colleagues. Another church body was piloting a broad church-transformation program with participants, both clergy and lay, from across a fairly wide geographic area and representing a spectrum of socioeconomic contexts, racial and ethnic backgrounds. Including a coaching component, designed in close discussion between an Auburn team and the program planner, has allowed for focused work with clergy leaders to develop and implement goals consistent with the objectives of the larger program and appropriate for, and organic to, their own local sites.

These and other examples provide a welcome if unsurprising outgrowth of Auburn's coaching philosophy and practice. The experience of coaching consistently results in stronger relationships and deepened community for the individual leaders, for their ministries, and for the broader contexts (be it local community or denominational structures). It is an instance—no, a model of incarnational learning at its most basic and profound:[4] meeting leaders and learners in their context in order to provide for a sustained commitment and relationship that responds to needs and opportunities.

For Auburn Seminary, the goal of its Coaching Institute, as well as its continuing education programs, is to support and develop bold religious leaders who are able to lead people and organizations forward with a sense of adventure and hope. Auburn's coaching expands the practice of lifelong learning by strengthening mind, heart, and spirit for the work of faithful and creative ministries.

Notes

1. The names of those involved have been changed.

2. For a description of Auburn's coaching method, see "Coaching Philosophy and Principles" at The Auburn Coaching Institute website, www.auburnsem.org/about/coaching.htm.

3. A readily available treatment of the concept and approach is available in Salvatore R. Maddi and Deborah M. Khoshaba, *Resilience at Work: How to Succeed No Matter What Life Throws at You* (New York: Amacom, 2005).

4. See "A Theology of Coaching for Pastoral Excellence" posted on the Auburn website, www.auburnsem.org.

CHAPTER 11

Why Would Laypeople Want Theological Education, Anyway?

Sally Simmel

> An education shaped by Christian spirituality . . . means being drawn into personal responsiveness and accountability to each other and the world of which we are a part.
> —Parker Palmer, *To Know as We Are Known*[1]

In this new world, this global village we inhabit, growing ever more complicated and accessible through science and technology, many of us think daily about the meaning and purpose of our lives. We are mindful of the decisions that need to be made to make sense of the world and our place in it. We can all tell stories of significant life experiences and the role we feel God is playing in them. A child is born, a child dies. A job is terminated; a new one is begun. We fall in love; we encounter something in nature that stirs us beyond anything we have known before. A parent dies and the loss lasts a very long time. We feel yearnings in our very soul for something yet unknown. We witness an incredible sunset or experience an amazing piece of art or poetry. We wonder about God's role in the universe and our role with God in the ongoing creation and sustaining of the planet. Even as we live in a post-9/11 world, with wars and natural disasters, worldwide economic changes, and climate and environmental issues, the search for meaning continues and each generation shares the universal concerns for life and common good.

Might this be yet another time in the global human journey when we need to hear the proclamation of God: "I am about to do a new thing; now it springs forth, do you not perceive it?" (Isa. 43:19a).

The situation is not the same as that mentioned in Isaiah. Then, God was bringing Israel out of Babylon. Now we are merely at the stage of perceiving the new act in which God is engaging. The world will always be dynamic. God will always be changing and creating.

This is the world to which we in continuing theological education introduce the questions of why and how to provide theological education for laity living into the worthy questions of faith for this time.

Who Are These People of God?—The Laity

Laity are those members of the church whom God has called to the church outside its walls. In unison they might say, "We write the laws of our lands and invent new technologies to serve humanity. We know how to clone animals and humans and measure germs on Mars. We rear and educate children. We work in corporations, governments, and health care systems. We build roads and homes. We write and produce movies and TV shows. In those endeavors, we seek to practice our faith. We need the wisdom of faith through deeper theological reflection to help discern the *how* and *why* of it all."

They might also say in unison that they are not theologians, while they in fact are *doing theology*. For the most part, that means they are not trained in theology for preaching, teaching, and Word and Sacrament ministry. That is a particular call. "Doing theology" does not merely mean studying tradition, doctrine, and Scripture so that one knows about those things. Rather, theology balances fact and theory with the lived experience of God each of us has. All experience has meaning and provides insight for the journey. To stay either in the academic mode or the experiential mode would deny the wholeness of each person, God, and the universe.

At a very early age, the people of God begin to speak to God, to recognize there is a God, even without fully understanding: "Now I lay me down to sleep, I pray the Lord . . ."

Theological Education for What?

To prepare for writing this chapter, I sent surveys to more than three hundred laypeople of several denominations, cultures, ages, and geography. The survey was simply to obtain some insights into questions, such as

- With what meaning-of-life questions are you currently wrestling?
- What kind of information, support, or challenges would assist you in clarifying your questions?
- If you were just starting on a new path in terms of your work or family, what kinds of faith-based education, reflection, or sharing would be helpful to you?
- How would you define theological education?
- Where and when have you experienced theological education?
- What has helped—or would help—you integrate such education into your daily life?
- What would be the most convenient way for you to access or do theological education and reflection for your daily life?

The response was encouraging in both quality and quantity. Researchers indicate a 5 percent response is necessary for reliable results. I had a 15 percent response. The respondents ranged in age from twenty-five to seventy-seven, with each decade in between represented. They live in Canada and from coast to coast in the United States. They are American Baptist, Presbyterian, Lutheran,

United Church of Christ, United Methodist, and Roman Catholic. Numbers of male and female respondents were evenly distributed, and about a 2 percent representation of people of color. I thank them all for sharing their stories, their issues, and their hopes for opportunities to reflect theologically on the lives God has called them to. All of that is scattered throughout this chapter.

Laypeople of all ages and cultures are searching for meaning and purpose. The church risks losing them if the only theological reflection available to them is the church school. A forty-three-year-old from the East Coast sums up some of the longing for meaning in life when she asks, "What is this deep longing I feel in spite of success and happiness? What is God's purpose for me? How do I know when God is speaking to me?" And from another person, "How do I do the integrative work of my life?"

Even in their mature years, people wonder about meaning and purpose as they remain vital but begin, as one sixty-something puts it, "to deal with end-of-life decisions for parents and in-laws. How, as Christians, do we make choices for ourselves and our loved ones?" Some issues in later life are about new relationships with children and grandchildren, meaningful retirement, or new directions for the vital years yet to come. Other issues are connected to new technologies that are frightening and often not understood by clergy or laity who are not working in the fields of science and technology. How do we bring the science and faith perspectives together in ways that assist Christians in making decisions?

According to the survey, mature Christians appear to be doing more inner work. The stress of earlier years—demanding jobs, making ends meet, raising families, and just staying on top of things—gives way to some space for moving from external demands to the inner work of letting go, making new choices, staying faithful, and contemplating God's work in and through these internal tasks. For many, theological reflection would provide time for sharing and engaging in activities that deepen their relationship with the sacred. This is true for some people of every generation.

The Knower

In *To Know as We Are Known: Education as a Spiritual Journey*, Parker Palmer designates a person on a journey of spirituality and education a "knower."[2] The term *knower* gives special meaning to the passage in 1 Corinthians 13:12: "For now we see in a mirror, dimly, but then we will see face to face. Now I know only in part; then I will know fully, even as I have been fully known."

That sense of knowing and being known stretches an understanding of the objectives of education. Theological education helps people move from being the *learner*—always a bit of a second-class position—to being a *knower*. Not once and for all, or of all things, but a knower of much and more as one continues the journey.

The knower, in this case the layperson discerning how to live faithfully in the world, has a worldview different from those who are called to work in the church as institution. For them, the church is not the center of their universe, and the majority of people they encounter are not of the same faith group or denomination as they. As they go about their daily work, in relationships, in neighborhoods, and in the larger community, they increasingly engage with people of little faith, no faith, and other faiths. Their lives are enriched by what they come to know from friends, coworkers, and acquaintances who are Hindu, Muslim, Buddhist, Jewish, or some combination of traditions.

Recently, I met a Zen priest who was also a member of a Quaker meeting. His regard for Buddha and Christ were not separable. In a pluralistic society, Christians need to invite people of all faiths into the conversation that educates about the world and the faith traditions out of which people live. In the places across the world where Christians find themselves, many of the church's dualisms do not hold up. If God created the whole world, how can something be sacred and something else be secular? Everything and everyone has a place in creation, whether one likes it or not.

Reflection and Conversation as Education

Breaking the mold of presenting education in a traditional class-room-lecture model may not be easy in some places, but it will be necessary if laypeople are to be included in the theological offerings of schools, seminaries, and independent centers.

Parker Palmer suggests an alternative theory about the nature of knowing is needed, not based on methods and models but on a transforming relationship between knower and knowledge. It means going back to recover a time when humans depended on emotion, intuition, and faith for their knowing, blending the reason, logic, and analysis of modern times. It allows sound fact and theory to spring from a truer passion and to work toward a truer end.

Survey respondents would support that kind of blending. They seem disinterested in fact and theory as a way to answer life's dilemmas. They spoke of theological education in language that is familiar to theological educators but often difficult to support and nurture. That is the challenge before us. How do we provide the spaces, the places, and the times for greater knowing that fits the yearnings of laypeople in this time?   When asked to define theological education, responses included the following:

- "Continuing growth in understanding of God's call in my life."
- "Serious exploration that examines (from a faith-based perspective) tradition and issues of contemporary life."
- "Very practical. Something like reflecting on what God's doing in the world, my world, your world."
- "Learning the stories, examples of Jesus's treatment of issues. Sometimes I'm not sure they (ministers) know the questions."
- "Study and meditation on the significant questions of life."
- "Research and study of faith and religious material, along with stories of how individuals act out their beliefs."
- "Preparation and support for one's faith journey."

- "Education that helps me think about my/our relationship with God. Teach us how to move into the future with God and prepare us to effectively live out our faith."
- "Hearing from those who have studied various religious schools of thought and hearing what they have to say about how to live life with meaning, and to please God."
- "Too often, it seems that we get caught up in the study of the history of religious thinkers and acts and miss the experience of God, which I believe is essential to theological education."
- "An attempt to provide answers to questions about the origins and reasons for human existence on earth. It raises questions that are not readily answered and challenges seekers to ponder such questions as why we are here (or why not), helping them understand humans' need to adopt faith positions."
- "Pushes seekers to examine the consistency between their religious teaching or faith positions and their daily behavior."
- "A process of learning about God and how God relates to the world. The process needs to include real experiences, not just intellectual, hypothetical situations."
- "Our lives in action, where we live, with our own questions—always questions."
- "Learning that brings us to a closer relationship with God."

The respondents would add to the teaching of fact and theory the element of reality and experience as a critical component of theological education for the whole of life. Theological education is not just knowing about faith and religion but also knowing how to apply it to living. Continuing education centers, seminaries, schools, and institutions that are interested in including laypeople in their processes and programs might want to consider ways of thinking and organizing to consider these real-life educational desires. In many religious traditions, theological education at its best is faith seeking understanding. According to Patricia O'Connell

Killen and John de Beer, "seeking God's presence involves theological reflection for the artful discipline of putting our experiences into conversation with the heritage of the Christian tradition."[3]

If You Build It, Will They Come?

If you build it—that is, theological education offerings that address the needs and issues identified above—will they come? The answer is, they will probably not come—at least, not at first. The average layperson who understands her- or himself on a spiritual journey, seeking a deeper relationship with God, has typically found less organized or structured ways to walk that walk.

Because of the clericalism that has accompanied centuries of organized religion, laypeople have learned their lessons well—they come second, behind clergy. Clergy are provided theological education, which is then "given" to the people. This system has dishonored the lived experience of all people, lay and clergy, individually and in community. As humanity moves to a global civilization, we can no longer afford to allow the purpose of education, as Palmer would point out, to be to control those who have less knowledge; instead, it must "come from a source of compassion."[4] Clergy must continue to have the theological education that prepares them for their particular calling, just as lawyers, doctors, plumbers, secretaries, and computer operators must have the education they need to prepare them for their calls. Beyond that, communal knowing—face to face, together for the journey— is needed.

Laypeople have also been led to believe that they need to "get it right" before they share their faith stories. Getting it right could be interpreted as another form of systemic clericalism. It takes us back to times when the priest or pastor had access to the faith and acted as intercessor. None of us will ever get it right, lay or clergy. We can only keep sharing our insights, our knowing, our truth, and keep moving, keep checking in, in a spirit of mutuality and accountability to one another and the faith. We check in and explore more deeply. We go out and live as faithfully as possible. We come back to the faith for more wisdom in order to go back out and act again. And, so it goes—all the days of our lives.

Several of those who replied to the survey would treasure theological education at the seminary or postseminary level at continuing education and retreat centers. The Education for Ministry project, offered by the School of Theology at the University of the South, Sewanee, Tennessee, is an example of a long-term process of theological education and reflection that combines theory and practice, giving equal weight to each.

Men and women, both clergy and laity, in all the generations represented in the survey would take advantage of continuing education that would allow more reflection and conversation-type knowing to take place in the congregation, involving both laypeople and clergy, and that explores God's activity in the world and their role as cocreators with God in sustaining a just world.

Others, especially those in their forties and fifties, would be eager to participate in occupation-based groups that might be designated as vocational theology groups, where particular issues might be addressed and in which participants share a common language. I met with a group in the high-tech industry not long ago and was amazed that they were applying their belief systems to such important issues as the ownership of intellectual property. The same yearning for connections between faith and work can be found in dozens of occupational fields as people meet together in homes and workplaces, because they find little understanding or support within their communities of faith.

One forty-four-year-old man spoke of dealing with the midlife work of "integration . . . of faith and work . . . of sacred and secular. The world I live in seems to be very fragmented; at times, my faith community seems to add to the sense of fragmentation." Such people explore their spirituality as a way of looking at how God is active in the situations in which they are involved. People in all occupations, in all life situations (including students, the retired, and the unemployed), in every level of work and economic situation have both joyful and tough issues to face on a day-to-day basis. Insights, stories, and examples from Scripture, tradition, and doctrine that have direct application are invaluable.

In an informal interview with a professional grant writer and consultant, I alluded to the idea of theological education for all interested laypeople. She asked, "Would a plumber want to go to seminary?" I wondered. The completed survey of a forty-one-year-old shoemaker gave me a partial answer. He was one of only a few people who had formal theological training in Mennonite and Roman Catholic settings. "Spiritual formation has always been the most helpful education for me. The major theme seems to be that God reveals himself through people that we come in contact with throughout our days."

I interviewed a thirty-something woman who feels genuinely called to teaching as a religious vocation as well as a professional career. I was impressed by her commitment to that call as she embarks on a part-time course of study in a theological school while continuing to teach high school full time.

Recently, I was engaged in a continuing education program in spiritual formation. In class we heard lectures on, among other things, Native American spirituality, Julian of Norwich, Thomas Merton, and Carl Jung. I now know the important dates in Thomas Merton's life, what he was doing when, and what influences shaped his life and thinking. I also know the soul struggles that brought him to a deeper knowledge of his own existence as connected to the entire universe. He shared in his autobiography *The Seven Storey Mountain* a lot of the searching that seems to be going on today among all people.[5]

Program participants could identify and connect with both the life and the teachings of Merton. Alongside the facts and the theory, we shared stories of our spiritual mothers and fathers, whoever they were and at whatever juncture in our lives they appeared—a gift of God to teach us about God and about life. Given a chance to tell the stories, we were amazed at what we had come to know, and from whom. One woman told of getting most of her knowledge about the Christian faith from books. She reached back to realize that her love of books came from the mother she had resisted for so many years. That led to more realizations about her mother's curiosity and courage and threw light on other participants' experiences with parents, siblings, and friends. From whence cometh the knowing? From angels God has sent along the way to teach what we need to know at that point in our lives.

Models and Methods

The spiritual journey of knowing includes both individual and communal acts. Jesus provided those opportunities by opening spaces for conversation with followers and seekers, for going deeper into their faith lives, and for hearing the word of God in order to come to know God. They met in homes, in small groups while fixing fishing nets, under trees, and in crowds. Their time together wasn't about learning facts and figures, dates and places, dos and don'ts. It was about knowing God and one another. Sometimes through silence knowing permeated their lives and inspired them to action, or miracles without fanfare caused people to gather in groups to talk about what was happening.

What do you suppose friends, neighbors, and onlookers talked about after the water was turned to wine or the blind man healed? What did they learn, what did they now know that was different? Parker Palmer writes, "If we could represent knowing for what it is—a way of creating community, and not destroying it—we would draw more young people into the great adventure of learning."[6]

Today people can be part of virtual groups on the Internet by way of blogs, Facebook, and YouTube, which may feel more comfortable and accessible to young people seeking community. We can create inner and outer space. We can explore individually or together, creating space, experiencing the moment. We can gather physically in a home, work, or school setting to share lives lived there. We can talk of what God is doing in our lives through and across the stages of life and in our different callings. We can test the knowing against reality, our own experience, and other world-views in order to act in a way consistent with our beliefs. We can participate in each other's education.

This knowing can also occur in more structured experiences. There are many books on theological reflection, both classical and new. In designing retreats a few years ago, I came across *The Art of Theological Reflection* by Patricia O'Connell Killen and John de Beer. The book is thorough in describing why theological reflection is needed and how to do that well with individuals and groups. Killen and de Beer include the following models, along with content and process.[7] All could be used in a retreat or continuing education context:

1. Beginning with a Life Situation (a real-life story)
2. Beginning with the Tradition I (piece of the Christian heritage)
3. Beginning with the Tradition II (a story from Scripture)
4. Beginning with Cultural Text I (literature, art, social conflict, and so forth)
5. Beginning with Cultural Text II (from cultural situation to tradition and experience)
6. Beginning with a Theme (birth, creativity, relationship, transition)
7. Beginning with Personal Positions (assessing in light of one's best understanding of one's religious heritage, lived narrative, and wisdom from the culture)
8. Beginning with Religious Experiences (encounters, interactions with life)
9. Reading Another's Theological Text (books, articles, in dialogue)

Everything anyone needs to know about putting together a full process, even a series of events, for theological reflection and conversation is contained in the pages of this book.

My survey respondents described the most convenient ways for them to engage in theological education and reflection in these terms:

- Conversation with networks related to my occupation
- Short courses in neighborhoods
- Conversations with good Christian friends and family
- Open exchange with others about their faith experience
- Conversations online
- Bible studies and retreats
- Reading
- College and seminary courses (weekends and evenings)

All Christians need a time and a place to think about their experiences, to make meaning from them, to find truth in them, and to take their beliefs into the world where they do their primary ministry and where God is already present and active.

Challenges and Directions

The continuing theological education needs of laity vary according to their situations in life, work, family, and community. That is no surprise. Most pastors and other people in church-related vocations appear to want "how to" education (how to do worship, stewardship, or evangelism, for example). Laity receive such training from their clergy and other leaders, of course, and in addition desire solid theological and biblical content that helps them cross over from Sunday life to Monday life. What is surprising is that, at least in my survey, there was no measurable difference in the needs expressed by members of various denominations.

This may be good news *and* bad news. Unlike the more predictable and compact list of theological needs of church professionals, the possibilities for educational programming for laity are awesome. All of life and faith is out there to chew on. That makes developing educational opportunities tricky. However, accepting the challenge means multiplying the number of people who are equipped for ministry in the world and in the church. People in church-related occupations may also be grateful for such offerings; many will appreciate a shift in emphasis for their own particular ministries. Continuing educators can enter the lay market in any number of places, slowly at first and then incrementally increasing or reframing offerings, testing, and checking with the audiences. I offer four strategies to help you get started.

Strategy 1

Involve laity in solid theological education (along with clergy, in many instances) where presenters and teachers pay special attention to applying their material to real-life situations. That will require a shift in teaching style for some presenters.

Strategy 2

Create reflection groups of people in similar occupations. Use a small group approach to provide information, support, accountability, and deep engagement in the issues of work and the marketplace. Often occupational groups are best done ecumenically; it strengthens relationships and better represents the day-to-day workplace connections of most Christians.

Strategy 3

Extend the groups mentioned in the first two strategies to include online conversations where possible. The Internet allows people to relate in real time and cyber time from anywhere participants find themselves working. Ethical and moral situations in which people find themselves on any given day can be discussed from a distance with trusted friends. A combination of face-to-face and online time probably appeals to many. The group can decide that for itself. Continuing educators need to be open to this type of format.

Strategy 4

Face squarely the challenges that this new group of participants will bring to traditional areas of your curriculum. For example, preaching events are popular for clergy. With laity, think about how pastors preach so that the Word can be heard. How do laity hear the preaching and then reword it for themselves? Who is responsible for the translating? Can laity and clergy do that together? How? Clergy and laity could participate in mealtime, evening, one-day, and weekend events.

There is no end to the corners of life that would benefit from theological reflection and education. In a post-Christian world, our faith should reach every aspect of work and family life, global economics, politics, and religion. Millions of laity are eager for the opportunity to expand their horizons, to think differently, to live differently. Learning happens in all of life and through all of life.

Why would laypeople want theological education, anyway? For life, of course.

Notes

1. Parker J. Palmer, *To Know as We Are Known: Education as a Spiritual Journey* (San Francisco: Harper, 1993), 14–15.

2. Ibid., 20.

3. Patricia O'Connell Killen and John de Beer, *The Art of Theological Reflection* (New York: Crossroad, 1997), 2.

4. Palmer, *To Know as We Are Known*, 8.

5. Thomas Merton, *The Seven Storey Mountain* (New York: Harcourt Brace, 1998).

6. Palmer, *To Know as We Are Known*, xvi.

7. Killen and de Beer, *Art of Theological Reflection*, 88–107.

CHAPTER 12

Linking Faith and Work: Continuing Education for Professionals

Robert E. Reber

For several years, Auburn Theological Seminary has worked with groups of Jewish, Christian, and Muslim attorneys and judges on issues of religious faith and the practice of law; health care professionals on discovering the unity of mind, body, and spirit; middle managers and chief executive officers on issues of corporate leadership and values in American society; and new directors of continuing education at seminaries and conference and retreat centers.

Auburn is an atypical seminary. Like other theological schools, its primary focus is strengthening religious leadership, but the school no longer grants degrees. Instead, it educates laity and clergy in a great variety of settings. The programs take place both on the campus shared with Union Theological Seminary in New York City and off campus at different sites around the country. A priority has been working with members of local congregations in those areas where they spend the most time and energy: the workplace, family life, and the larger community.

Getting Started

In its work with the professional groups, Auburn began slowly and deliberately to identify individuals within particular professions that might meet with staff for exploratory conversations. Professional and lay religious leaders put the seminary into contact with individuals in their congregations who seemed to be open to and interested in how their religious faith and values relate to their work and the larger society in which they find themselves. Generally speaking, the staff never made cold calls to anyone. Others initially introduced Auburn's educational interests and staff to men and women in different professions.

A specific example of what I am talking about is the beginning work with attorneys. In an informal conversation, a rabbi who is on Auburn's board of directors and the dean decided to ask two attorneys whom they knew—one Jewish, one Christian—about developing programs that would focus on issues arising from what it means to be a Jew or a Christian and a lawyer. They had a hunch that the two would respond favorably and that the interreligious dimension would make it even more appealing. They made it clear that a careful planning process would be set up to involve attorneys with staff in making decisions about the purposes, design, leadership, schedule, and venue for any possible program.

The response of the two attorneys was overwhelmingly positive. They agreed to be cochairs and to help identify other attorneys who might agree to be part of a planning committee. Twenty men and women met for an exploratory meeting where people became acquainted and learned more about Auburn. Over the next six months, they developed a three-part program, "Faith and the Practice of Law." The larger committee of twenty agreed to having a subcommittee of six work out details and then test them with the larger group. In total, five meetings were held—three of the larger group and two of the smaller one. The planning process was a highly significant educational experience. Participants got to know one another better, explored the territory of religious faith and law, and gained considerable ownership of the program.

This same kind of planning process was replicated in working with health care professionals, middle managers, CEOs, and directors of continuing education. The staff identified, with the help of others, who was interested; had an exploratory meeting to share information and get acquainted; asked who else might be interested; and called together a larger group to test interest in the proposed programs and to be a part of a planning team over a six- to twelve-month period. During the initial steps, it was very important that participants be asked to come to only one meeting and that those in attendance would decide whether they wished to be involved further. Also, we had to be very clear about Auburn's interests and why we would want to engage them in developing an educational program. Laity are a bit wary of theological schools and centers that have paid little attention to them, especially when it comes to focusing on their professional lives and workplace issues.

Examples of Programs Developed and Carried Out

In what follows, I first give examples of programs developed and carried out by the different professional groups and then address what has been learned that may be helpful to those who are responsible for continuing theological education for laity and clergy.

The programs for lawyers have involved several hundred people over the last fifteen years and now include judges. In increasing numbers, men and women, young and old, in different areas of practice have served on planning committees and participated in programs. The Louis Stein Center for Law and Ethics at Fordham University Law School and the Finkelstein Institute of the Jewish Theological Seminary joined in as partners. Muslim attorneys are now coming to programs and taking part in the planning. In addition to the annual three-part series for local attorneys and judges, a major conference, "The Relevance of Religion to a Lawyer's Work," was held and involved attorneys across the country. A more recent conference, "Rediscovering the Role of Religion in the Lives of Lawyers and Those They Represent," included teams from local communities across North America. The teams were made up of attorneys, religious leaders and educators, and professors of law and ethics. One of the goals was to help get programs going in local and regional areas. The papers presented at both conferences resulted in special publications of the Fordham Law Review.

Among the topics of different programs have been "Faith and the Practice of Law: An Overview," "Law and Religion Today: Challenges in Faith and Practice," "Keeping Faith and Your Legal Practice," "Conflicts between Religious Beliefs and the Lawyer's Role," "Faith/Religious Perspectives and the Work of Judges," "With God in My Briefcase: Putting Your Religious Values to Work," and "Quinlan to Cruzan: Forging a Consensus on End of Life Decisions."

The programs for health care professionals involved physicians, nurses, clergy, psychologists, mental health care workers, psychoanalysts, psychotherapists, counselors, social workers, medical and seminary students, chaplains, and practitioners of holistic medicine. The overall theme was "Discovering the Oneness: Mind, Body, and Spirit." Programs have been varied and based on different formats: large conferences, weekly seminars, and public lectures. Partners with Auburn in the planning and sponsorship have been the Blanton-Peale Institutes of Religion and Health, C. G. Jung Foundation of New York, Interweave Center for Holistic Living, the program in religion and psychiatry at Union Theological Seminary, the Center for Contemporary Spirituality at Fordham University, the Department of Religion at Rutgers University, the Temple of Understanding of New York, and the Psychotherapy and Spirituality Institute of New York.

The topics of particular programs have included "Oneness and Soul: What Can Science Say?" "Experiencing Oneness of Body, Mind, and Spirit," "Prayer and Healing," "Music and Meditation," "Principles of Wholistic Medicine," "Mysticism and Matter: Levels of Consciousness in the Spiritual Journey," "Traditional Christian Salvation and Psychosomatic Medicine," "Sacred Dialogue in Healing," "Meditating for Health and Wholeness in the Workplace," and "Integrating Spiritual Direction with Individual Psychotherapy."

Working with chief executive officers (CEOs) of major corporations on issues of corporate leadership and values in American society has been an exciting and challenging venture. Both Christians and Jews have been involved from the profit and not-for-profit sectors. The first program was "Ethics and Corporate Leadership in America," and others have been the "Ethics of Executive Compensation," "Human Rights, Religious Values, and International Trade," and "Market Pressures, Accounting Principles, and Ethical Failures."

The programs are planned by a small group of CEOs and take place in different corporate headquarters. Participation is by invitation and limited to sixteen to twenty CEOs. The standard format includes a meal (usually breakfast or dinner), a half-hour presentation, and a good hour and a half of off-the-record discussion.

A vision statement was adopted by the planning committee. The purposes of the "Chief Executive Officer Seminars on How Religious Values Impact Us" are: to discuss a range of religious/ethical issues that CEOs face; probe religious/ethical values that may inform our decisions; explore the impact these issues have on corporations and the larger society; and participate in discussions that are mutually beneficial with peers.

The group has also developed guidelines to ensure that seminars accomplish this vision. The following stipulations guide planners:

1. Only CEOs of major institutions in the greater New York City area are to be invited;

2. Each event should involve no more than fifteen to twenty participants;
3. Participants should represent diverse constituencies with respect to religious affiliation, both profit and not-for-profit sectors, gender, and age;
4. All conversations are to be considered off the record and confidential;
5. Presenters should be leaders in their field;
6. When possible, study papers for background reading are to be provided in advance.

In addition to the CEOs, Auburn established a program that involved a broader cross section of corporate managers. Again, with the help of corporate officers, a small group of Jews and Christians was invited to sit down with Auburn staff to talk about the interests and needs for such a program on religious and ethical values and corporate life. Two exploratory meetings were held before deciding on a four-part program series for the first year. This group decided to alternate holding the programs in a synagogue and a church on Monday evenings from 6:00 to 8:30, with a buffet supper, presentation, and discussion. Titles of the programs have been "Being Practically Faithful in the Workplace," "Being Faithfully Visible in the Workplace," "Being Spiritually Disciplined in the Workplace," and "Being Just and Faithful in the Workplace."

The Colleague Program for New Directors of Continuing Theological Education emerged out of discussions among directors active in the Society for the Advancement of Continuing Education for Ministry (SACEM). Auburn Seminary convened a group of directors to consider the need for a training program, and the group recommended that one be launched. Begun in 1995, the Colleague Program was funded in part by the Henry Luce Foundation and designed for small groups of no more than twelve newly appointed directors of continuing education in seminaries and independent centers in the United States and Canada. Colleagues met four times over an eighteen-month period for three-day gatherings. Since most participants began their jobs with little or no experience in continuing education, the Colleague Program created opportunities for them to learn from one another and from seasoned professionals about a field that has been neglected in theological institutions and centers.

What Has Been Learned?

What has been learned from working with these diverse professional and occupational groups? Here are some general recommendations for continuing theological educators who would like to get involved in similar ventures:

- People are eager to explore the relationship between their faith and their daily lives; the church or synagogue does not usually offer the time and space to do this. Most people are called to live primarily outside the walls of these institutions. The more we see how our faith relates and speaks to our whole lives, the more we will become committed as people of faith and as stewards of all creation.
- Time and energy must be given to planning educational programs with people. Ultimately, continuing theological educators want people to own and take responsibility for their own lives and the life of faith. When a program fails because of a lack of response, it is almost always because people representing the group to be served were not involved in planning the why, what, how, who, when, and where.
- In working with professionals, or any particular group, it is important to begin by asking them as members of congregations or particular religious faiths. This has been a key factor in Auburn's work. The common denominator of religious commitment has been a critical basis for getting together. That does not mean that there is always clarity or agreement about what we mean or understand religious faith to be, but it is a primary factor that draws people. In

fact, our interfaith advisory committee at Auburn said that knowing that these would be interreligious was particularly appealing.

- Tap into the growing body of articles and books in the field of religion, law, medicine, business, and ethics. In the last fifteen years, numerous books and articles have been written on faith and the workplace, spirituality and daily life, a holistic approach to living, and so forth.

- Develop programs that have some sustained educational thrust over time and that allow for a lot of give and take among participants and leaders. You may have to begin with a one-shot program, but one good experience can pave the way for many more.

- Recruit participants through letters of invitation signed by members of the planning committee who suggested them. One person inviting another with similar background or interests to join him or her in the program is a powerful appeal and gives the program immediate credibility in the eyes of the invitee.

- Network with other individuals, institutions, and community organizations. When an idea for a program or work with a particular professional group comes up, ask who else might you work with. None of us can afford to go it alone. We need each other in order to demonstrate real collaboration in a world often fragmented and divided. As I indicated earlier, we may not know who is best situated to help us with a particular goal but, most likely, somebody we know does!

- Money is not the issue. Once a key group is involved in planning and deciding with you, they are almost always willing to give or help you get the funding that is needed. This has been my experience for more than thirty-five years. The real challenges are our imaginations and our willingness to take risks and to engage in new ventures.

A quote by theologian and philosopher Martin Buber that was shared with one of the professional groups has become a rallying point of inquiry as Auburn moved ahead to explore the connections between faith and work and daily life: "We shall accomplish nothing at all if we divide our world and our life into two domains: one in which God's command is paramount, the other governed exclusively by the laws of economics, politics, and the 'simple self-assertion' of the group. . . . Stopping one's ears so as not to hear the voice from above is breaking the connection between the existence and the meaning of existence."[1] Professionals and laypeople in congregations are eager to explore "the connection," and we need to provide opportunities for them to do so.

Notes

1. Martin Buber, *The Way of Response*, ed. N. N. Glatzer (New York: Schocken Books, 1966), 34.

Additional References on Faith and Work

Allegretti, Joseph. *Loving Your Job, Finding Your Passion: Work and the Spiritual Life*. New York: Paulist Press, 2000.

Ball, Milner S. *The Word and the Law*. Chicago: University of Chicago Press, 1993.

Diehl, William E. *The Monday Connection: A Spirituality of Competence, Affirmation, and Support in the Workplace*. San Francisco: HarperSanFrancisco, 1991.

Haughey, John C. *Converting 9 to 5: A Spirituality of Daily Work*. New York: Crossroad, 1989.

Kraemer, Hendrik. *A Theology of the Laity*. Philadelphia: Westminster Press, 1958.

Martin, W. Steele. *Blue Collar Ministry*. With Priscilla C. Martin. Herndon, VA: Alban Institute, 1989.

Muller, Wayne. *Sabbath: Finding Rest, Renewal, and Delight in Our Busy Lives*. New York: Bantam, 2000.

Nash, Laura, and Scotty McLennan. *Church on Sunday, Work on Monday: The Challenge of Fusing Christian Values with Business Life*. San Francisco: Jossey-Bass, 2001.

Pierce, Gregory F. A. *Spirituality at Work: 10 Ways to Balance Your Life on the Job.* Chicago: Loyola Press, 2001.

Pierce, Gregory F. Augustine, ed. *Of Human Hands: A Reader in the Spirituality of Work.* Minneapolis: Augsburg, 1991.

Rion, Michael. *The Responsible Manager: Practical Strategies for Ethical Decision Making.* San Francisco: Harper & Row, 1990.

Salkin, Jeffrey K. *Being God's Partner: How to Find the Hidden Link between Spirituality and Your Work.* Woodstock, VT: Jewish Lights, 1994.

CHAPTER 13

Bending Over Backward to Prepare Nontraditional Students

Marvin L. Morgan

I grew up on a farm in North Carolina. Work on the farm often required that my father, six brothers, two sisters, and I do work that involved bending over for long periods of time. We pulled corn off the tall stalks by hand, working in teams. One team of four people would break off the ears of corn and place them in small piles between the corn rows. In a ten-acre field, the teams would make several hundred piles of corn, with more than fifty ears of corn in each pile. Because the piles were located between the cornrows, the ears on the bottom were always down in a trench six to eight inches deep. Those of us who collected rather than pulled the corn would spend hour after hour bending over to pick up the ears of corn that the pickers had stacked throughout the field. After bending over for many long hours, our backs ached profoundly, causing us to receive the midday and evening periods of rest with great joy.

Another back-bending task we performed with great frequency was picking cotton. We had no mechanical picker; we picked cotton the old-fashioned way, with our hands. Each year we raised several acres of cotton. When I was a child, I can remember thinking that the acres of cotton on our farm would have multiplied to a number no person could count, if God had not shown mercy by providing a large grove of trees at the edge of the farm. I will always believe that the grove of trees, and it alone, convinced my father that it was time to stop planting. To harvest the cotton, our entire family spent hour after hour, day after day, bending over the short cotton stalks, picking the cotton, one boll at a time. Strapped over our shoulders were burlap sacks that we dragged along the ground from one end of the field to the other. As we worked in a bent over, stooped down position, our backs ached indescribably. In fact, it was not unusual to need the helping hand of another person just to stand upright at the end of the cotton row.

The backaches of those harvest seasons rushed back to me later in life when my mother gave me some parental advice. After patiently listening to my lament over having failed to finish a particular task, she said, "Marvin, in order to achieve some of life's most important goals, you have to bend over backwards." In turn, her words reminded me of Langston Hughes's poem, "Mother to Son":[1]

> Well, son, I'll tell you:
> Life for me ain't been no crystal stair.
> It's had tacks in it,
> And splinters,
> and boards torn up,
> and places with no carpet on the floor—Bare . . .
> Don't you set down on the steps,
> 'Cause you finds it's kinder hard . . .

Although I did not fully understand the long-range implications of my mother's advice, I am quite certain of one thing. Because of my experiences in the cornfields and cotton fields of North Carolina, I know that bending over requires considerable effort. Therefore, bending over backward surely must require extraordinary effort, a high level of commitment, and a degree of tenacity far beyond the norm.

A Continuing Revolution in Zion

Charles Shelby Rooks, former associate director and later executive director of the Fund for Theological Education (FTE) published a book in 1990, *Revolution in Zion: Reshaping African American Ministry, 1960–1974*. He wrote that, following his call to the position of associate director of the FTE in September 1960, an event that he experienced as divinely ordained, he "set out to organize a revolution."[2] He referred not to just any revolution but rather to a "revolution in Zion," a revolution in the African American church.[3] His was to be a "religious revolution" that would result in the infusion of new, well-trained leaders in African American churches who would be committed to bringing about social justice in those churches and in the lives of church participants and their families.

Using the Fund for Theological Education as his "base of operations or staging area,"[4] he assumed primary responsibility for developing leadership for Protestant churches in the United States and Canada.[5] This was a noble endeavor. The Fund, organized in 1954 "to strengthen Protestant churches and theological seminaries, by recruiting prospective ministers from among the most talented college graduates of the time," had already become recognized as a key contributor to leadership development for Protestant churches in the six years preceding Shelby Rooks's arrival.[6]

Nevertheless, Rooks's tenure with the Fund spans a period when revolutionary ferment was everywhere in the nation and was having an impact upon most major institutions of that period. The FTE was no exception. Although he was concerned about leadership development for all Protestant churches, Rooks chose as his primary focus the recruitment of the most able African American college students for the profession of Christian ministry, a decision that is easy to understand. Identifying and providing financial resources to "support their graduate theological education" was a visible sign of his high level commitment to this endeavor.[7] His hope was that a new pool of well-trained church leaders "would enable African American churches to develop their potential for changing the conditions under which their members and the people in their communities lived."[8]

Several FTE programs were implemented. One program, the Trial Year in Seminary, provided full scholarships to more than sixty students per year as they studied theology and reflected upon possible careers in ministry. Another was the Rockefeller Doctoral Program that succeeded in producing what appeared to be an overabundance of doctors in religion. However, these were not African American doctoral scholars. To meet this unique need, the Doctoral Scholarship for Black North Americans program was established. This program was designed to enable the Fund, and indirectly the churches, colleges, and seminaries, to "compete with other occupations for the most promising college graduates of that era."[9] Finally, this same goal was further achieved through the Protestant Fellowship Program (PFP). In 1960 Rooks was called to this program to serve as staff person.[10] The primary purposes of the PFP were threefold: (1) to support the education of thirty-five to forty people per year who were committed to Christian ministry—it was hoped as pastors of local churches, (2) to engage in research about ministry in African American churches, and (3) to stimulate and organize a broad range of activities that would strengthen the mission and ministries of those churches.[11] With this broad range of initiatives, Rooks set out to lead a "revolution in Zion."

Between 1960 and 1988 the number of African American seminary students increased from 387 to 3,379; the number of African American faculty serving at predominantly white institutions increased from 6 to 186, and the number of African American doctoral students increased from 18 to 89.[12] Today, many of these same FTE program participants are making major contributions to black religion as faculty members, college and university presidents, writers, researchers, and pastors.[13]

The lists of names and accomplishments read like volumes of *Who's Who of World Religions*. In many ways, Rooks and the FTE "leaned over backward" to identify and train new leaders for the black church. What they have succeeded in doing, and what is evident even until this day, is nothing short of a revolution that has changed, for the better, the influence of African American religious leaders throughout the world.

One line Rooks wrote regarding the need for continued student recruitment may prove to be his most prophetic expression. Notwithstanding these leaders' many accomplishments, Rooks wrote that "the revolution will never be complete."[14] He could not have been more correct. Like most revolutions, there are within the revolution in Zion other bases of operation or staging areas, with different sets of players whose stories have not yet been told. The following is an attempt, somewhat comparatively, to tell the rest of the story.

A New Stage, but the Same Zion

Eleven years after Shelby Rooks left the FTE, inspiration for further revolutionary action in Zion came to James H. Costen, who at that time was immediate past president of the Interdenominational Theological Center (ITC) in Atlanta, Georgia. ITC is the largest and strongest predominantly African American theological center in the United States. Jim Costen's professional sojourn at Johnson C. Smith Theological Seminary (JCSTS), Atlanta, and later at ITC, began as he studied for the Bachelor of Divinity degree, now known as the Master of Divinity degree, which he received with highest honors in 1956. His professional career at these institutions spans a twenty-eight-year period, 1969–1997. He was the dean of JCSTS following its move from the Johnson C. Smith University campus in Charlotte, North Carolina, to the ITC campus in Atlanta. He served with distinction in this position for fourteen years. Then in 1983 he was named president of ITC. During his fourteen-year tenure as ITC president, Costen developed a legacy worthy to become the standard by which the work of all future education administrators may be measured.[15] His tenure represents the most prosperous years in the history of this unique institution. While many of his accomplishments are unique, the primary concern here is with his support of continuing education for nontraditional students.

Costen would be one of the first education administrators to agree that the best and the brightest students are special and should be encouraged to pursue graduate theological studies. He would also agree that such special students are better able to reach their highest potential when education administrators, judicatory leaders, and directors of major foundations put forth extraordinary effort and, yes, bend over backwards to help with their professional preparation. However, Costen also asked rhetorically, "Is it possible for effective strategies that are applied at the highest levels of professional preparation, with appropriate contextual modifications, to be equally effective when applied at other levels, even remedial levels of preparation?" And so to his second question, "Should graduate theological schools and foundations provide special assistance to the best and the brightest students while failing to do the same for others who have not yet received high honors?" he answered a resounding "No!"

A sentence in Matthew's Gospel referring to the matter of tithing in the practice of Hebraic Law addresses the human tendency to do good in one area of life while neglecting to do good in another: "These ought ye to have done, and not to leave the other undone" (Matt. 23:23 KJV). The FTE should have done precisely what was done for the best and brightest students of that era. However, Jim Costen had the wisdom, foresight, and personal sensitivity to recognize that another group of special learners was urgently in need of continuing education for ministry. These were pastors and lay leaders who did "not qualify to enter a graduate professional school." These special learners were "already established, accepted, and respected leaders in their communities."[16] Many of them were "gifted, highly articulate preachers in their pulpits but were often extremely limited" in their other pastoral skills.[17]

Costen was convinced that a continuing education program at ITC could help these pastors and other church leaders provide the high quality leadership capable of addressing the social, economic, moral, and spiritual needs of contemporary society. This need for more professionally trained African American clergy was not a new phenomenon. However, because of the increasing demands being placed upon clergy and lay leaders to get on with the business of "equipping the saints," there was a sense of urgency to remedy this shortage and to begin the task immediately. Costen sought to meet these and other needs of the African American churches through the development of the continuing education and lifelong learning certificate program at ITC.

As revolutionary ferment again roiled the waters surrounding Zion, Jim Costen was clearly captain of the ship. Equally apparent was that his cocaptain and primary point person for matters related to continuing education was Mance C. Jackson, then associate professor of Church Administration and Leadership Education at ITC. He was, and not surprisingly, a product of the FTE's Protestant Fellowship Program. Jackson, an ordained clergyperson, pastor, and presiding elder in the Christian Methodist Episcopal Church, also served as part-time director of continuing education. He shared and implemented Costen's vision for the future of continuing education at ITC. Jackson and Costen were in close collaboration every step of the way as they worked to firmly establish continuing education and lifelong learning as one of the key priorities of the seminary.

All conditions seemed ripe for continuing revolutionary activity in Zion. It is estimated that in the early 1980s more than 80 percent of the pastors serving the approximately sixty-five thousand African American congregations in the United States lacked professional theological education. A minimum of two thousand ministers was needed each year to fill vacant pulpits, in addition to the scores of individuals needed to fill non-parish-related ministry positions. However, the average annual number of African

American seminarians graduating from theological schools in the United States was 350. Having no other seminary-trained clergy to fill the additional 1,650 pulpits each year, congregations looked within their own ranks to find those individuals who had acknowledged receiving a call to the vocation of ministry. Who would step forward to provide professional theological training to these non-college-trained pastors and church leaders? If not the ITC, then who? If not in the 1980s, then when?

Many other factors seemed to indicate a need to devote special attention to continuing education and lifelong learning at the ITC. Costen and Jackson recognized that the very low level of alumni support being received at that time reflected the high level of frustration alumni were experiencing over critical leadership development issues within their local churches.

The first few years of the Costen presidency had been devoted to the demanding tasks of fundraising and staff and faculty development in support of the basic degree programs of the seminary. Dollars for the support of theological education were limited, and the competition with the seminaries of historic, prestigious universities and highly influential mainline denominations was fierce. While the ITC directed most of its resources to strengthening its basic degree programs, little if any resources remained to respond to alumni requests for continuing education opportunities.

The requests were many and quite varied in scope. For example, there were local pastors whose judicatories required that they complete a minimum number of hours of continuing education each year. They could, and often did, register for courses at other institutions. However, they expressed a desire to return to their alma mater, the ITC, for what they perceived to be more relevant continuing studies. These same pastors and others served local churches where laypeople volunteered for a myriad of leadership positions. Many new skills were needed as laypeople volunteered to serve as directors of Christian education, superintendents of church schools, youth directors, church school teachers, and so forth. The pastors looked to the ITC for help in training and equipping these volunteers.

Finally, there were public issues such as aging, domestic and world hunger, increasing crime rates, the peace movement, and the nuclear arms race. Other issues were concerned about substance abuse, racism, sexism, homophobia, human rights, medical and legal ethics, economic development with justice, peace with justice, toxic waste disposal, prayer in public schools, public versus private schools, and so forth. This host of issues confronting congregations needed to be addressed from religious perspectives. Pastors were being challenged to become what ITC's next president, Robert M. Franklin, calls "public theologians," and they were ill-equipped to do so.[18] Seminars, institutes, workshops, lecture series, and minicourses would be excellent ways to train these pastors so that they could, in turn, train their congregations to deal with these many public issues. Responding to these many needs was essential if ITC was to maintain the allegiances and confidences so carefully developed while these alumni were enrolled in degree programs.

To fulfill effectively this broad range of training needs, ITC would need a comprehensive, multifaceted continuing education and lifelong learning program. The goals and objectives for the program would need to be stated in such a convincing way that the staff of a major foundation would be totally assured of its positive impact and long-term benefit to our beloved Zion. Costen and Jackson were equal to the task. They proposed a fourfold agenda for the continuing education and lifelong learning programs: (1) a three-year program of continuing education for ministers (including military chaplains) with seminary degrees, (2) a three-year program of lifelong learning for ministers without seminary degrees, (3) a three-year program of lifelong learning for church lay workers through a lay school of theology, and (4) short-term learning experiences for ministers, laypeople, and special interest constituencies.

Continuing Education for Ministers with Seminary Degrees

The program of continuing education for ministers with seminary degrees would support the graduates of ITC's degree programs with ongoing classes. A survey was conducted among ITC alumni to determine the topics they wished to have covered in continuing education events. In response to the survey, the decision was made to offer two continuing education institutes or modules per year over a three-year period. These would consist of a three-day seminar each fall and a one-week-long seminar each summer. These were to be held on the ITC campus. The proposed topics for the fall sessions were biblical studies (year 1), systematic theology (year 2), and church history (year 3). The instructors were to be members of the ITC faculty, faculty from other institutions, and guest lecturers. The summer sessions were to focus upon the participants' ministry style and techniques as applied when working with different segments of the congregation. The proposed focuses were senior citizens (year 1), young adults (year 2), and youth (year 3).

Lifelong Learning for Ministers without Seminary Degrees

The program of lifelong learning for ministers without seminary degrees was based on the assumption that non-college-trained clergy have essentially the same professional training needs as those who are qualified to enter graduate degree programs. However, the concern was that these participants might lack certain basic liberal arts competencies. The intent was to offer at convenient hours (evenings and Saturdays) some of the same courses offered in the seminary's master's degree programs. Students were to meet on Tuesday evenings, Thursday evenings, and on Saturdays and were to take courses such as "Introductions to Old and New Testament," "Systematic Theology," and "Church History."

These courses were to be taught by members of the ITC faculty or by qualified guest lecturers. Following the completion of twelve ten-hour courses (a duration of about three years), the participant would be issued a certificate of completion. One continuing education unit would be granted for each course.

Lifelong Learning for Church Lay Workers through a Lay School of Theology

Given the broad range of ministries within and beyond the local church that laypeople provide, the need for special training opportunities among the laity would appear to be obvious. Nevertheless, very few continuing education courses were available at that time that were designed to equip laypeople for the broad range of ministries in which they were engaged. The ITC's proposed Lay School of Theology was intended to be a three-year course of study that would parallel the program for ministers without seminary degrees. Some of the courses were designed to prepare participants for ministries traditionally rendered by the laity. However, other lay ministries required the same theological competencies as those services provided by the clergy, for example, Christian education and church music. The proposed program was also designed to help laypeople more clearly articulate their faith, lead worship services, and provide spiritual guidance to others. Lay participants would receive a certificate of completion after finishing twelve ten-hour courses. One continuing education unit would be granted for each course.

Short-term Learning Experiences

The final component of ITC's fourfold agenda for continuing education was to sponsor a variety of special educational events. The ITC is located within the rich academic environment of the Atlanta University Center, only a few miles from the heart of Metropolitan Atlanta. It is uniquely situated to address the many public policy issues that affect the African American church and community. The proposed seminars, workshops, and short-term intensive courses were intended to facilitate ongoing dialogue among theologians, physicians, ethicists, psychologists, psychiatrists, politicians, and various segments of the business community. Continuing education sessions were designed for one-hour luncheons, half-day and daylong "intensives," and weekend retreats. Anticipated participants were to consist of people from various professions, public housing tenants, unemployed and underemployed individuals, welfare recipients, and families of incarcerated persons. These events were intended to enhance contact and interaction between all components of the seminary and the surrounding community.

Martin Paul Trimble, program officer and, later, religion/program associate with the Pew Charitable Trusts in Philadelphia, became a critical supporter of the program. The program as initially proposed was too broad to be successfully coordinated by a part-time director. After consulting with Trimble and receiving some helpful advice, Costen and Jackson requested and received in 1987 a modest planning grant from the Pew Charitable Trusts, which provided valuable time for the completion of data gathering and the careful refinement of their original proposal.

Utilizing the data gathered from surveys and consultations with judicatory leaders, college and university presidents, and members of a very gifted central advisory committee, ITC implemented a program that focused on the second and third agenda items outlined above: educating clergy who had not received graduate training and educating laypeople. These two branches of the program have been since 1991 jointly known as the Certificate in Theology program. Although some participants are college graduates, an earned college degree is not a prerequisite to enroll in the program. Refinement of the program required two years of intense development work and involved some false starts, some trial and error, some moderate successes, and certainly some failures. However, Costen and Jackson were determined to persevere and Trimble was equally determined to be generous with his patience.

In the spring of 1990, with a $300,000 grant from the Pew Charitable Trusts to be received over three years, ITC gained renewed capabilities and much needed reassurances to further the revolution in Zion. On more than one occasion during this protracted planning process, Trimble played key roles in helping to assure the eventual acquisition of funding.

However, ITC faculty began to express some concerns regarding the very limited amount of time they could commit to teaching remedial courses, over and beyond their regular course loads. The evening hours, weekend schedules, and modest stipends dampened their enthusiasm for traveling great distances to teach certificate-level courses. Therefore, twelve members of the faculty were asked to deliver lectures before a video camera and to present essentially the same material they covered in their graduate-level classes. For each course, twelve forty-five-minute lectures were recorded. These videotaped lectures could then be delivered to seminary-trained local instructors who were hired to teach courses at extension study sites. The local instructors were asked to acquaint themselves with the content of each course and then to show major portions of the videotaped materials to those people attending the weekly class sessions. The local instructors served as discussion facilitators and provided many of the other services for students that would ordinarily have been provided by the ITC faculty.

This redesigned Certificate in Theology program was based on some key assumptions regarding the ways learning occurs. The hope was that learning and significant sharing of information would take place in at least three ways. First, through the videos, the students would be introduced to the latest thinking and ideas of the ITC's distinguished faculty, without having to travel to the Atlanta campus. Second, seminary trained local instructors would be available to clarify the content of the videos and lead class discussions. And, third, by participating in numerous classroom discussions, these students would learn valuable lessons from each other because of their many years of service within local churches and communities.

The initial extension study sites were established at Edward Waters College in Jacksonville, Florida, and at Stillman College in Tuscaloosa, Alabama. These college campuses were chosen because of their on-campus resources and in hopes that some certificate students would enroll in undergraduate courses. However, this synergy did not materialize. Therefore, when ITC received requests to establish extension study sites in cities and small towns where the seminary had not cultivated any close relationships with local colleges, ITC administrators felt free to modify their approach.

In 1991, in recognition of the need for a full-time staff person to move the program forward, Mance Jackson relinquished his role and I was called by ITC to serve as Director of Continuing Education and the Certificate Programs. Beginning this same year, classes were no longer limited to college campuses, as study sites were established in the educational wings of local churches, community centers, public schools, Baptist association assembly halls, and so forth. Wherever the minimum of twenty students could be recruited, competent seminary-trained local instructors and coordinators hired, and adequate class meeting space found, ITC moved quickly to establish new extension study sites. During the period 1992–1999, the program grew from forty-five students meeting in three cities to more than six hundred students meeting in forty-two cities. Study sites were established throughout the United States and also in Canada, Bermuda, the Bahamas, and Japan. To date, nearly two thousand students have earned the Certificate in Theology from the ITC. Of this number, approximately thirty students who already held bachelor's degrees have enrolled in one of the master's level programs at the ITC. Many of these former certificate students have distinguished themselves as exceptional degree program participants.

Not unlike the students who were helped by the FTE's Protestant Fellowship Program, many of the students who earned the Certificate in Theology are now serving in local churches where they are making outstanding contributions to the quality of life in and beyond Zion. Positive changes have been made in the ways they do ministry. They now serve with increased competence and renewed confidence in their own abilities, and are thereby better able, with the help of God, to offer hope to others. They greatly appreciate the seminary's willingness to meet them where they were so that they could move to higher levels of competency in ministry.

Often when they arrive at their classes, these students are bent over with fatigue, having already worked a full day in secular jobs. Nevertheless, they meet for three to six hours weekly. They meet in Tupelo and Marks, Mississippi; in Grambling, Louisiana; in Hamilton, Ontario, Canada; in the Hamilton Township of Bermuda; and in Yokohama, Japan. Wherever they meet, they do so at the end of long, hard days. When they come to the end of the program, perhaps they realize what the staff and official boards of the FTE and ITC already know—that "in order to achieve some of life's most important goals, you have to bend over backwards."

A Challenge to All Seminaries and Theological Centers

The FTE stood alone as it recruited the best and brightest students and encouraged them to pursue ministry-related careers in the 1960s and early 1970s. Similarly, the ITC has enjoyed very little company among mainline members of the Association of Theological Schools as it has provided certificate-level courses to predominantly African American constituents in local, national, and international settings. Providing training for nontraditional theological students is demanding, even backbreaking work when done by only a few, but would be far less demanding and infinitely more productive if done by many.

For better or worse, ours is a market-driven society that rewards those who respond positively to the market. The demand
for theological training is great among clergy and other church
leaders who have not yet been able to pursue formal college or
seminary training. Throughout the history of Christendom, untrained men and women have been inspired, called, commissioned, and ordained to engage in ministry. They are going to
minister to others, rightly or wrongly, whether or not seminaries help to equip them. They are going to seek training in unac-
credited Bible colleges, in denominational academies, and often at
the feet of untrained instructors unless the seminaries respond to
their critical training needs.

The challenge for every seminary is to interpret its mandate
to provide theological education as all-inclusive. In compliance
with their historic mandates, seminaries must continue to train
those individuals who have already earned college degrees. Admission standards for graduate level theological studies are clear
and appropriate. Nevertheless, other prospective students are calling upon the seminaries to show greater flexibility in the types of
courses offered, in the times and places courses are offered, and
in the use of media through which they are delivered. A willingness to be flexible in these and other areas may enable seminaries
to bend over backward in efforts to serve more effectively those
students who do not fit traditional models. By accepting the
challenge to train all students, the gifted and the remedial, all accredited theological seminaries may become part of a new, more
inclusive staging area for the ongoing and essential continuing
revolution in Zion.

Notes

1. Langston Hughes, "Mother to Son," *Collected Poems of Langston Hughes*
(New York: Random House, 1995).

2. Charles Shelby Rooks, *Revolution in Zion: Reshaping African American
Ministry, 1960–1974* (New York: Pilgrim Press, 1990), 14.

3. Ibid., 6.

4. Ibid., 15.

5. Ibid., 14.

6. Ibid., 15.

7. Ibid., 14.

8. Ibid.

9. Ibid., 24.

10. Ibid., 34.

11. Ibid., 24.

12. Ibid., 174–76.

13. Ibid., 23.

14. Ibid., 174.

15. Clinton M. Marsh, "The President's Legacy," *The Journal of the Interdenominational Theological Center* 24 (Fall and Spring 1996–97): 113–29.

16. James H. Costen, "A Proposal for the Creation and Development of a Continuing Education and Lifelong Learning Program at the Interdenominational Theological Center" (presentation, the Pew Charitable Trusts, Philadelphia, May 1984), 1. All quotations used with permission.

17. Ibid., 1, 2.

18. Robert M. Franklin, *Another Day's Journey: Black Churches Confronting the American Crisis* (Minneapolis: Augsburg Fortress, 1997), 122–24.

CHAPTER 14

Multifaith Continuing Education: Leading Faithfully in a Religiously Diverse World

Justus N. Baird

As a rabbi who directs a multifaith center in a Christian seminary, I often get asked about multifaith education. People ask me, "What curriculum should I use?" or "How can we teach our students about other religions?" Even more often I am asked, "Do you know a Muslim I can invite to speak at our program?" But rarely am I asked, "Why should we be doing interfaith education at all?" A rabbinic colleague of mine put it to me this way: "I just can't articulate why interfaith is important to focus on," he said. What worries him most about serving his congregation is not how much his congregants know about other faiths. "Other than making sure we can all just get along, why does this matter?" he asked. Let's be honest: most of us know precious little about our own religious traditions, so why should we spend our valuable time learning about other faiths?

The aim of this chapter is to articulate what multifaith education is and why it should be part of any continuing education program and to address some of the challenges that confront multifaith education. Part one answers the "Why do interfaith?"

question articulated by my colleague and makes the case for including multifaith learning in any continuing education program. Part two defines multifaith education and describes various approaches to multifaith education. Part three articulates the challenges and barriers to multifaith education.

Because of the wide variety of approaches to and motivations for interfaith work in the world, it is worth disclosing my personal and theological perspective. I am a rabbi, trained at Hebrew Union College-Jewish Institute of Religion. I proudly identify as a Reform rabbi. I am married to a Conservative rabbi, and most of my in-laws are Orthodox. My extended family, like most American Jewish families, also includes non-Jews. I work in a Christian seminary: Auburn Theological Seminary in New York City, which was founded in 1818 and is affiliated with the Presbyterian Church (U.S.A.). I get paid to direct the Center for Multifaith Education at Auburn. In my spare time, I serve as the part-time rabbi for a small synagogue on the New Jersey shore. I do not embrace a "why don't we all just get along" attitude toward interfaith work, and I do not believe that the world would be a better place if people of faith would just focus on a few so-called universal teachings from their religious traditions. I do not want there to be one religion in the world; in fact, I think that would be a disaster, and my own understanding of God's will, which is rooted in Jewish tradition and the Hebrew Bible, is that God doesn't want there to be one religion either.

Articulating a personal theology of difference, or a theology of religious pluralism, is an important task for anyone who engages in multifaith work. It is impossible to work closely and deeply with people of different faiths without doing some serious thinking about how those faiths and their adherents fit into one's own religious worldview. For me, the narrative of the Tower of Babel is the cornerstone of my own theology of difference. Here is the short version of an already short nine-verse story (Gen. 11): Once upon a time all humanity spoke the same language. "Come, let us build a city and tower into the sky and make a name for ourselves," they conspire. God notices the skyscraper and proclaims, "If this is how those humans are going to act when they speak the same language, then we must confound their speech so they won't understand each other and then scatter them around the earth."

One important message of the Tower of Babel is that when humans all work together as one, with the same language (or culture or religion), bad things happen. Our desire to control and our ambition for power take over, and we try to compete with God. Rather than asking, "Why can't we all just get along?" maybe we should be asking, "What terrible things might happen if we did all get along?" This is paradoxical thinking, so let me offer a couple analogies. Ecologically, habitats are healthy when they are biologically diverse and unhealthy when a single species dominates (think kudzu). Can you imagine a world where there is only one kind of tree? Or think politically: what happens when power is concentrated in a single party?

God knows that unchecked human power is a bad idea. By confounding our language and scattering us around the world, God sets up a divinely inspired system of checks and balances. This is a theology of difference: that the reason we humans are so different from each other—linguistically, religiously, culturally—is to protect us from trying to become God. God wants multiple and different faiths to thrive, just as God wanted humans to have different languages—because God is just too great for any one faith to capture God completely.

Having disclosed my own perspective on multifaith work and a theology of difference that informs that work, let me now make the case for multifaith education.

The Case for Multifaith Education

The case for multifaith education stands on three things: the news, the pews, and religious views. First, the news. News headlines are dominated by events that are, at least in part, the result of religious ignorance or misunderstanding. Consider the following news cycles making headlines as I prepared this chapter, each of which has a significant interfaith component: the 2008 presidential race, including confusion over the religious background of presidential candidates Barack Obama and Mitt Romney and the way both John McCain's and Barack Obama's pastors were part of the news coverage; international conflicts including the Afghanistan and Iraq wars, saber rattling with Iran, and the Israeli-Palestinian conflict, each conflict colored by so-called fundamentalist Muslims; and a federal raid of a large compound in Texas run by the Fundamentalist Church of Jesus Christ of Latter-day Saints, followed by an embarrassing reversal of many of the charges by the Texas Supreme Court. None of these stories is exclusively about religion, but each one has a religious component.

Because news stories like these are the primary source of information about other religious traditions for most Americans, it is not surprising that so many of us are misinformed or have biased opinions about people of different faiths. Is Judaism well represented by the news of a federal raid on the kosher slaughterhouse in Postville, Iowa, or by stories about the Israeli-Palestinian conflict? Is Christianity well represented by headlines about Ted Haggard, Jeremiah Wright, or pedophile priests? Religion's high profile in the media puts the responsibility on religious leaders to offer quality instruction about other religious traditions to their flocks. If we don't answer this call for multifaith learning, we will raise another generation of people of faith schooled in misunderstanding, stereotypes, and bias.

But news headlines make the case for multifaith education in other ways as well. News stories are a constant reminder that religion and misunderstanding about religion play a role in conflict around the world. In places like the former Yugoslavia, India, Israel, Iraq, Iran, the Sudan, Myanmar, and Northern Ireland, conflict is fueled by the relations between faith communities. On 9/11 Americans learned that such conflict is not confined to foreign shores. Humanity's ability to resolve conflict is in part predicated on our ability to create better understanding between peoples of faith; our own security—our physical safety—is directly related to building relations across religious divides.

Even news stories that appear to have nothing to do with religion are an impetus for multifaith education. Global warming, torture at Abu Ghraib, and poverty: injustices like these are opportunities for people of different faiths to engage in cooperative action to promote justice. The news is a daily reminder that the world remains a broken place. People of faith have a responsibility to take part in repairing the world by reaching across religious divides and working together on issues of shared concern. For all these reasons—the misunderstanding and bias created by learning about other faiths from the news, the role of religion in conflict that affects our security, and the reminder of injustices that demand cooperative action—the news is a major part of the case for multifaith education.

The second reason to engage in multifaith education is the pews. "Pews" refers to the religious diversity in our neighborhoods and in our congregations. Although reliable figures are hard to come by, many have claimed that the United States is the most religiously diverse country in the world.[1] What is not disputed is the incredible growth of religious diversity in the United States since the Immigration and Nationality Act of 1965. In 2008 researchers at Harvard University's Pluralism Project listed more than 1,600 mosques, 2,200 Buddhist sanghas, 700 Hindu temples, and 250 Sikh gurdwaras in the United States. How many times have we driven by these structures in our own neighborhood without ever bothering to stop in?[2]

The religious diversity in our neighborhoods spills over into the pews of our congregations. Each time I lead prayers or give a sermon in my own synagogue on the Jersey shore, I have to think about how the prayers or the sermon will be understood not only by my Jewish congregants but also by the many non-Jewish people in the room. These are not curious visitors—these are the partners and spouses of congregants, many of whom regularly come to the services. And almost half of the people in the pews of

American congregations grew up in a different denomination: the 2008 U.S. Religious Landscape Survey by the Pew Forum on Religion and Public Life reported that 44 percent of Americans have left the denomination of their childhood for another denomination, another faith, or no faith at all. Most clergy find a wide variety of backgrounds represented in the pews: lifelong adherents, less affiliated newcomers shopping for a religious community, and people of a different faith altogether. Family members of different faiths turn up during a visit to the hospital, at weddings, and at funerals. Do clergy know enough about other religious traditions to serve nonadherents well? Do lay leaders know how to embrace people from other religious traditions without saying embarrassing things? Can congregations serve families made up of a variety of religious affiliations? To effectively serve our communities—to lead our congregations faithfully—we must have a better working knowledge of other faith traditions.

These are the two high-profile reasons for engaging in multifaith continuing education—the news and the pews. The third reason, religious views, is more subtle and personal: engaging in multifaith education enriches one's own faith. Those who spend time learning about different religious traditions report that they come to understand their own tradition better and that they are stretched to grow spiritually. A familiar maxim teaches that "to know one religion is to know none." Religious traditions did not evolve in a vacuum—they are interrelated, and many aspects of our faith traditions cannot be understood without knowledge of other religions.[3] Learning about other religions helps us make sense of our own. Encountering other faiths also directs our attention to muted theological strands in our own tradition. Religious practices or ideas that are strongly emphasized in one tradition may be more hidden in another.[4] We can experience what theologian Krister Stendahl called "holy envy";[5] that is, we can appreciate new languages to praise God while being faithful to our own tradition.

This is the case for multifaith education: the news, the pews, and religious views. No longer can we ignore the religious diversity that influences our world and reaches deep into our communities. Because of a great lack of education about other faiths, stereotypes and misunderstanding continue to proliferate, which fuels conflicts around the world and at home. Religious leaders and laypeople must better understand other faith traditions in order to serve their own communities and engage in righteous acts with others. And as we travel the path toward greater understanding of other religions, we will grow in our own relationship to God. For these reasons and many more, multifaith education should be part of any continuing religious education program.

What Does Multifaith Education Look Like?

Having stated the case for multifaith education, we turn now to what multifaith education looks like. Multifaith work happens in the open space between religious communities; there is generally no one and no organization in charge. In addition, there are competing narratives of what multifaith work is about and competing visions about why we should, or shouldn't, engage in multifaith education.

A brief word about terminology: in the first section, I used the words *interfaith* and *multifaith* interchangeably. Both of these words are adjectives that generally mean involving people of different religious faiths. Their connotations can be different, however. The word *interfaith* is used to mean "between faith communities or between individuals of different faiths" as in the phrases *interfaith dialogue* and *interfaith marriage*. The word *multifaith* is used here to mean "many faiths." The phrase *multifaith education* thus means learning about multiple faiths. My own use of the term *multifaith* does not suggest any form of syncretic spirituality or what Syracuse University professor of religion and media Gustav Niebuhr calls "spiritual Esperanto."[6]

Often the first word heard after the word *interfaith* is the word *dialogue*. Interfaith dialogue plays an important role in multifaith education, but there are many ways other than interfaith dialogue to learn about—and work alongside—other faith traditions and the people who follow those traditions. Interfaith dialogue is best seen as one of many different approaches to multifaith education. Multifaith education includes a broad range of intentional activities that meet the goal of learning about multiple religious traditions. The chart on pages 254–256 presents a brief description of various approaches in use today, along with the advantages, risks, and examples of each approach.

Challenges to Multifaith Education

Multifaith continuing education faces four key challenges: (1) theological and religious challenges; (2) fear, especially of conversion or intermarriage; (3) politics and history; and finally, (4) ambivalence. Any successful multifaith continuing education program must respond to these four challenges in some way. The final part of this chapter outlines these challenges and offers brief responses to each one.

For some, especially for those who tend toward conservative or literalist approaches to their religious traditions or who have strong convictions that their religious tradition is right for everyone, multifaith work raises serious theological and religious issues. When I teach clergy about engaging across lines of faith, I work to bring these theological issues out into the open. I challenge them to engage purposefully theological questions like the following:

- Did God intend for there to be so many religious traditions?
- What is the relationship between the God you worship and the God others worship?
- How do other faiths fit into your understanding of salvation and eschatology?
- Should people of faith try to convert each other?
- What does God expect of you when you interact with members of another faith?

These questions do not have to be answered prior to engaging in multifaith education, but exploring the questions is an important part of the learning process for those who are theologically oriented. Multifaith work tends to challenge theologies people espouse but haven't examined in detail. Taking time to study and reflect, individually or with a trusted partner, is an important part of the multifaith education process and helps to resolve theological dissonance.

A second major challenge that interfaith education faces is fear, especially the fears of conversion and intermarriage. Many Christians, especially those from more mainline denominations, may not relate to these fears. But such fears can run deep for members of minority religious traditions. When your religious community represents less than 2 percent of the population in the country (a demographic reality for all the religions in America except Christianity), you often feel at risk of being proselytized. Christianity has a reputation of being a proselytizing tradition, so participants engaged in multifaith education need to know up front how the facilitators of a program will respond if someone engages in proselytizing behavior. Parents may fear that their children, if exposed to the religious teachings of another tradition, will be enchanted and decide to convert. For these families, staying home seems like a safer alternative.

Intermarriage is also a major fear. In the American Jewish community, where intermarriage rates have held steady around 50 percent for many years, there is fear that interfaith activity, especially among young people, will only lead to more intermarriage (which is generally seen as a sad or even tragic event by members of the Jewish community, although different attitudes do exist). In addition, religious leaders may argue that interfaith education leads to loss of identity, saying, "My congregants already have enough interfaith interaction in their daily lives—every place they go, from work to school to the public square, is full of interfaith interactions. What my flock needs is a deeper experience of their own religious tradition." These fears of conversion, intermarriage, or loss of identity, which are rarely discussed during polite interfaith

Figure 14.1. Methods, Pros and Cons, and Examples of Multifaith Education

Methodology	Pros and Cons	Examples
Dialogue • "Two-way communication between persons who hold significantly differing views on a subject, with the purpose of learning more truth about the subject from one another."[7] • Dialogue is defined by the intentionality of the communication rather than the content of the conversations. Tougher subjects are best reserved for groups that have developed trust. • Dialogue can be a one-time event or an ongoing process; it can happen between people who have never met or between people with deep relationships.	*Good for* the talking and listening oriented. *Difficult for* large groups. *Watch for:* • selection of participants and group balance; • dynamics that affect who speaks and who does not; • clear role of facilitator.	Dialogues can be bilateral (Christian-Muslim or Hindu-Jewish), trilateral (Christian-Jewish-Muslim), or open. Some dialogues occur among elite leadership and others are grassroots.
Text Study • Small groups or even pairs of individuals reading and then discussing a specific text, usually scripture. • Often themed: sitting together, participants engage in the text, ask questions of each other, and reflect on how studying together broadens one's understanding of the theme. • Useful tool to approach difficult subjects.	*Good for* those who have a high regard for scripture and the intellectually oriented. *Difficult for* those who prefer religious practice or social action to study. *Watch for:* • privileging scripture over commentary; • projecting a single way of reading the text; • the process of selecting texts; • "experts" dominating the conversation.	Most multifaith text study happens as part of a larger interfaith program, but one example of specialized multifaith text study is scriptural reasoning.
Experiential • Attending or observing religious practices, such as communal prayers; life-cycle events like a baby naming, baptism, coming-of-age ceremony, wedding, or funeral; or home-based rituals such as a Shabbat dinner, Passover seder (ritual meal), Iftar (break-fast meal) during Ramadan, private worship in a Hindu home, or family rituals around Christmas or Easter.	*Good for* creating memories, images, and experiences. *Difficult for* those who fear interfaith interaction. *Watch for:* • boundary between observing and participating; • religious restrictions (for example, some Jews who strictly observe Jewish law will not go into the sanctuary of a church, especially if it contains images or icons)	Experiential learning can happen informally between neighbors or formally as part of a class. See description in column 1 for examples.

Description	Notes	Examples
• To be a guest during one of these sacred moments is to learn how an individual, family, or community lives out the religious tradition.		
Cooperative Action • May take the form of (1) shared political action on issues of common concern, combining resources to offer more effective social services, or (2) joining together to engage in volunteer service. • Finding overlap in mission between faith communities can be a fertile starting point for interaction. For some, engaging in service and action across lines of faith brings a unique sense of holiness to the work.	*Good for* hands-on action, building relationships. *Watch for* political tradeoffs involved in building coalitions.	Congregation-Based Community Organizing (CBCO) Greenfaith—an interfaith coalition for the environment Interfaith ministries offering social services Interfaith service days
Interfaith Travel • Usually has an education and dialogue component. • Shared experiences and memories that inevitably result from traveling are the real benefit of interfaith travel. • Trust develops quickly on the road, and after a few days of polite conversation, participants are ready to explore deeper issues and ask tougher questions that would normally be held back from a local interfaith exchange. • Participants who engage in interfaith travel develop relationships that are likely to have a deep impact on their understanding of another faith tradition.	*Good for* a broad audience—who doesn't like to travel? *Difficult for* people with limited financial resources. *Watch for:* • dietary requirements; • balancing scheduled with unscheduled time; • logistics and fears when visiting conflict regions.	Muslims and Jews visiting southern Spain Christians, Jews, and Muslims visiting the Middle East Christians and Buddhists visiting Far East Some travel agencies specialize in such trips.
Sharing Sacred Space • When one religious community borrows or rents the space of another religious community.	*Good for* "walking the walk" of religious tolerance. *Difficult for* groups that have vastly different prayer-space needs. *Watch for* stakeholders who oppose the move but are hesitant to say so.	Such sharing of space is now common across the U.S. One example: Muslims and Methodists built houses of worship side by

• The practical and theological issues that arise from such sharing have to be dealt with by each community. • Some communities wisely turn a relationship that began as an economic exchange (space rental) into an opportunity for deeper interfaith learning and action.		side in Fremont, CA—a collaboration featured in the documentary film *Fremont, USA*.
Formal Education • Americans grow up with surprisingly little knowledge of other faiths since very little formal education in religion is offered in the U.S. at the primary and secondary school level. Religious congregations have not filled the gap; offerings usually focus on converting others or integrating new members. • Many have turned to the religious studies faculty at colleges and universities, either by enrolling in coursework or by taking advantage of continuing education programs. • There is a greater need for quality youth and adult education about other religious traditions.	*Good for* those who love classroom or academic learning. *Difficult for* having a meaningful exchange, since the learning is usually *about* the "other" instead of *from* the "other." *Watch for* secular faculty who may not be able to convey the lived religious experience of the community.	Center for Religious Inquiry in New York, Minneapolis, and Los Angeles Continuing education programs of colleges and universities
Youth Education • Youth could be a part of any of the interfaith activity described above, but separate youth programming is important. • High school teens, who tend to be suspicious of organized religion and curious about other religious traditions, are especially ripe for multifaith education. • Interfaith programming that helps youth learn how their religious tradition differs from others allows teens to strengthen their own faith while asking deeper questions of identity and can help them grow from a childlike understanding of their faith to a nuanced adult perspective of their faith.	*Good for* youth who are bored with their religious education, the strongly affiliated, and skeptical teens. *Watch for:* • concerns about interfaith dating; • leaving parents out of the process.	Face to Face/Faith to Faith (Auburn Seminary) Abraham's Vision (for Jewish and Muslim day schools) Interfaith Youth Core

program planning meetings, can present a serious challenge to interfaith education. One effective response to these fears is to ask respected individuals who have experienced multifaith education to discuss their own fears going into the process.

A third challenge is politics and history. Religious communities have been interacting ever since there were religious traditions, and the history of those interactions is present in the room during any interfaith experience. Jewish participants may feel that Christianity has historically been a bully to Jews, from the Crusades to the Holocaust. Muslim participants may be concerned about discrimination or feel that Americans are Islam phobic and that the West is out to recolonize Muslim countries. Christian participants may feel concerned about the political actions of Muslim countries or feel ashamed of Christian history. Current political events also have a huge influence over the tone of interfaith interactions. The topic of Israel and Palestine is generally the hottest issue for any interfaith group in our time, but other political issues such as American policies towards Muslim-majority countries, media portrayal of religion, and prayer in public venues may also be on the minds of participants. Interfaith programs that address these issues directly risk being overtaken by grandstanding ideologues, and programs that avoid all political questions risk being irrelevant. To avoid both pitfalls, leaders should establish clear educational goals and provide skilled facilitation.

The fourth, and perhaps greatest, challenge to multifaith education is ambivalence. Outside of the minority of individuals from each faith community who are naturally drawn to interfaith work, either by personality, theological curiosity, or the promise of universal truths, many people feel ambivalent about engaging in multifaith education. For some, it is a question of priorities. A December 2007 study by the Center for the Study of Theological Education at Auburn Seminary asked 2,300 graduates of seminaries and rabbinical schools to rank fourteen areas of study in order of relevance to their professional life and work. "World religions" was ranked number thirteen (only congregational administration was ranked lower). Ouch. Educators and clergy who are confronted by challenges like declining membership, overprogrammed families, and lack of financial resources may argue that multifaith education sounds nice, but it is just not a critical priority. Part one of this chapter is a response to this ambivalence; the news, the pews, and our religious views challenge us to engage in multifaith education or be content with mediocre religious leadership that is unable to help people of faith navigate the challenges of our time.

These four challenges—religious and theological concerns, fear of conversion or intermarriage, politics and history, and ambivalence—must be dealt with each time the opportunity for multifaith education reaches new people. My colleague's question, "Other than making sure we can all just get along, why does this matter?" must be answered over and over again. But the multireligious world we now inhabit demands that we find ways to overcome these challenges. Collectively, we have a long history of using our religious traditions to wage holy war—a history that continues today. We have much less experience using our religious traditions to wage holy peace. People of faith can make major contributions toward improving the world we live in. While much good can come of the individual, communal, and denominational work we do within our own faith community, I sense that God is calling us to do our good work across lines of faith as well. People of faith will not be successful at sharing the task of repairing the world if we remain utterly ignorant about each other's faith traditions and religious lives. By making room in continuing education programs for multifaith education, educators and religious leaders can make a huge impact on the knowledge and attitudes that our communities have toward other faiths, and by doing so, bring more peace and justice into the world.

Notes

1. Diana L. Eck, *A New Religious America: How a "Christian Country" Has Become the World's Most Religiously Diverse Nation* (San Francisco: Harper,

2001) is probably the best known source that makes this claim. Despite detailed research and anecdotes about religious diversity in the United States, little comparative data from other nations is available to support the claim that the United States is the *most* religiously diverse nation.

2. This religious diversity is spread across every state in the nation, but the nation is still predominantly Christian. The 2008 "U.S. Religious Landscape Survey" by the Pew Forum on Religion and Public Life reported that 78 percent of Americans claim some form of Christian identity, 16 percent described themselves as unaffiliated, and just fewer than 5 percent claimed a non-Christian religious identity. The United States is both predominantly Christian and religiously diverse.

3. Examples are plentiful. One straightforward example in which Islam influenced my own religious tradition: the early mystical work *Duties of the Heart* by Bachya ibn Paquda (eleventh century) contains many teachings and stories attributed to anonymous sages that can be traced to Islamic Sufi traditions.

4. More than once I have heard a Sunday school teacher describe Judaism as the religion of law and Christianity as the religion of love. Such generalizations are at best unhelpful, but the kernel of truth behind the statement is that the rabbinic tradition has developed a rich legal process and Christian theologians over the centuries have spilled much ink on the subject of love. A Jew learning about Christian views on divine love will be reminded of God's *ahavah* (love) for the world, expressed in the daily Jewish liturgy and throughout the Hebrew Bible and rabbinic texts. And a Christian learning about *halakhah* (Jewish law) will be reminded of the Christian legal tradition that dates back to the emergence of Christianity and continues today.

5. Leaving room for "holy envy" was one of Stendahl's three rules of religious understanding presented at a 1985 press conference in Stockholm in response to vocal opposition to the building of a temple there by the Church of Jesus Christ of Latter-day Saints. The other two rules were: (1) when trying to understand another religion, you should ask the adherents of that religion and not its enemies; and (2) don't compare your best to their worst.

6. See Gustav Niebuhr, *Beyond Tolerance: Searching for Interfaith Understanding in America* (New York: Viking, 2008), xxiv. Similarly, Wayne Teasdale coined the term *interspirituality* to mean "the assimilation of insights, values and spiritual practices from the various religions and their application to one's own inner life and development" (George Cairns and Wayne Teasdale, *The Community of Religions* [New York: Continuum, 1996]). Insights, values, and spiritual practices have moved across religious traditions for as long as there have been religions. The core distinction between multifaith work and interspirituality is this: multifaith work happens within multiple religious traditions and their associated communities, structures, and histories. Interspirituality describes the phenomenon of individuals or small communities mixing and matching insights, values, and spiritual practices from multiple religious tradi-

tions to create an "it works for me" spirituality, not unlike the practice of visiting the by-the-pound section of the candy store to fill a bag with one's favorite sweets.

7. Leonard Swidler, Khalid Duran, and Reuven Firestone, *Trialogue: Jews, Christians, and Muslims in Dialogue* (New London, CT: Twenty-Third Publications, 2007), 7.

CHAPTER 15

Educating Religious Leadership for a Multireligious Society

Robert E. Reber

The religious landscape of North America is rapidly changing. The religious pluralism of the world is increasingly at our doorstep. No longer are Buddhists only in Japan or China, Muslims in Egypt or Indonesia, or Hindus in India or Thailand. Adherents of these faiths as well as others now reside in many communities across North America. What is new is not the number of traditions but their proximity.[1] In numerous cities and towns one can find churches, synagogues, mosques, and temples within easy walking distance of each other. We are living in an ever-growing multireligious environment, whether in New York City, Hartford, Washington, D.C., Atlanta, Toledo, Indianapolis, Chicago, Columbus, Cedar Rapids, Houston, Denver, San Francisco, or Los Angeles.

Christians, accustomed to dominating the religious sphere in the United States, respond in a variety of ways to this new reality of religious pluralism. Some withdraw, even move away to another community. Others ignore it. Others increase their efforts to convert non-Christians. Some are threatened by religious pluralism while others are intrigued and open to learning more about this new reality. Issues of identity come to the fore for every religious tradition as it lives alongside different traditions. Each faces the question of what it means to live as a religion within a family of religions.

Uncharted Waters

Having lived and worked in one of the most multireligious areas in this country has raised directly for me the issue of what is my responsibility as a continuing theological educator in a historic Presbyterian institution that is committed to developing religious leadership for the future of various religious traditions and American society. For many, confronting the reality of religious pluralism is not a strongly felt need or interest. To move into an arena pretty well ignored by many continuing and adult education enterprises is full of risks and promises. The territory is rather uncharted in terms of developing educational programs for both clergy and laity. There is considerable history of Jews and Christians, and more recently Muslims, working together, but little to go on when one seeks to engage Buddhists, Hindus, Jains, Sikhs, Wiccas, and Baha'is.

My first effort in multifaith programming was almost eighteen years ago when we at Auburn Seminary invited a team of educators from the Multi-Faith Centre in Birmingham, England, to lead a workshop in the United States, over a seven-day period, on multifaith dialogue in a multicultural society. The team included laypeople from the Buddhist, Hindu, Jewish, Muslim, Sikh, and Christian communities. They had been working together for several years to bring about knowledge and understanding that fosters multifaith and intercultural relationships and contributes to the quality of life in local settings. It was an extraordinary occasion that left workshop participants dizzy with ideas, exhilarated by relationships and stories, and challenged to take seriously their own society and particular community settings.

During the intervening years, Auburn Seminary has involved representatives of twelve different faith traditions in planning and carrying out programs that have included visiting various religious centers; partnering with others in holding multifaith festivals of ritual, music, dance, fellowship, and education; sponsoring programs for women of faith on death, healing and the afterlife, raising children in today's world, women mystics of different traditions, and feminine images of the divine; developing a yearlong series on spirituality and various religious traditions; holding public lectures by scholars from different traditions; and planning an ongoing program called "Building Bridges: Understanding Our Neighbors' Faiths." To give you an idea of what is involved in developing an interreligious educational program, I will describe this last one in more detail.

Under the sponsorship of the Long Island Multi-Faith Forum, Auburn Theological Seminary, and the Long Island Council of Churches, I chaired the education committee for three years that developed the Building Bridges program. Members from each of the following traditions have been active members: Baha'i, Brahma Kumaris, Buddhism, Christianity, Hinduism, Islam, Jainism, Judaism, and Sikhism. In the beginning committee members spent considerable time getting better acquainted and exploring what educational programs might be needed on Long Island. We talked to religious leaders, educators, and members of different religious communities, and we reviewed regularly our ideas with the representatives of twelve faith traditions who made up the Long Island Multi-Faith Forum and the members of the Interreligious Task Force of Auburn Seminary.

Building Bridges

As an education committee, we identified four main objectives of the "Building Bridges: Understanding Our Neighbors' Faiths" program:

- Educate communities about religious diversity in their world.
- Encourage neighbors to reach out to one another in friendship and respect.

- Expand horizons of knowledge about beliefs and customs of our neighbors.
- Explore ways to make our communities more just and peaceful for all peoples.

We wanted the program to be flexible in its length and to occur in a variety of settings, such as religious communities, congregations, high schools and colleges, civic groups, hospitals, professional organizations, senior citizen centers, and so forth. We thought it was important for the programs to be interactive, use different teaching methods, and offer ongoing possibilities for people of various faith traditions to work together, to better understand each other, and to address issues that could make for a qualitative difference in the lives of their local communities.

We came up with a program that would have four key components: a twenty-minute audiovisual that gives an overview of how multireligious Long Island is; a panel presentation by representatives from different faith traditions; an open question-and-discussion period; and a booklet on each faith tradition that includes follow-up contacts and bibliographic suggestions. All of this proved to be a big undertaking and required that we obtained modest grants to underwrite the production of materials.

The first thing the committee tackled was developing a four-page folio on each of the twelve faith traditions represented on the Long Island Multi-Faith Forum. In addition to the nine already represented in the membership of the education committee, we included Native American spirituality, Unitarian Universalism, and yoga spirituality. Lucinda Allen Mosher, a longtime student of world religions and a graduate student at General Theological Seminary, volunteered her time as writer and editor. She began by asking committee members what would be important to include in the folio. Members came up with key symbols, origins, sacred writings, key beliefs and practices, holidays, how they are organized, what they do for social action and community outreach, and Long Island contacts for more information and local leadership in particular traditions. She interviewed religious leaders, read materials they suggested, and drew on her own rich background in the study of world religions in drafting the folios. Each step along the way, members of a specific religious tradition reviewed the materials and made suggestions. Then the document was presented to the entire education committee for review and vote. Finally, the twelve four-page folios were reviewed and voted upon by the Long Island Multi-Faith Forum. This process was time consuming but absolutely critical for creating documents that were both affirmed and owned by each particular religious group as well as understood and affirmed by the twelve traditions in the Multi-Faith Forum. The folios were printed by the Long Island Multi-Faith Forum as "An Introduction to Your Neighbors' Religions" and are now available online and can be downloaded.[2]

The next major task was developing an audiovisual presentation. The education committee met with Michael Fairchild, a well-known photographer and frequent contributor to *National Geographic*, to explore what was needed to show and tell people how the religious landscape had, in fact, changed on Long Island. Over a period of two months, Michael took pictures of the places of worship, rituals, and community activities of all twelve religious traditions. A script was developed with the input and critique of Multi-Faith Forum members, and they helped obtain a broad selection of recorded music and chanting that could be used. The end product is a DVD that features a spectacular kaleidoscopic view of the religious and cultural diversity of Long Island. The video was updated about two years ago and made much more user friendly for intergenerational audiences.

Staging live panel presentations on what it means to live out one's faith on Long Island required training people to be open, interactive, spontaneous, and free in a public setting, rather than simply giving a minilecture about what a Buddhist, Hindu, Jain, Sikh, Christian, or Jew believes. We generated a long list of possible questions for moderators of panels to use to get the discussion going, including the following:

- What is a big challenge you face in raising your children in your faith tradition?
- What misunderstandings have you encountered about your faith from others on Long Island? Where do they occur?
- What does your religious tradition say about other religious traditions?
- In what ways might communities on Long Island affirm publicly that religious pluralism is a reality and is to be valued?

The training sessions were designed to be practice sessions for potential panelists and moderators, and to be fun! The process involved an orientation to the Building Bridges program, listing suggestions of dos and don'ts for panelists, getting volunteers of at least four different traditions to be on a panel, having an actual panel discussion, letting the audience address questions to the panel, and then getting feedback from panelists and the audience on how it went. More than one hundred people from the twelve traditions have now participated in these training sessions and have been panelists. The education committee keeps notes on who did well, what needs improving, and when various people are available. All of us have learned a lot about each other's faith and some of the deepest concerns and hopes that people have.

Panel members are all volunteers. Most are laypeople living, working, and raising families on Long Island. All treasure their own communities while cherishing American society and its values, which protect and affirm religious diversity. All are informed about their own religious tradition and eager to share its values and customs with others. All are genuinely interested in learning about other religious traditions and building bridges of understanding.

About twelve years ago "Building Bridges: Understanding Our Neighbors' Faiths" was publicly launched. The brochure about the program has been widely distributed and requests continue to come in. Approximately 250 presentations have been made to date. So far, it has been an exciting and challenging venture for the Forum. The entire planning, designing, and training process took more than three years and was an incredible educational journey. Changes continue to be made and materials updated.

Key Learnings

Below I identify eight key learnings that may be helpful to anyone in adult, continuing, professional, or religious education who develops programs that address questions and concerns emerging from our ever-growing religiously and culturally pluralistic society. For these learnings, I am indebted to individuals from a variety of religious backgrounds with whom I worked for seven years in planning and carrying out numerous interreligious, educational programs.

1. Be clear about why you want to engage the multireligious community in developing educational programs. Most of these communities are still in minority positions, and members will want to know why you are interested in working with them. As a member of a dominant religious community, I believe I am called by God to help build a human community that seeks to relieve suffering and cares for the planet. I need their help in bringing about a better understanding of their traditions in my own community and in building a just and peaceful society for all people who value religious and cultural pluralism. I am firmly convinced that plurality in a positive sense means becoming a community of communities, a concept that received considerable attention in the World Council of Churches. Many other reasons can be added. The point is to be clear about why any of us are doing what we are doing!

2. Take time and care to find out what religious groups are in your community. Identifying religious groups in your community is not an easy task. Many are not organized in the ways Christians and Jews are. Often, neither an overarching organizational structure nor a directory or listing of all the religious traditions in a particular area exists. On Long Island, we looked in the telephone directory, contacted school systems, drove around neighborhoods, went to media outlets, and called the Center for the Study of World Religions at Harvard Divinity School. This center, through the Pluralism Project, has developed a database that includes many communities across the United States and lists of the religious groups that exist within them. There is an increasing number of interfaith organizations that have membership lists, and they can be very helpful in identifying groups.

3. *More often than not, there will not be an expressed interest or felt need for interfaith educational programs.* It does not work for program directors to just set up programs and hope that somebody comes. We have to create a climate, build expectations, and develop a constituency base. We have to involve others in an educational partnership with us. Many immigrant religious communities have continued to be strangers in this land because members of the dominant group have not reached out to welcome or get to know them. Those in the dominant community need to take the first step. I remember the surprise and delight of a Jain family when I went to their home to introduce myself and indicate something of my interest in their religion and culture. I discovered later that they had been in this country for twenty years and no Christian had ever come to their home except to try to convert them.

4. *Building mutual trust is a challenge for all of us.* Do not ever assume that trust is there. Considerable patience, understanding, time, and caring are required. Trust is not built overnight or in one event. We have to get to know each other by sharing our religious convictions, why our faith is important to us, what fears we have, and what we hope for ourselves and the world in which we live. This says a lot about the type of educational programs that are needed. Do they provide a safe space for sharing and interaction between and among participants so that trust may emerge?

5. *Part of the task of theological education is to become mediating centers.* As educational institutions we can provide a place where

people of vastly different religious traditions may come to understand and experience the multifaith and multicultural society that is growing every day. E. Allen Richardson in *Strangers in this Land: Pluralism and the Response to Diversity in the United States* says that our society needs "mediating institutions that provide middle ground between public and private life, between values of homogeneity and diversity. . . . Mediating institutions deal with the question of identity by maintaining a balance between competing ideologies of pluralism and assimilation. They affirm the value of ethnicity and at the same time offer a vehicle for helping members of tightly knit ethnic communities to overcome their apprehension of the experience of public life."[3] To be a mediating center is an extraordinary demand of our educational enterprises, but a very critical and important one. If theological educators are committed to adult and continuing education that makes a qualitative difference in the lives of individuals and their communities, should we not take up the challenge that Richardson offers?

6. *The planning process is crucial and demanding.* In planning educational programs with representatives of the constituency to be served during the past thirty-five years, I have found there is none more exacting than the interfaith domain. It is a rocky road and full of hazards. Who represents whom is a tough question to answer. Those who are Christian need to remember that considerable diversity exists within any particular faith tradition, just as there is within Christianity. Whenever possible, care must be given to have broad representation from within as well as among the various traditions. For example, in New York City the Muslim community is very complex and diverse and is made up of people from the African American and Anglo communities, the Middle East, Africa, Asia, the Caribbean, and Eastern Europe. There are Sunnis, Shiites, and Sufis. Whom we invite into the planning process will affect the focus and outcome of educational programs that we offer. Planning is not just what we do to make education happen but is also a part of the educational process itself and can have a powerful impact on those involved.

7. We must give primary attention to involving laypeople from the various religious communities. To a large extent interreligious dialogue and programming in this country has been in the hands of paid professional religionists. The base of involvement desperately needs to be expanded to include the vast number of people from various religious traditions who have not been invited into the multifaith educational arena and who have enormous influence in private and public life, whether at home, at work, in the larger society, or in their own particular faith community. In my experience, I have found that we must insist on this. Otherwise our educational programs will have little impact within and among these communities. Every step along the way, we should commit ourselves to involving laity as well as religious professionals in our work as program planners and educators.

Particular attention must be given to involving women, who constitute the majority of the faithful in most traditions and yet are often excluded from interfaith dialogue. Ursula King points out this appalling truth: "Such narrowness is evident with regard to the marginalization, invisibility and exclusion of women, for wherever interreligious dialogue has developed, women seem to have little part in it, at least at the official level. Proof is found in every single book on interfaith dialogue, religious pluralism, the theology of religions, or the 'wider ecumenism' of global inter-religious encounter."[4]

8. Nothing sells itself better than a program that meets head-on an emerging public need and interest with a well-developed program and committed leadership. "Building Bridges: Understanding Our Neighbors' Faiths" is a great example of this. It has continued to grow and improve for more than twelve years. The model can be adapted to different settings. New people are continually being recruited for leadership. Training and support are ongoing. Enthusiastic participants are spreading the good news about the program and, in effect, recruiting new audiences and groups to benefit from the program. Many are not only excited about Building Bridges but also motivated to learn more about the other religious traditions as well as their own.

For Christianity in the United States, this is a new, historic moment in which Christians can now recognize an increasingly multireligious society. Many of us would not have dreamed of having a Muslim, Buddhist, or Hindu living in our neighborhoods a generation ago. However, the first mosque in this country was built seventy-five years ago in Cedar Rapids, Iowa, and now the Muslim faith is growing faster than Christianity and is expected to be the majority faith worldwide in this century. Perhaps even more important for us today than the opportunity of knowing about different religions is the possibility of encountering people of different faiths. Former Harvard University comparative religions professor W. C. Smith's words of almost fifty years ago have even more validity today:

> The religious life of [humankind] from now on, if it is to be lived at all, will be lived in a context of religious pluralism. . . . This is true for all of us: not only for [humankind] in general on an abstract level, but for you and me as individual persons. No longer are people of other persuasions, peripheral or distant, the idle curiosities of travellers' tales. The more alert we are, and the more involved in life, the more we are finding that they are our neighbours, our colleagues, our competitors, our fellows; Confucians and Hindus, Buddhists and Muslims are with us not only in the United Nations, but down the street. Increasingly, not only is our civilization's destiny affected by their actions, but we drink coffee with them personally.[5]

We continuing theological educators are no longer in a position to plead ignorance, to content ourselves with caricatures of people of religious traditions other than our own, or to avoid engaging our religiously plural world. Our responsibility as educators is to develop programs that celebrate religious pluralism, foster understanding, respect differences, and promote justice and peace and a sustainable planet for all peoples. The goal is not to make us one, not to engage in syncretism, but "to generate a strong social fabric through the interweaving of commitments"[6] that will move in the direction of a community of communities.

Notes

1. Diana Eck, *A New Religious America: How A "Christian Country" Has Become the World's Most Religiously Diverse Nation* (San Francisco: HarperCollins Publishers, 2001).

2. Materials and copies of DVDs ($35 including postage) may be requested by calling the Long Island Council of Churches at (516) 565-0290 or by going to the Long Island Multi-Faith Forum website, www.ncccusa.org/ecmin/licc/multiforum.html.

3. E. Allen Richardson, *Strangers in This Land: Pluralism and the Response to Diversity in the United States* (New York: Pilgrim Press, 1988), 202.

4. Ursula King, "Feminism: The Missing Dimension in the Dialogue of Religions," in *Pluralism and the Religions: The Theological and Political Dimensions*, ed. John May (London: Cassell Academic, 1998), 42.

5. Wilfred Cantwell Smith, *The Faith of Other Men* (New York: Harper & Row, 1963), 11.

6. Diana L. Eck, *Encountering God: A Spiritual Journey from Bozeman to Benaras* (Boston: Beacon Press, 1991), 195.

CHAPTER 16

Connected Learning for Ministry in a Technological Age

A. Christopher Hammon

The following story was told by a student in the Global Online Doctor of Ministry Program at Drew University Theological School, where I am a member of the faculty. I share it here, with her permission, because it represents the experience of many of Drew's online students.

Evy's Story

The idea of online community was an anathema to me. For years, I spoke against the notion that relationships could be formed by engaging through the Internet; then came a Doctor of Ministry program where the major contact between students would be online. After ten months of meeting one another, through our Web cams, rapidly firing off responses to questions, arguing over meaning of words, and learning how to accept our differences, we came together.

From the moment we met in person, I experienced a profound difference. As someone who has been physically challenged since eighteen months of age, I have had to consistently prove myself.

Throughout my life, I had to be at the top of my class just to be noticed. Being average has never been acceptable for me because that meant I faded into the background or never made it to the "playing field."

During our first hours together, I kept looking for those glances; the ones that try not to notice my physical disability but say "I am uncomfortable." To my great surprise, there were none. For the first time in my life, I did not have to prove myself first; prove that I was worthy; prove that I, too, belonged in the group. There was a startling acceptance that occurred, solely because we first met online. I had to let go of my bias that said valid relationships could not be formed through the Internet.

Our group quickly gained a reputation: we did everything together, and we mostly did it loudly! While other groups were meeting one another on an individual basis, we put our tables together so that we could all talk at once—the same way we had communicated through chat sessions and threaded discussions. The learning curve was limited; we didn't know what each other looked like or sounded like, but that was overshadowed by our instant understanding of one another's individual language. We came to the Doctor of Ministry program as individuals, but by the summer intensive session, we were the Global/Online Class of 2010 Doctor of Ministry Cabal.[1] Our postmodern curriculum, accompanied by postmodern learning tools, had formed us into a postmodern community that extended far beyond learning and extended our reach far beyond our expectations.

Why Lifelong Learning Online?

In the midst of the current whirlwinds of change that are energized by the shift of worldviews, the collapse of distance, the paradigm shifts in how people work and learn, and a blurring information explosion, the challenge to be constantly engaged in learning is paramount for all professions, including the various disciplines of pastoral ministry. For providers of lifelong ministry for ministry, the challenges for offering just-in-time learning that is available, affordable, and meaningful in terms of practical value is even greater. Many sources, including a 2001 report issued by the Alban Institute,[2] recognize the need to develop new and innovative pathways for ministers to learn and connect and to develop safe environments in which to explore innovative approaches for lifelong learning.

I teach both online and offline as part of the Global Online Doctor of Ministry program at Drew University's Theological School. The campus is just over a seven-hundred-mile commute each way from Louisville, Kentucky, where I live and direct the online lifelong learning for ministry program of the Wayne E. Oates Institute. The Oates Institute offices are located at Deer Park Baptist Church, but the campus with classrooms and resource library is located at www.oates.org.

When the Wayne E. Oates Institute moved into offering lifelong learning for ministry in the online environment in 1998, we saw it as offering a venue that enabled us to respond to concerns among our constituents about opportunities available for those not located near urban centers and participation costs in terms of time and money for traveling to traditional offline events. More than ten years later these concerns are still voiced by many of our constituents and members of our learning community as significant.

Since the Oates Institute is involved in providing continuing education programs to professional practitioners in the very high-touch field of ministry, the words we heard from many were that the online environment would never be as good as the offline environment of the traditional classroom. As the Oates Institute board contemplated the plunge into the online environment, the question asked by many was, "Will chaplains, counselors, and pastors participate in these opportunities?" Wayne E. Oates spoke up to suggest that we were asking the wrong question. "What we need to be asking is: How do we teach them?"

We initially focused on holding online conferences and workshops for our constituents following a distance education model through which we extended our conference hall into the global village, allowing participants to attend the presentations from wherever they may be. All they needed was a computer with a Web browser and an Internet connection. By making the presentations asynchronous so that participants could access them at their convenience, we enhanced the schedule flexibility of the conference and opened the opportunity for using the scheduled gathering times to focus on dialogue between the presenters and participants.

Connected Learning: Some Definitions

Distance Education: An approach that emphasizes transmitting knowledge and skills from teachers to students who are not present in the same geographical space. This is also known as distance teaching. In general application, this has served as a virtual microphone in the classroom, enabling institutions of learning to broadcast information to a larger audience.

Distance Learning: The practice of learners reaching out to geographically distant resources, including teachers and mentors, to stimulate their learning process. This opportunity has rapidly accelerated the practice of informal lifelong learning among many adults. They have increasingly turned to the resources of the World Wide Web as needed to learn about products, places, health, interests, ideas, and technologies. This opportunity has taken the concept of the community library as a learning resource to a new level.

Connected Learning: A collaborative learning process that uses cyberspace to connect learners with their inner selves, other learners, teachers, mentors, facilitators, and learning resources while transcending the need for participants to share the same time or space. Connected learning is made possible by the convergence of new technologies and new educational methodologies that connect learning opportunities with practice in order to meet individual needs within a diverse community of colleagues.

We moved from using the *distance education approaches* into using *distance learning approaches* also by continuing to make conference presentations and other resources available to our members and constituents. Resources available in the growing global online library met the needs of people who were seeking specific types of resources. Both of these approaches were quite successful in making lifelong learning opportunities available in very cost-effective ways. We frequently hear stories from our members about how our online offerings are saving them three- to four-hour commutes each way to more traditional offline learning opportunities; particularly those living west of the Mississippi River in the United States, in Australia, and in countries in Africa. But we still were not meeting all of the challenges for lifelong learning that we saw among those in ministry or even those of our constituency.

Over the past ten years, Vicki Hollon, my colleague at the Oates Institute and at Drew, and I have engaged the ministry of teaching others to use the online environment and discovered that there is a willingness to learn and a willingness to participate in online opportunities. But we have also discovered a lot more about offering lifelong learning for ministry opportunities online. Most significant, we discovered that online learning has several advantages over offline learning (traditional face-to-face). This is particularly true for lifelong learning where the goal is educating reflective practitioners, such as those engaged in ministry. These key advantages are the opportunities for getting to know one another from the inside out, geographical diversity in perspective, sustained peer reflective learning, and the opportunity to blend all of these to form ongoing learning communities.

In the midst of our collaborative doctoral research exploring the use of the online environment for lifelong learning for ministry, however, we discovered even greater opportunities offered through connected learning. While seeing *distance education* and *distance learning* as good uses of the online environment, we sought to tap the expertise of practitioner experience as a primary learning resource. What caught our attention were (*a*) the emerging opportunities for peer reflective learning as a way to address the learning challenges facing midcareer ministers and (*b*) the development of ongoing, geographically dispersed learning communities made possible by the convergence of new educational methodologies and educational technologies.

Learning Challenges
Facing Midcareer Ministers

Our concern for the learning challenges facing midcareer pastors, chaplains, and counselors—especially those more than ten years away from their most recent professional degree—grew out of our research regarding current cultural transitions. In our report "Learning Challenges for 21st Century Ministry," prepared as part of a Louisville Institute-funded project, we identified three congruent forces interacting to energize the current condition of cultural transition. One force we observed was the changing worldviews—how people perceive and give expression to their understanding of reality. Worldviews shaped by complex systems theory, emergence theory, and postmodern relativity are supplanting the reductionist approaches of Enlightenment Rationalism and the modern era's pursuit of absolute truth. A second force we saw was the further collapse of distance and the cultural convergence brought on by the evolution of digital technologies and communications networks, such as the Internet and global cell-phone networks. The third force was the paradigm shift being experienced in the way people work and learn. Hierarchical, vertically structured, competitive organizations are being replaced by new collaborative team approaches with group empowering, project oriented, wiki-connected, open source structures. All three of these cultural shifts are intimately interrelated forces, each being energized by and energizing the others. This cultural transition is likened by many to be a watershed time in human history similar to that experienced in the sixteenth century.

As the known world transitions into the world still being discovered—the emerging world in which all of us are living, working, and ministering—people are faced with the incredible challenge of learning, unlearning, surviving, and adapting all at the same time. While caught up in reconstructing styles and ministries to adapt to the emerging transitions within their communities, congregational leaders also have to assimilate significant amounts of new knowledge, revise some of their basic assumptions, and re-construct their theological and philosophical models while they also continue to serve as a leadership bridge spanning old and new worlds and ways of thinking.

These transitions are particularly challenging to those whose primary professional training was completed prior to the begin-ning of the twenty-first century, when these change forces reached critical mass and began significantly reshaping the ways that all of us relate, conduct business, learn, create, and recreate. Since Pulpit and Pew's findings indicate that more than half of all pastors are over age fifty and have more than twenty years of professional ex-perience, staying up-to-date through lifelong professional learn-ing is critical.[3] In addressing the issue of Internet safety among youth, John Pallfrey and Urs Glasser call attention to the risk to youth due to the learning gap among teachers, parents, and com-munity leaders in understanding these new technologies and en-vironments for learning, connecting, and creating.[4]

We identified six key learning challenges facing congregational leaders as a result of these cultural transitions. One is learning to accept that a disciplined approach to lifelong learning is a signifi-cant part of one's professional practice. While basic professional training remains a necessary part of professional preparation, a professional's overall knowledge base is doubling in fewer than four years. Much of what people have learned through their basic professional training has a limited shelf life and may be outdated early in their career. In today's world, if one is not engaged in con-tinuous learning while in the midst of doing, then one is falling behind. Leonard Sweet writes:

> Where education was once thought of as a period of preparation for a lifetime of work, it is now seen as a lifetime of preparation for various work assignments. Perhaps the most important law of ecology is this: $L \geq C$. It means that to survive, an organism's rate of learning must be equal to or greater than the rate of change in the environment. That is why the "learning organization" metaphor must be as applicable to

church life as it is to corporate life. . . . If ministers are not constantly learning and unlearning, they are becoming less and less qualified to serve as effective disciples of Jesus Christ.[5]

Generally speaking, this could be said of any religious tradition: If you are not continually learning, you are less and less qualified to serve as an effective disciple of your tradition. The primary challenge for congregational leaders is putting this discipline into practice in the face of competing priorities, which means that both the leader and his or her congregation need to see this discipline in learning as a priority to invest in.

A second challenge in today's culture is learning new approaches to learning: learning to learn collaboratively (cocreative learning communities and Peter Senge's "Learning Organizations"), learning to learn from reflecting on experience (Donald Schon's "Reflective Practitioner"), learning to learn by reflecting on the learning process (double-loop learning and triple-loop learning, Chris Argyris and Don Schon), and learning to make use of new technologies for learning.[6]

Third, after years of analytically trying to break things down into smaller units and reduce complex concepts or relationships in order to comprehend their independent essence, congregational leaders are now challenged to see the whole as a dynamic interconnection of relationships. This living systems orientation applies not only to the natural world but also to the social world of families, communities, nations, and congregations. This is understood and promoted in the emphasis on family systems theory and organizational behavior.

Fourth, congregational leaders are challenged to learn how to experiment with innovative and creative approaches, to take risks, and to fail. Fear of any kind of failure in ministry cripples one's ability to develop necessary new approaches and solutions for current situations. It also curtails the opportunity for learning that comes from pushing beyond the comfort zone. Openness to experimenting with approaches and willingness to risk are essential ingredients for creatively addressing change and innovating new ministry approaches.

Fifth, what educators and leaders have learned in recent years about multiple learning styles and multiple intelligences requires that we learn to be inclusive of multiple ways of learning, understanding, and expressing meaning. For many congregational leaders, who are often deeply embedded in valuing the Western cognitive tradition and the primary expression of ideas and emotions through propositional statements in the form of words, part of this challenge is learning to be sensitive to hearing, empowering, and providing opportunities for those who have other learning styles and preferences, other ways of viewing the world, and other forms of intelligence.

Sixth, in this age of computer-mediated communications and information technologies, we must be willing to learn to use new tools, connect in new ways, and work in new environments. This requires the willingness to take risks, to ask for help, to see ourselves as students, and learn from kids. Many of today's tools are much more powerful in their capacity to produce than yesterday's tools, and they provide significant opportunities for those in ministry to work smarter, more creatively, and more productively. While the tools are powerful and the new environments they make possible provide advantageous opportunities, the tools are also more complex to use. Developing the skills to use these tools and to work in these new environments frequently involves hands-on trial-and-error learning. This often involves a role reversal as older people learn from younger people, and for many who are accustomed to being the expert, this reversal can feel very vulnerable. In addition, many may feel the added anxiety of job insecurity. These fears are something that must be overcome.

Failure on the part of congregational leaders to successfully negotiate these learning challenges puts us in the church at risk of being an irrelevant voice for the gospel in twenty-first century culture.

Connected Learning as an Approach to Lifelong Learning for Ministry

Distance education and distance learning are not new innovations for addressing the challenges of time, distance, and availability. One common practice for overcoming these hindrances has been to employ an ancient information technology known as a book. While this technology has become more widespread and more cost effective through the years, books (or journals) alone do not provide the interactive environment that facilitates the social process of learning and reflecting on best practices among peers. The merger of new educational methods and new information technologies is causing a variety of educational paradigm shifts that are generating a number of new opportunities for addressing the issues of concern that Hollon and I identified.

Connected Learning as Paradigm and Opportunity

There is some ambiguity among educators regarding clearly accepted definitions for nonlocalized learning. For our purpose, Hollon and I accepted the conventional perspectives that *distance education* refers to those approaches that emphasize transmitting knowledge and skills from teachers to students who are not present in the same geographical space. This is also known as *distance teaching*. In general application, this has served as a virtual microphone in the classroom, enabling institutions of learning to broadcast information to a larger audience. We also acknowledged that *distance learning* refers to the practice of learners reaching out to geographically distant resources, including teachers and mentors, to stimulate their learning process. This opportunity has rapidly accelerated the practice of informal lifelong learning among many adults as they have increasingly turned to the resources of the World Wide Web as needed to learn about products, places, health, interests, ideas, and technologies. This opportunity has taken the concept of the community library as a learning resource to a new level.

Since neither *distance education* nor *distance learning* adequately described the opportunity made possible through this convergence of technologies and methodologies, we chose the term *connected learning* to convey the idea of online collaborative learning, a learning process that uses cyberspace, itself a metaphor, to connect learners with their inner selves, other learners, teachers, mentors, facilitators, and learning resources while transcending the need for immediacy (synchronicity) in either time or space. *Connected learning* is the opportunity to connect learning opportunities with practice to meet individually defined needs within a culturally diverse community of colleagues.

Mary Field Belenky and collaborators add further insight to the meaning of connected learning over separate forms of learning when they noted the nature of the deep relationships that characterize connected learning: "Connected knowers begin with an interest in the facts of other people's lives, but they gradually shift the focus to other people's ways of thinking. . . . Faith told us that deep relationships offered her a chance to really get to know another view of the world."[7]

Another key insight Belenky and collaborators contributed to our understanding of connected learning is found in this comment: "The connected class provides a culture for growth. In a connected class no one apologizes for uncertainty. It is assumed that evolving thought will be tentative . . . [we can] speak with certainty but we can also try to construct a different sort of authority, based on personal individual experience and acknowledging 'the uncertainties implicit in an approach which values the personal.'"[8]

As we continued to explore what the online environment offered in merging the new educational methodologies—such as Malcolm Knowles's approaches to andragogy extending to the new experiential, participative, image-driven, collaborative pedagogies of digital natives—with emerging information technologies, our collaborative doctoral research revealed several opportunities connected learning provided that are more difficult to achieve in traditional offline settings. These opportunities make connected learning much more beneficial for meeting twenty-first-century learning challenges than just approaches that overcome time, distance, and availability hindrances. The most significant of these are in keeping with the educational shifts taking place: diversity of decentralization, increased interaction, opportunities for reflective and peer group learning, collaborative learning, and opportunities to develop lifelong learning communities.

Connected Learning as Diverse, Decentralized Learning

Learning is rapidly being decentralized and breaking away from the traditional centers for education. Several key benefits come out of this, and one is that learning is getting closer to the field of practice. For congregational leaders this means having the opportunity to pursue theological training and continuing education while remaining on the job, potentially far away from sought-out educational centers and having the benefit of a practice-oriented learning lab. Leonard Sweet observed, "Learners increasingly expect to learn in their homes and to receive academic credit for their efforts . . . the future belongs to those educational institutions that come to learners."[9]

A significant benefit of this decentralization is the inclusion of diverse cultures, perspectives, and ethnic backgrounds as a more common experience. In our research, we discovered that simply having people from different regions sharing their perspectives and best practices brought a new level of learning to pastoral leaders, chaplains, and counselors. In learning activities that brought participants into the conversation from various countries, ethnic backgrounds, and denominational bodies, we found a much richer level of dialogue than we encountered when participants were from one region, one denomination, or one ethnic heritage.[10]

Perhaps the most significant thing we noticed, however, was that geographical and denominational diversity also brought increased levels of openness and vulnerability.[11] This inclination of people to share more openly in the online environment has been observed by numerous studies seeking to address both the benefits and the risks of that behavior. What caught our attention was the openness and honesty of dialogue among clergy in light of the studies by William Lord and John Bryan identifying clergy resistance to being vulnerable with other clergy as a hindrance to continued learning.[12] As a participant in one of our online research groups commented, "I appreciated everyone's insight and honest comments. I thought many of the heartfelt conversations revealed a real need for open dialogue. I wonder how much of that would have occurred in a face-to-face meeting." In our research, open dialogue didn't occur in the offline (face-to-face) groups.

Connected Learning as Interactive, Individualized Learning

Mass production approaches to education, based in a pedagogy of information transmission and age-based curriculum, were a by-product of the industrial revolution. The capabilities of the digital revolution have introduced a paradigm shift to interactive, individualized learning approaches. Don Tapscott, author of many books on information technology, proclaimed that the digital revolution provides students and educators with "a new, more powerful, and more effective learning paradigm."[13] He noted several paradigm shifts in this movement: (*a*) the move from sequential, linear learning to nonsequential, interactive, hypermedia learning; (*b*) a shift from instruction-oriented learning to construction and discovery, which is also to say "a shift away from pedagogy . . . to the creation of learning partnerships and learning cultures";[14] (*c*) the move toward learner-centered education and away from teacher-centered instruction, focused on the experience of the learners, the merger of learning and entertainment, and the stimulation of learner motivation (note that this also encompasses awareness of the learner's responsibility to identify his or her learning needs and to take charge of creating learning situations for meeting those needs); (*d*) an emphasis on learning how to navigate information and learning how to learn, including how to synthesize and assimilate, in lieu of just absorbing the material.

Opportunities coming out of this shift include developing learning approaches that help individual congregational leaders to identify their specific learning needs and to meet those needs in light of their own circumstances, gifts, and personal learning styles. The possibilities for connecting with others with similar learning needs are expanded as congregational leaders learn to connect as peer learning groups transcending geographic regions. Models made possible and energized by the digital revolution are providing significant new opportunities and networks for connecting learners with teachers, resources, and other learners. Tapscott quotes Seymour Papert, author of *The Connected Family: Bridging the Digital Generation Gap*, who observed, "What I see as the real contribution of digital media to education is a flexibility that could allow every individual to discover their own personal paths to learning. This will make possible the dream of every progressive educator to come true: In the learning environment of the future, every learner will be special."[15]

Tapscott, author of *Growing Up Digital* and *Wikinomics: How Mass Collaboration Changes Everything*, has contemplated how the digital revolution has changed and will continue to change the learning experience of the next generation of congregational leaders. He accurately projected that

> the ultimate interactive learning environment will be the Web and the Net as a whole. It increasingly includes the vast repository of human knowledge, tools to manage this knowledge, access to people, and a growing galaxy of services ranging from sandbox environments for preschoolers to virtual laboratories for medical students studying neural psychiatry. Today's baby will learn about Michelangelo tomorrow by walking through the Sistine Chapel, watching the artist paint, and perhaps stopping for a conversation. Students will stroll on the moon.
>
> To glimpse the new pedagogy that has emerged from the advent of these technologies one needs only to observe a teenager engaging the

world of interactive gaming within the matrix of a multiuser simulated environment. It is a world of trial and error, learning combined with information sharing at multiple levels, combined with shared reflection on experience. It is a world of interactive role playing with varying degrees of "reality" and fantasy. It is a world of multicultural relationships and interactions involving trade and the negotiation of contracts both real and virtual. It is a world that requires acquiring information and mastering skills toward developing expertise.[16]

Connected Learning as Reflective Learning in Practice

The new information technologies offer numerous opportunities for practitioners to engage in reflective learning. The awareness provided by the studies of Donald Schon, Chris Argyris, and others demonstrate that the best practices or solutions often emerge within specific problem situations. The new technologies provide the opportunity for practitioners and their colleagues to gather and evaluate a situation in a very timely way. This gathering of multiple outside perspectives can help clarify how a problem is understood, expand the number of possible solutions, and enhance one's perspective on a given situation. The new technologies have the potential to enhance reflection on prior experience and provide a method for accountability and awareness of one's underlying assumptions and how those assumptions shape which solution approaches are considered and which are resisted. A connected network of colleagues offers the potential for a support system in the midst of a learning experience or when implementing a difficult solution.

Donald Schon's studies regarding the emphasis on continuing education adds another dimension to this struggle between updating the professionals' knowledge and improving professional practice. In Schon's critique of the traditional model for continuing education he calls attention to the emphasis on practitioners returning to the academy for the latest updates to their knowledge base. Schon observes:

In the varied topography of professional practice, there is a high, hard
ground overlooking a swamp. On the high ground, manageable problems lend themselves to solution through the application of research-
based theory and technique. In the swampy lowland, messy, confusing
problems defy technical solution. The irony of this situation is that the
problems of the high ground tend to be relatively unimportant to individuals or society at large . . . while in the swamp lie the problems of
greatest human concern.[17]

New educational methodologies that developed over the past
twenty years, particularly with reference to adult learning, recognize that (a) the convergence of learning and doing is critical to
innovative adaptation and problem solving in a rapidly changing
world and (b) practitioners are the most qualified experts in their
particular context. The new information and communications
technologies developed during the same time frame include technologies for voice, video, and data creation, storage, and presentation as well as communications networks such as the Internet and
wireless networks. The energy generated by the merger of these
two forces, new technologies and new methodologies, has accelerated the paradigm shift in how people work and learn. It has also
created a remarkable new environment in which to address key
challenges facing continuing education providers.

Our approach to using connected learning for lifelong learning for ministry has brought congregational leaders, chaplains,
and counselors together in online, facilitated conversations where
we have asked these participants to first reflect on the course materials and presentations in light of their own experience and
contexts: What rings true for them and what doesn't? What has
worked for them and what hasn't? Just because a perceived "expert" said it doesn't make it true for the participant's context or
in the participant's experience. There is no more one right answer
or one size fits all. Then we ask participants to share their thinking with others in the group so that they can reflect through dialogue among themselves. We ask each of the seminar participants

to think about the reflections of others in the group, again in light of his or her own experience and context.

When asked how this learning approach contributed to reflective learning, we received the following responses. One pastor said, "Since thoughts in both e-mail and the discussion group had to be written . . . there was some thought before expressing a response." A second commented, "The process caused me to have to do connection between the heart and the head. . . . The diversity of the group offered thoughts that fed a need for understanding, but then forced me to reflect on what I was reading to give application to my own situation." Other reactions include such comments as, "As people are all thinking about similar things and reflecting on their own experiences, their thoughts and ideas caused me to do more inner work of my own." "This was one of the best educational experiences in which I have ever participated. It provided a variety of viewpoints and life experiences from participants. It elicited my own life experience as a base for further reflection and learning and offered an opportunity to gain insights from others." "It really made me think seriously and reflect on how I can better myself by this reflective learning and not be so afraid to challenge new openings such as this learning experience but 'take the bull by the horns' and get going." "I was given permission to explore, not only in words on the computer screen, but in my day-to-day ministry and to apply/formulate/evaluate my attitudes, opinions, actions and interactions with the aging population. My sensitivity and my abilities were increased with this new learning and I felt empowered to go out with a new approach, a new plan and to start something right away in a practical accomplishment."

Connected Learning and Opportunities for Lifelong Learning Communities

Learners have a long tradition of gathering in community for the benefits of shared resources, shared dialogue, and shared support around a common commitment to learning. Modern universities are just one example of this. The connected world of cyberspace has presented a new dimension for human social organization around learning. Community formation in virtual reality has already shown that it has significant potential for redefining community around shared values and interests rather than geographical proximity.

For a world that realizes the value of diverse perspectives for constructing understandings of problems and developing solutions, forming learning communities in cyberspace presents several key opportunities. One is the chance to form an ongoing community among practitioners who are in the field working and moving from place to place throughout their careers. While the seminary campus provides a special learning community environment during a minister's basic professional training, ministers tend to relocate several times during their careers, typically from small, rural congregations progressively toward larger metropolitan congregations. My current group of Doctor of Ministry students at Drew, the D.Min. Cabal, reflects this range of congregational placements; group members are geographically dispersed from the East Coast of the United States to the West Coast and north to Canada. Our membership at the Oates Institute, those who participate in and facilitate our learning events, come from throughout North America and eight other countries. Members pay an annual fee with the option to sign up for any of the seminars the institute offers during the year (with the recognition that we offer forty to fifty online seminars per year, seminars are limited to twelve participants, and those registered are expected to participate). It is a growing learning community where quite a few have been members since we went online in 1998, many have been members more than five years, and most have been members more than one year.

As a result of offering an ongoing schedule of online learning opportunities throughout the year, we at the Oates Institute have seen the formation of a growing learning community whose members continue to connect with each other through participation in various seminars. This focus on developing a learning community rather than on program events is a significant new understanding of the relationship of online learning community to specific learning experiences, and it demonstrates the cyberspace parallel experience to that of residential academic degree programs where students come to know one another and form community because they are sharing multiple classes. We are seeing this in comments that connect with prior seminars people have participated in together and with their recollection of nontopic details, such as details about children, spouses, and placements. As their connections with one another have grown stronger, we have also seen increased levels of interaction and openness in sharing.

A second opportunity is expanded connections through a wider series of personal networks not limited by geography or mobility. Practitioners have discovered that in learning communities where everyone shares proximity there is a greater tendency to know the same people and resources. Learning communities in cyberspace tend to bring greater geographical diversity and provide expanded opportunities to connect with other people and resources they were not previously aware of or did not previously have access to. When joined together as a collaborative learning community they generate significant potential for innovation and creativity.

In a world where lifelong just-in-time learning is the new norm, the opportunity to stay connected as part of an ongoing learning community, even as you move from place to place, is a significant advantage. It used to be that one pursued an education at an educational center that was perceived to prepare one for a lifetime of work. This is no longer true, not even for ministers. One only needs to look at the continuing transitions in understanding family systems theory as it applies to an understanding of families and congregations over the past two decades to get a sense of learning that continues over a lifetime. Or if you observe the changes in how the day-to-day business of a congregation is conducted, you get another perspective. Or if you look at the emerging worldview of digital natives who now constitute a portion of five-generation congregations as part of the modern-postmodern digital spectrum, you get still another perspective. Don Tapscott observed, "For young boomers . . . life was divided into the period when you learned and the period when you did. You went to school . . . and learned a competency . . . and for the rest of your life your challenge was simply to keep up with developments in your field. But things changed. Today many boomers can expect to reinvent their knowledge base constantly. Learning has become a continuous, lifelong process."[18]

Tapscott also noted that Richard Soderberg with the National Technological University expressed it well when he said, "People mistakenly think that once they've graduated from university they are good for the next decade—when they are really good for the next ten seconds."[19]

As a minister working in pastoral education in the online environment, I can share that the Internet approaches we used at the Oates Institute in 1998 are now four generations of evolution obsolete, and we are continuously updating and implementing new technologies. That doesn't begin to take in the development of new narrative and postmodern clinical approaches to pastoral care and counseling or the evolution of twenty-first-century leadership approaches in light of global wikinomics, social networking, crowd sourcing, Theory U, and so forth. Staying current requires a day-in-day-out, just-in-time learning approach (learning too much in advance requires too much additional effort to unlearn when it finally comes time to do). This approach benefits from my participation in several online learning communities where I can consult colleagues to quickly learn what I need to know.

A Word of Caution about Connected Learning

As many organizations look to online opportunities as an avenue for economically extending their educational programs to larger audiences, it is important to note that connected learning is time intense for faculty. On the one hand, this reality will provide comfort to faculty members who fear the loss of jobs as more and more courses go into the online environment. On the other hand, this fact will be a discouraging word to institutions thinking that online opportunities enable an increase in the faculty-student ratio or that it will reduce the time faculty members commit to a course.

While the Oates Institute has discovered that connected learning provides outstanding opportunities for meeting today's learning needs and overcoming many of the challenges to meeting those needs, especially for those in ministry, we have discovered that small groups and facilitation are key factors. In our experimentation with various approaches and durations, we have discovered that three-week, asynchronous seminars limited to twelve participants work very well.

But We Ain't Seen Nothin' Yet

As I consider the direction things are going for the online environment and lifelong learning for ministry, we are barely through the door for a whole new world of connections and opportunities between learners, learning communities, and lifelong learning providers. At the Oates Institute, with a meager annual budget, we provide forty to fifty online seminar opportunities per year, several peer learning group certificate programs with online practicum components, a variety of brief learning opportunities and conversations, annual online conferences, ongoing support for several clergy peer learning groups, and opportunities for our learning community to create their own learning events and conversations. We also publish an online professional journal featuring regular articles, special issues, and a growing group of regular columnists, along with republishing Wayne Oates's out-of-print books.

Web 2.0 and social networking technologies are leading to the formation of many new learning-centered Facebook and MySpace groups, to the developments from the open source community with dynamic learning platforms such as Moodle, to virtual campuses located in virtual worlds such as Second Life. With these innovations, a new generation of learning tools and opportunities have come on the scene. The question is how fast can we as lifelong learning for ministry providers learn and create new, innovative opportunities. How creative is our imagination?

Providers of lifelong learning for ministry need to keep four dynamics on our radar. The first is the recognition that the traditional institutions for theological education are no longer advantaged. Anyone can form a learning peer group using a Yahoo Group or a Facebook Group; no experience and very little computer or Internet skill are required. The ready availability of Moodle and of low-cost service providers to host a group means that the larger institutions who could afford the licensing fees of Blackboard, WebCT, or Angel no longer have an advantage. Moodle, which stands for Modular Object-Oriented Dynamic Learning Environment, is an open source application available free to any organization or individual who wants to use it and who will invest a bit of time learning how. Not only is Drew University now using Moodle for all of its online classes, but the Oates Institute also has its own Moodle installation for many of our online seminars and classes. The bottom line is that large institutions and large institutional budgets no longer provide technological advantages for providing online opportunities. The advantage now goes to the imaginative and the creative.

A second dynamic to watch is the demand for lifelong learning opportunities created by the significance of emerging cultural transitions. Phyllis Tickle has nailed this era in her 2008 book, *The Great Emergence: How Christianity Is Changing and Why*. She sees this era as the next five-hundred-year transition in the church's history; an era of upheaval and transition in the church's life comparable to the Protestant Reformation.[20] Rex Miller, in *The Millennium Matrix: Reclaiming the Past, Reframing the Future of the Church*, has identified well the recognition that the medium is the worldview. For the first time in the history of the church (civilization, for that matter), Miller observes that church members reflect the world-views of three primary communications eras: print (modern), broadcast (postmodern), and digital (convergent).[21] The church currently has a crisis regarding numbers of congregational lead-ers who are prepared to minister across the breadth of this world-view spectrum, which reveals three approaches to discerning what is and what is meaningful, three perspectives on what it means to participate and to belong, and three sets of expectations for what they seek from their faith community. In the past, the primary fo-cus of seminaries has been to provide basic professional training for ministers. In today's world the focus needs to shift to lifelong learning for ministry to enable ministers to adapt to twenty-first century needs and to continue to develop their practical ministry skills in a rapidly changing world and church. Those of us in theo-logical education are already starting to see teaching congregations and parachurch organizations rise to meet this need, one that is going unmet by the seminaries. The demand for opportunities to learn how to adapt and how to lead in this time of change is about to accelerate.

A third dynamic to watch is the effect of the current economic downturn, which is both cutting budgets available for continu-ing education and prompting many to seek retooling for career change or adjustment. Already universities are seeing increased demand for online courses, even from their residential and par-ticularly from their commuter students. Since most individuals and organizations are aware that learning still needs to happen, the focal point for the budget cuts is travel costs. We have already seen this among Oates Institute members, and we are doing it ourselves. While I will be attending a number of conferences and seminars during the next few years, almost all will all be online to cut travel costs.

The fourth dynamic may be the most significant for the future. So far in online lifelong learning for ministry, digital settlers and early adopter immigrants are the ones exploring and taking ad-vantage of this new world of opportunity. On the threshold are the first wave of digital natives who are completing their basic professional training and going into practice. Digital natives are those who have grown up with computers and connective technologies. When they want to know something, their first impulse is to Google it. They have grown up in a world where knowledge is constantly changing and reality is constructed within the community's conversation and creativity. They already think in terms of lifelong, just-in-time learning. They think in terms of collaborative, experiential, and participative learning. And they transition seamlessly between online and offline environments. What we as providers of lifelong learning for ministry do not provide they will create. Resistance is futile. Our most exciting era yet is just ahead—as long as we keep learning, adapting, and creating at an accelerated pace.

Notes

1. Class wiki, used with permission.

2. James P. Wind and Gilbert R. Rendle, "The Leadership Situation Facing American Congregations: An Alban Institute Special Report" (Herndon, VA: Alban Institute, 2001).

3. Becky McMillan, "The View from Pulpit & Pew: Provocative Findings on Pastoral Leadership in the 21st Century" (paper presented at "Coloring Outside the Lines," Society for the Advancement of Continuing Education for Ministry, Lake Junaluska, NC, February 2003), 2, http://www.sacem.com/sacem2003-mcmillan.pdf (accessed July 31, 2003).

4. Urs Glasser and John Palfrey, *Born Digital: Understanding the First Generation of Digital Natives* (New York: Basic Books, 2008), 109–10.

5. Leonard I. Sweet, *Eleven Genetic Gateways to Spiritual Awakening* (Nashville: Abingdon, 1998), 47–49.

6. Peter M. Senge, *The Fifth Discipline: The Art and Practice of the Learning Organization* (New York: Doubleday/Currency, 1990); Donald A. Schon, *Educating the Reflective Practitioner* (San Francisco: Jossey-Bass, 1987) and *The Reflective Practitioner: How Professionals Think in Action* (New York: Basic Books, 1983); Chris Argyris and Donald A. Schon, *Theory in Practice: Increasing Professional Effectiveness* (Oxford, England: Jossey-Bass, 1974).

7. Mary Field Belenky and others, *Women's Ways of Knowing: The Development of Self, Voice, and Mind* (New York: Basic Books, 1986), 115.

8. Ibid., 221.

9. Sweet, *Eleven Genetic Gateways*, 49.

10. A. Christopher Hammon and Vicki Lynn Hollon, *Thriving in the Whirlwind: Connected Learning as an Approach to Lifelong Learning for Ministry* (PhD diss., Theological School of Drew University, 2004). Available online.

11. Ibid.

12. William Lord and George Brown, "Where and How Religious Leaders Learn," in *A Lifelong Call to Learn: Approaches to Continuing Education for Church Leaders*, ed. Robert E. Reber and D. Bruce Roberts (Nashville: Abingdon Press, 2000), 89–101.

13. Don Tapscott, *Growing Up Digital: The Rise of the Net Generation* (New York: McGraw-Hill, 1998), 142.

14. Ibid., 143.

15. Ibid., 146.

16. Ibid., 142.

17. Schon, *Educating the Reflective Practitioner*, 3.

18. Tapscott, *Growing Up Digital*, 145–46.

19. Ibid., 146.

20. Phyllis Tickle, *The Great Emergence: How Christianity Is Changing and Why* (Grand Rapids: Baker Books, 2008).

21. Rex Miller, *The Millennium Matrix: Reclaiming the Past, Reframing the Future of the Church* (San Francisco: Jossey-Bass, 2004).

Additional References

Hammon, A. Christopher, and Vicki Lynn Hollon. "Connected Learning: An Emerging Opportunity for Lifelong Learning for Ministry." *The Clergy Journal* (October 2004), 7–10.

Palloff, Rena M., and Keith Pratt. *Building Learning Communities in Cyberspace: Effective Strategies for the Online Classroom.* San Francisco: Jossey-Bass, 1999.

———. *Lessons from the Cyberspace Classroom: The Realities of Online Teaching.* San Francisco: Jossey-Bass, 2001.

Tapscott, Don. *Wikinomics: How Mass Collaboration Changes Everything.* New York: Portfolio-Penguin, 2006.

PART IV

Development, Management, and Promotion of Programs

CHAPTER 17

The Politics of Moving Continuing Education to the Center of the Institutional Mission

Donald C. Guthrie and Ronald M. Cervero

At a time when the necessity for lifelong learning has been recognized throughout society, there is a significant opportunity to negotiate a more central role for continuing theological education within the broader enterprise of theological education. It has become axiomatic to believe that lifelong learning is a necessity because of the mind-numbing scope and pace of change in our culture. However, there is more to continuing theological education than keeping up with the latest content, technique, or motivational innovation. Continuing theological education, like all educational endeavors, is about people. Moving continuing theological education to the center of the institution's mission, therefore, is about people. Real people with real interests, real power, real experiences, and real perspectives. It's about how these real people do the best they can to teach others about God, train practitioners to reconcile those who are unable or unwilling to be reconciled, and advance the message of faith, hope, and love in which they believe. Continuing theological educators should take the lead within their theological institutions to promote such a person-centered perspective among their colleagues and leaders.

As continuing theological educators promote such a perspective, they will quickly find that some will wholeheartedly endorse its implementation across the institution's spectrum of services. These stakeholders will enthusiastically support this person-centered movement because they embrace change rather than fear it. Others, however, will be less excited about this movement. These stakeholders will seek to maintain the status quo of the institution, perhaps because the uncertainty inherent in change is threatening to them. Either way, problem solving, persuading, bartering, and negotiating will be necessary as continuing theological educators engage their colleagues and leaders about the centrality of continuing theological education to the institution's mission.

If these communication strategies (for example, persuading and negotiating) will be at the core of what continuing theological educators employ as they promote their vision and model their agenda, they would do well to increase their understanding of such strategies and of the political process in general. The political process, after all, is just as real as the people who engage in it. Indeed, the political negotiation in which continuing theological educators engage within their institutions is the same political process they should draw attention to in the continuing education programs they develop.

Continuing theological education is necessary because wise action requires that informed practitioners understand how the ever-evolving relationships among educational stakeholders determine the content that is usually the focus of educational efforts. Distributing content, however, represents only part of continuing education's equation. If continuing educators hope to truly help those for whom their programs are intended, they must engage in political advocacy, not simply to advance their own interests but so that the interests of those whom they seek to serve are represented. This is particularly true if the clients are those who live at the margins of society and therefore do not enjoy positions of power or have relationships with those who do. Continuing *theological* educators are in a strategic position to serve those that tend to be marginalized and others who minister to them, and thus demonstrate they have heeded God's mandate to identify with the alien and stranger.

This chapter discusses how continuing theological educators can increase their political awareness and negotiation skills. Through an analysis of two case studies, we will describe how to develop these skills in continuing theological education planning contexts by (1) naming the political context for continuing theological education; (2) identifying potential stakeholders within the church, seminary, conference center, and other educational settings; (3) discussing the interests of and the political relationships among these stakeholders; and (4) suggesting potential negotiation strategies so that continuing theological educators may observe this process within their own and other related institutional contexts.

Seeing the Political Context for Continuing Education

Continuing theological educators do not typically work in situations characterized by symmetrical power relations within which all interests are equally important and negotiation proceeds on a consensual basis. Rather, the most common situations are marked by asymmetrical power relations, which both threaten and offer opportunities for their continuing education program. In response to these realities, continuing theological educators need to see that their work is a form of political action. Because of this, it is important that continuing theological educators can read the political relationships in their social and organizational contexts in order to understand how they constrain and enable their work.

Power Relations Frame the Contexts for Continuing Education

The starting point is that continuing education practice, like any other human activity, must be located in a set of social dynamics. As stated above, this work nearly always involves working with other people, so one has to think about it in terms of "the enduring social relationships" that support or constrain educators' working relations and actions.[1] The fundamental enduring social relationship that structures the context in which planners routinely work is power: who has it and what do they do with it.

Sociologist Anthony Giddens argues that power, which is the socially structured capacity to act, and not just a matter of personal attribute, is a central feature of these relationships. He says that "action only exists when an agent has the capability of intervening, or refraining from intervening, in a series of events so as to be able to influence their course."[2] While action is the result of human intention, the ability to act is structurally distributed. Thus, power is the capacity to act, which is distributed to individuals by virtue of the organizational and social positions that they occupy.[3]

Interests Produce Continuing Education Programs

Interests, which direct the actions of all people, are complex sets of "predispositions, embracing goals, values, desires, expectations, and other orientations and expectations that lead a person to act in one direction or another."[4] Interests, then, are the motivations and purposes that lead people to act in certain ways when confronted with situations in which they must make a judgment about what to do or say. Quite simply, people's interests directly produce continuing education programs. We believe that, more fundamentally, educational programs are causally related to the exercise of power in relation to people's interests, which always matter in determining program purposes, content, and formats. That education programs are causally related to these interests is not a superfluous claim, for continuing theological educators must ask: If programs do not depend on people's interests, upon what do they depend? Perhaps more important, if programs were not causally related to people's interests, why would it matter which educational programs were constructed?

Negotiation Defines the
Practice of Continuing Education

In order to make the direct connection between the continuing educator and the organizational context, we argue that negotiation is the central form of action that they undertake. Continuing educators always negotiate in two dimensions simultaneously. First, and most obviously, their actions construct an educational program. For this, we draw upon the conventional usage of *negotiation*, which is defined as "to confer, bargain, or discuss with a view to reaching agreement" with others.[5]

Within this conventional usage, educators not only bring their own interests to the negotiation process, but they also must constantly negotiate between others' interests to construct the educational program. Second, and at a more fundamental and encompassing level, educators also negotiate about the interests and power relations themselves. People's interests and power relations are not static, but are being continually acted upon by the negotiation practices themselves. Continuing theological educators' actions, while directed toward constructing educational programs, are also always reconstructing the power relations and interests of everyone involved (or not involved) in the planning process.

Matching Negotiation Strategy
to Organizational Context

Figure 17.1 offers a conceptual scheme that delineates four different ways that power relations and interests structure the situations in which continuing theological educators carry out their work.[6] It presents a template for how continuing educators should read situations resulting from particular configurations of power relations and interests.

The four-cell design of figure 17.1 on page 306 is created by crossing the type of *power relations* in which continuing educators act (from symmetrical to asymmetrical) and the relations among

Figure 17.1. Negotiation Strategies in Continuing Education Practice

Interests	Power Relations	
	Symmetrical	*Asymmetrical*
Consensual	(1) Problem solve	(2) Network
Conflictual	(3) Bargain	(4) Counteract

legitimate actors in the organizational context (from consensual to conflictual). In terms of power relations, some may be symmetrical, in that the continuing theological educator's capacity to act is equivalent to other relevant actors, while others may be relatively asymmetrical, in that his or her capacity to act is not equivalent to other relevant actors. In the figure's second dimension, the people who have a legitimate stake in the continuing education program may have *interests* that are largely the same (consensual) or different (conflictual). The distinction is important because when people have conflicting interests, those with the greatest amount of power will often exercise it to achieve their interests.

In the face of the four different situations laid out in the figure, different negotiation strategies will be necessary: problem solving (cell 1), networking (cell 2), bargaining (cell 3), and counteracting (cell 4). The major point of this figure is to recognize that it is not possible or responsible to act the same in all situations, because what would protect democratic planning in one situation may actually prevent it in another. Of course, the figure cannot be a complete mapping of all situations that educators face in practice, since situations do not typically fall neatly into one cell or another. Rather, it is meant as a framework to focus attention on what really matters as educators nurture a substantively democratic planning process.

In cell 1, in which little or no conflict or differences in power exist among those planning the program, *problem solving* is the most appropriate strategy. Discussions and dialogues among the interested parties can be conducted in an open atmosphere of trust, with everyone seeking to arrive at optimal solutions to issues about the purposes, content, audience, and format for a program.

Cell 2 is more complicated because the setting is differentiated by a division of labor in which power is distributed asymmetrically, although everyone involved is cooperative and shares a similar set of interests related to the program. In these situations, the most appropriate strategy is to *network* among all the parties that have information and authority to construct the program. Networking means knowing who has what information relevant to the program, who has a legitimate stake in the outcome, and how to involve them in the relevant parts of the planning.

Although the power relations among which planners must act are relatively symmetrical in cell 3, different actors have competing interests and are willing to use their leverage to further those interests. In these settings, planners must use their position of power in the overall strategy of *bargaining* among the competing interests. Short-term compromise becomes the typical negotiating strategy and can be a responsible approach as long as all affected parties are legitimately represented.

In the situations covered by cell 4, competing interests are held by people working among asymmetrical power relations that are rooted in organizational and social structures. Strategies most likely to address inequalities of power are related to political and community organizing, which require educators to *counteract* the effects of established interests. This may take a variety of forms, from providing information to affected groups to more active interventions.

Although the figure suggests a most appropriate strategy for each cell, continuing theological educators need to draw on the entire repertoire of strategies across the situations. These strategies should be seen as cumulative in that each one, while most appropriate in its own context, can be called upon at more complex levels, as well.

Case Studies

The following case studies illustrate how continuing theological educators could account for the stakeholder interests and power relationships during a program planning process so that they might choose appropriate negotiation strategies. Each brief scenario is followed by a discussion of how the continuing theological educator might negotiate through the process, depending on how stakeholder interests and power relationships are interpreted. A seminary provides the context for the first case, and the central character is the associate dean. The second case involves a conference center director and a judicatory representative.

The Associate Dean and the Foundation Grant

Suppose that a seminary's president decides to pursue a large grant from a major foundation that will enable the seminary to expand significantly its continuing education program. The president assigns the responsibility of assembling the proposal research and writing team to the dean. The dean invites several administrators, faculty members, and local church representatives to a meeting to explain the opportunity and to select a chairperson for the project. The dean invites suggestions from the group about who should serve as chairperson, but suggests that the associate dean is most qualified and experienced. Everyone agrees with the dean's suggestion. The associate dean assumes responsibility for the supervision of the project, although the dean asks the associate dean for regular updates on the project's progress.

How should the associate dean proceed as she steers the project? How does she identify who has an interest in the project and what those interests are? How does she weigh the relative merit and importance of the interests? How does she assess the power relationships among the interested parties? Notice in this scenario that the interests among the principal planners appear to be consensual and that the power relations among the principal planners appear to be asymmetrical. If this were generally true, the suggested strategy for the associate dean would be to *network* (cell 2) with team members and others who may be able to provide helpful information or special skills during the planning process.

The associate dean's networking could take the form of casual conversations, e-mails, letters, telephone calls, or meetings. Since she can assume the support of the dean and the president, the associate dean can use this representative power as she networks to persuade those with greater power to support the project and provide information or skills during the planning process. Having the support of superiors and communicating that support to others in strategic ways will help the associate dean make the best use of those who can help her most within the organization, who might otherwise see the project as being low priority for the institution.

However, what if there were great interpersonal conflict among the principal planners or significant differences in perspective about the project's legitimacy? For instance, what if everyone agreed with the dean's suggestion about the associate dean's leadership, because to disagree with the dean's perspective meant certain professional difficulty for the administrators and faculty members on the team? What if the president were the only one who thinks the project is worth everyone's time and energy, but to disagree with him is tantamount to professional suicide for the administrators and faculty members? What if one of the seminary's large donors pushed the project on the president, so that the president is not free to disagree and reject the project, even though he knows it will consume large amounts of his overworked staff's time?

If any of the elements of this scenario were true, one could conclude that the interests among the principal planners would be conflictual and the power relations asymmetrical. Therefore, the associate dean may want to consider how to *counteract* (cell 4) the power and interests of those involved so that a more democratic planning process would occur. We are not suggesting the associate dean engage in unethical actions to subvert authority or merely negotiate her own interests during the planning process. She, like other continuing theological educators, must operate within the constraints of her theological convictions when applying the delicate counteracting strategy. She must consider what are the potential personal and institutional costs if she decides to counteract, for instance, the overbearing desires of the donor so that the broader interests of the seminary are served. To what extent will she go to protect her job or maintain her convictions? As she deliberates such potentially explosive matters, in whom can she confide as she weighs the options?

The Conference Director and the Judicatory Representative

Suppose a conference center director receives a call from a prominent local pastor who represents the regional judicatory. The pastor would like to meet with the conference director to discuss how the center might create and deliver a series of continuing education workshops for newly ordained pastors in the judicatory. The judicatory has experienced a recent influx of new pastors, who are fresh out of seminary and possess little parish experience. The series is to cover planning church budgets, leading stewardship campaigns, assimilating new members, and maintaining family unity in the midst of ministry. The pastor mentions that while the judicatory has the ability to pay a significant sum to the conference center for the workshops, it does not possess the personnel to help develop the plan. The center needs the money. The judicatory needs the training.

It appears that this scenario provides the conference director with an opportunity to *problem solve* (cell 1) with the pastor, because they, as the principal planners, share a relatively equal capacity to act and consensual interests. The conference director and the pastor could begin by assessing what the new pastors already know. This could be done by written surveys, face-to-face or phone interviews, focus groups, or some combination of these and other data gathering methods. Next, the planners could identify and prioritize the purposes, goals, and hoped-for outcomes of the program. They could then move to select the most appropriate methods and resources they will employ for the workshops. Finally, they could design or identify evaluative tools so that the effectiveness of the training could be determined.

What if, however, the interests of the two planners were decidedly at odds while their capacities to act remained relatively equal (cell 3)? In this scenario, although the professional interests of the pastor and the conference director intersect, their personal desires for the partnership's outcomes remain in conflict. Prior to the meeting with the conference director, the pastor had successfully persuaded the judicatory to adopt his training plan for the new pastors, which includes the topics he thinks are most needed. The conference director does not necessarily disagree that the chosen topics would be helpful to new pastors. He does, however, believe that the pastor has overemphasized the pragmatic areas of ministry and overlooked the spiritual areas. For example, the conference director prefers including more topics that cover establishing personal and corporate spiritual disciplines in ministry; cultivating healthy work and rest patterns; and nurturing the spiritual development of the pastor's family.

Are the planners consigned to disagree silently about the content of the workshops as they simultaneously smile and wince at each other during the planning meetings? Or should they voice their workshop preferences and the rationales behind them to one another, and agree to disagree? According to the suggested strategy in cell 3 (*bargaining*), the planners could voice their interests; provide evidence for inclusion of their preferred workshop topic; and seek to arrive at a mutually agreeable solution that encompasses the interests of both legitimate perspectives. This outcome is ultimately more satisfying, because the participants will enjoy the benefit of the series' negotiated content and the continuing theological educators can build on this success for future mutually productive endeavors.

Notice how in each scenario, the same story, when interpreted from the perspective of differing power and interests, suggests very different negotiation strategies. We doubt that many scenarios exist where employing one negotiation strategy will produce the most desirable outcome. Scenarios with clear-cut problems and strategies that produce pure solutions do not exist in an imperfect world. However, as continuing theological educators consider the interests and power relations of program stakeholders, identify those interests, and discern which negotiation strategies to employ during the planning process, they can more accurately account for the interests of all stakeholders, because they recognize the planning process in the context of political reality.

Cultivating Wise Action

We believe that this approach to planning requires the continuing theological educator to move beyond merely employing techniques and to move toward cultivating a way of seeing the planning process as a context full of power relations and interests. Accordingly, we advocate that the continuing theological educator continually assess stakeholder interests, power relations, and negotiation strategies. If wise action is the goal and method of continuing theological educators, recognizing the political context of the planning process will enhance the possibility that such action is realized. Such recognition begins by asking wise questions. The following list summarizes the key questions continuing theological educators should address when assessing any program planning process.

Planning Process Questions
for Continuing Theological Educators

1. Who has an interest in the program, issue, or meeting?
2. What are the interests? How do they relate to one another?
3. What is the relative merit and importance of each interest?
4. What are the power relationships among the interested parties, including yourself?

5. Which negotiation strategies would be most appropriate, given the interests and power relationships among the stakeholders?
6. How do your theological and ethical convictions inform your choices and decisions?
7. How do people learn more effectively whether one is focused on knowledge, understanding, skills, attitudes, or values?

Addressing these questions will direct continuing theological educators toward the heart of continuing education—people. Keeping people at the heart of continuing theological education promotes the mission of the educator's institution, addresses the needs of the institution's constituents, and promotes the institution's mission of service derived from its service of God.

Notes

1. Jeffrey C. Isaac, *Power and Marxist Theory: A Realist View* (Ithaca, NY: Cornell University Press, 1987), 51.

2. Anthony Giddens, *Central Problems in Social Theory: Action, Structure, and Contradiction in Social Analysis* (Berkeley: University of California Press, 1979), 256.

3. Isaac, *Power and Marxist Theory*.

4. Gareth Morgan, *Images of Organization* (Beverly Hills, CA: Sage, 1986), 41.

5. Webster's *New World Dictionary* (1976), s.v. "Negotiation."

6. Ronald M. Cervero and Arthur L. Wilson, *Planning Responsibly for Adult Education: A Guide to Negotiating Power Interests* (San Francisco: Jossey-Bass, 1994); Cervero and Wilson, eds., *What Really Matters in Adult Education Program Planning: Lessons in Negotiating Power and Interests, New Directions for Adult and Continuing Education* 69 (San Francisco: Jossey-Bass, 1996); and Cervero and Wilson, "Working the Planning Table: The Political Practice of Adult Education," *Studies in Continuing Education* 20 (1998), 5–21.

CHAPTER 18

Getting from Here to There, Wherever That May Be: Program Planning, Design, and Evaluation

Janet L. Maykus

Program planning, design, and evaluation all must be completed within the confines of a specific place and time. What may have worked at one time in one place may or may not fit a new time and place. Therefore, to begin at the beginning is important.

Learn Where You Are

Before you can plan programming for an agency or institution, you must know the culture of the place in which the program is to take place. Spend time making a nest. This advice flies in the face of popular culture that thrives on speed. Look around and observe those who enter your office. Read all the materials you can find about your organization and its history. Discover what sorts of programs have been planned before your arrival. Ask questions. Do people in your constituency enjoy meeting together? Are online services desired? If online services are offered, are they utilized? Do people enjoy coming to your facilities, or are other facilities better able to meet the needs of those who come? Do groups want didactic material? Do groups enjoy conversational methods of learning? What role do the arts play? What about service work? Are there places for mentorship? Is your constituency conservative, moderate, liberal, or a combination thereof? If it is disparate, do these groups work well together? Do you want to serve a local constituency or a larger one? How do people in your organization view lifelong learning? What is your organization's hope for the future?

If you can imagine a question about an organization's culture, the answer may have an effect on your program planning. Do not hesitate to let your thoughts run free with questions, and ask a wide variety of people for answers. Do not stop with your supervisor or the person in the office next to yours. If you are able to talk to the person who held your position before you, ask her about the strategy that was used for program planning. This does not mean that you will need to follow in this path, but it never hurts to learn from others' experiences. If people call asking about your events calendar, ask for a moment of their time and query them about the best time of year for them to attend workshops; then ask if they prefer one-day or multiple-day workshops. The point of all this asking is to allow a community to assist in planning its programs.

When I came to my current position at Austin Presbyterian Theological Seminary, an active continuing education program was not in place, and I was charged with finding a way to make one. I created a survey for ministers and laypeople. The survey was administered to many people within the seminary's local constituency. Our constituents were rich in opinions and suggestions. From the information I gleaned we created a yearlong calendar that addressed every suggested topic. I was certain we would have a dynamic year of one scintillating continuing education event after another. However, only three of the classes had enough registrants (at least five people) to go ahead.

I was fortunate to have forgiving supervisors. In my rush to create something wonderful, I failed to consider a picture that included more than the desires of those who might or might not attend a continuing education event at my institution. Almost everyone wants to learn new things related to their interests. I failed to ask how often those interviewed actually attend continuing education events. I did not ask if those surveyed have funds to pay for courses. Nor did I ask the ministers surveyed if their congregations appreciate time spent away for continuing education. Nor did I ask if those nearby prefer to attend events out of town. Suffice it to say, I forgot to ask questions over which I had no control but whose answers could direct the style and type of programs we might offer. Finally, I forgot to keep at the foundation of all planning the mission and vision of our organization.

Know Who You Want to Become

Mission and vision are essential tools to use in program planning and development. Know the history of your institution; where it has come from shapes its current culture. Institutions exist for particular reasons; know what those reasons are. If your institution is primarily concerned about the work of ordained clergy, then investigate what the needs of ordained clergy are and put together programs for them. If your institution is more concerned about the lifelong learning of the laity, then do likewise for them. The vision of your organization will tell you where it wants to go. Visions can be approached more easily in the arenas of lifelong learning than in the realms of degree-granting programs. It is less stressful for an organization to offer an innovative or unexpected program or course through its lifelong learning departments than through its academically accredited programs. For instance, if your institution's mission is to serve the church in a particular denomination and its vision is to become a leading source for education for clergy and laity of this denomination, then you might find yourself being the first person on staff to create programs for clergy and laity. Your institution can find out if clergy and laity learn well together or if, on the whole, they prefer to have educational opportunities separate from one another. Your task will be to evaluate and disseminate what you learn to others in your organization.

Prudence Is Practical

Approach your work with enthusiastic caution. Enthusiasm breeds enthusiasm. If you find your work dull, chances are others will too. This neither means that directing a continuing education program will be the most thrilling of calls nor that the courses offered should reflect only topics that grab your interests and desires. Administering exceptional lifelong learning opportunities is a call of service. Most of the hard work is done behind the scenes, little of it is ever known to the rest of the world, and the results (your events) should seem to take place effortlessly, so that only those who have conducted this work will ever know the energy and time that went into any endeavor.

Caution keeps you from cascading down the perilous mountainside of "mission creep." Many good ideas are out there. An equal number of committed people are ready to promote and execute their ideas under the title of your institution. Evaluate ideas for classes, online seminars, retreats, lecture series, or MP3 recordings carefully. Although the content is interesting, is it in line with the overall context in which you find yourself? If it seems a bit dissonant, is that because this idea is something that might help your organization reach a new growing edge that is in sync with your vision, or does it simply not fit? If good suggestions do not fit, refer the person eager to offer the course to another institution where you think it might blend.

As you plan your calendar, be realistic about who you are. I am inundated by electronic spam and postal mail promoting continuing education events and tips and tricks that promise to teach me how to increase the size of my program. Not every institution can create or accommodate large events. When it comes to lifelong learning, bigger is not always better. Generate a culture that focuses on elegance rather than size. Attend to the details. Make certain your speakers are qualified, clear about the mission and vision of your organization, have the necessary equipment, and are able to relate to those in attendance. If you record events, publish them only if the sound or audiovisual quality is very good. Details such as air temperature, comfort of chairs, hospitality of front desk workers, food quality, and audiovisuals can make or break your event. In other words, make certain what you do, you do well.

Time and Money

Good continuing education programs take time to plan and execute. Planning is your foundation, therefore it must be solid. Do not plan more than you have money, staff, and energy to undertake. If you apply for grant funding, you must account for the time and energy the grant itself will take from your other work and plan your schedule accordingly. All grant proposals should be written well. Even if you are not awarded a particular grant, grant committees often remember a well-written grant proposal and may include you in subsequent requests for proposals based on previous applications. Once a grant has been awarded, adequate time must be given to investigating and writing annual reports.

One of the often overlooked truths about planning for and executing well-run continuing education events is that the same effort goes into creating an event for ten as it does for one hundred. Those who do not plan and execute these events sometimes have trouble understanding this, especially if you do your job well. Well-run events seem to happen effortlessly, so you might encounter people who have great suggestions for events they believe have to happen in the very near future, yet they have no plans to assist in executing the events. Unless the events have some sort of urgency, such as declaration of war, a recent major social injustice, and so forth, it might be best to table the suggestions until you have the time and resources to devote to planning and marketing the programs.

Making Grants

Some continuing education programs offer grants. These grants may allow people to participate in programs of the organization's design, the participants' design, or both. If your institution decides to make grants available, a few concerns must be addressed. It is important that you be clear in all materials what your expectations are. Even if you ask for a complex proposal, your instructions should be simple. Simplicity and clarity will save you a great deal of work trying to explain yourself to every interested caller. You must consider how you will account for funds. Decide if you are going to award the funds in one check or if you will set up an account for the winners and reimburse them for their costs. If the grants will be used for self-designed programs, how much reporting do you expect for the participants? State when you expect reports, the length of the reports, and the questions you want your reports to answer.

In all materials you must state how awards will be made. Is there a deadline for applications or do you have a rolling application acceptance? Are awards given on a first come, first served basis or do you read all the applications at a set time and award the best proposals? Whatever you set in place, follow it. You must be fair and honest in what you do. How you set your schedule is at the prerogative of your institution, but having an application deadline and a set beginning and ending time of grants awarded is administratively simpler. An established time frame is also easier for an institution to budget for funds that go out on a regular cycle.

Getting the Word Out

People attend continuing education events for a variety of reasons. Some are required to attend by denominational judicatories. Others need intellectual stimulation. Some are lonely and look for friendship and camaraderie among the other attendees. Others are looking for ways to revitalize their commitments to their calls. Some need administrative and management skills but others may want to learn how to increase stewardship and attendance. Others are compelled by a "big name" speaker. You cannot meet everyone's needs and desires at every event. Therefore, market your chosen events with a clear, concise description of what you offer. In your marketing materials, list dates, times, speakers, places to stay, where and how food is offered, cost, and the other things attendees can expect when attending. If each participant will receive a book or relevant handouts, be certain to state that in marketing materials. If the schedule includes ample free time for self-guided activities, state that. If you know the instructor will ask for physical participation (for example, walks or sitting on the floor), be certain to list the necessity of comfortable clothes suited for the activities.

If the programs you offer are online courses, audio or video material available on discs, or downloadable in an MP3 format, then marketing materials should include the same sorts of information you would provide for your on-site events. Who is speaking, when was it recorded, what do you hope your listeners or viewers will learn? Is it possible for those who purchase these items to register for a certificate of completion in order to qualify for denominationally required hours of continuing education? Do study guides accompany the audio or video? Finally, if something is not of good quality, do not post it on the Web; your audience is global.

Many directors find marketing a stumbling block. Advertisements in most denominational and national publications are prohibitively expensive. Have no fear! Most of your events probably should not be marketed in these publications. Unless you are holding an event of national importance, with a named speaker known to draw hundreds, in a place that can accommodate hundreds in a comfortable fashion, you should market in other venues. Use your website. Keep it fresh and inviting. Use e-mail announcements. Create pleasant-looking, crisp and informative bulletins about upcoming events. Keep your e-mail list current, and add to it as you learn new e-mail addresses. Send announcements to everyone on your list, even if you know certain people are not appropriate targets for particular events. They may pass your announcement on to someone else before pressing the delete icon. Use your institution's newsletter, magazine, annual brochures, and other publications. Make certain that at least the titles of your events or the website where your products can be purchased are listed. Include a contact person, phone number, e-mail address, and any other social networking site you use.

Evaluation Is Good

Every event you hold, every item available for purchase, should be evaluated by those who attend or who buy what you have for sale. Evaluations are some of the most helpful tools available to you. But you have to evaluate what you want to know and what you have the ability to change. When I first arrived at my position, I inherited an evaluation tool that asked numerous questions about the physical plant and food service. These questions occupied the majority of space on the evaluation. Although I did want to know about the space and the food, I could do little to effect change in those areas of our institution. I decided to re-create the evaluation tool to learn what I wanted to know. The primary objective of evaluations is to determine if the program objective was met, so I asked questions such as:

- Did the event meet your expectations?
- How was the speaker?
- Was there enough time for discussion?
- Did you learn things that will help you in your ministry . . . if so, what and how?
- Were you comfortable in your room?
- Was the food healthy and tasty?
- How did you learn of this event?

In this manner, I gathered information that helped me design future events, information that I could pass on to those who manage the physical plant and food service, and information that helped me maximize my next marketing efforts.

You will gather more evaluations if you block out time in your event for evaluation completion. Most people are willing to complete an evaluation if their responses can remain anonymous. Provide a space for participants to list their names and contact information in case they wish to engage you in further discussion. If people say they want to be contacted, contact them.

If you need to collect your evaluations when people are not on site (for example, if you offer grants to individuals or groups who do not come to your campus), you might want to use one of the many online survey sites. Most of these sites have different levels of use. Some sites allow people to create their own surveys and use their sites free of charge; these will be short surveys of usually ten questions or fewer. If your survey is more complex, you will pay a nominal fee for use of the survey websites. Once the survey is designed, the process for using it is simple. Your office sends an e-mail with a link to the survey to those who participated. It is important to ask participants to respond before a certain date. You will need to send your request e-mail to event participants at least two times.

If you are conducting online courses, include the evaluation as part of the course. When people complete their courses, the last page should be your evaluation. Once the evaluation is completed, participants may request a statement of completion from your office. Evaluations can give you information about how your program is operating on different types of computer systems and how intuitively designed it is.

Read your evaluations, but wait until a day or two after the event. You will be tired, and it might be difficult to hear negative responses. At the point of fatigue, people are more inclined to disregard criticism. Attend to what is stated in evaluations. If people take the time to write remarks about what transpired for them, these remarks will help guide you in your next endeavor. Evaluations are not tests. Even if overall remarks are less than favorable, you have not failed, unless you disregard the evaluations. The manner in which course evaluations are used in continuing education differs a great deal from the manner in which course evaluations are used in degree-granting programs. Therefore, if you find yourself in an academic institution, do not fret if you use your evaluations in different ways than your colleagues.

Evaluation results may provide information that will be helpful in upcoming events (for example, in the afternoon the room gets very hot, so arrange for different afternoon meeting space if the air cannot be changed), and it may provide information that will help you design similar future events (for example, the speaker was wonderful, but there was not enough question-and-answer time). Take the evaluations seriously, but do not react in a knee-jerk way to your upcoming calendar event. If people responded negatively to a speaker you have scheduled to teach again later in the year, do not cancel the event. Take time to talk to the speaker, let him or her know what the evaluations revealed, and strategize together how to make the next event better.

Evaluations take you back to planning and to design. Each of these areas relies on the other for maximum effectiveness. Attending to the necessities of each component will keep your program fresh and flexible and meet the rapidly changing needs of those in ministry. Growing and maintaining an excellent lifelong learning program is more akin to gardening than to the running of trains. There are seasons for all types of learning and for information. *Try* to stay attuned to the rhythms and cycles of these seasons. Today's minister is called to be a dedicated generalist. It is impossible for a seminary or divinity school to meet all the needs of what future ministers will need to know. You have the opportunity to help them fill in their blanks. The joy of your position is that you do not have to have all the answers for your constituency; rather, you have the pleasure of being a guide to help them find what they need.

More in-depth resources are available on each of the subjects I have discussed in this brief chapter. A favorite of mine is *Projects That Matter: Successful Planning and Evaluation for Religious Organizations* by Kathleen A. Cahalan, published by the Alban Institute in 2003.

CHAPTER 19

Learning as a Model for Developing and Promoting Lifelong Learning for Ministry

Dent Davis

> "Who are you?" said the Caterpillar. . . . "I hardly know, Sir, just at present," Alice replied rather shyly, "at least I know who I was when I got up this morning, but I think I must have been changed several times since then."
>
> —*Lewis Carroll*, Alice's Adventures in Wonderland

Call it what you want: continuing education, spiritual formation, coaching, or lifelong learning, the work is changing for those engaged in noncredit learning for ministry, whether in seminaries, retreat centers, or denominational offices. Past approaches are becoming more problematical as new challenges emerge. Programs with topics that once generated large, enthusiastic audiences have waning attendance. Educational institutions are insisting that the noncredit parts of their programs generate more revenue and reduce expenses, a difficult challenge when participants often have limited incomes. Because of increasing economic challenges, most organizations working in noncredit learning have to do more with fewer resources and work harder to satisfy the growing needs of diverse constituency groups.

Challenges also present an opportunity to look at noncredit learning in new ways. For example, the explosion of Internet technologies presents a world of possibilities for developing innovative learning experiences. Today's more global, multicultural environment demands educational programs that are both inclusive and able to address the complex needs of diverse groups of participants. In addressing these challenges there are no silver bullets, much less golden parachutes. The only answer to keeping one's equilibrium in times of constant change is to switch from being an expert who has the answers to being a learner who asks the right questions. In today's world we are all learners, maybe even novices. Learning takes persistence and hard work, said Jackson Carroll, sociologist of religion at Duke Divinity School, when addressing the challenges of sustaining vital pastoral leadership in a study sponsored by the school's Pulpit and Pew. He observed that "those who practice excellent pastoral leadership . . . are not so much a 'learned' clergy as a 'learning' clergy."[1] Carroll went on to say, "The willingness to be a learner, formally and informally, is, I believe, a sine qua non of excellent pastoral leadership, and will only grow in importance."[2] The same could be said about continuing educators.

Instead of the comfort of being an expert in one's field today, this time of extraordinary change is making much hard-earned expertise obsolete by tomorrow. Although learning is key, it is no longer possible, if it ever was, for one person, program, or institution to learn fast enough or broadly enough to be continuously effective. Collaboration is no longer just a nice idea; it is essential to survival. Learning, both individually and collaboratively, provides a new perspective for planning a specific educational program and for communicating, marketing, or promoting that program. In this chapter I use the term *lifelong learning* to describe noncredit learning for ministry. This is the term we use at Columbia Theological Seminary, and it also emphasizes the importance of learning in program planning and marketing.

Planning Programs for Lifelong Learning

Most noncredit educational programs for ministry developed in the shadow of the educational paradigm that emerged from the post–World War II era with its strong institutional emphasis. The culture of twentieth-century education builds on an assumption that experts know what needs to be taught, have a structured and systematic way to teach it, and have a way to document and measure its achievement. Although this view still dominates, noncredit learning cannot operate on the same assumption because the focus of noncredit learning for ministry is on ministry practice, and ministry is practiced in a host of different contexts, each uniquely affected by many ongoing changes. In today's world, expertise is short lived and constantly changing. As adult educators working in a postmodern, increasingly global, rapidly changing world of diminishing resources and increasing needs, we have to learn to "make the road by walking," in the words of Paulo Freire and Myles Horton.[3] We have to "learn our way through" the uncertainties of these times.[4]

Program planning in noncredit continuing education for ministry has also been based on the assumption of strong institutional leadership. Whether a retreat center, a seminary, or a denominational program, planners have normally identified what learning programs they thought were important to offer and communicated those offerings to potential participants through brochures, announcements, and more recently the Internet. Traditionally, marketing and program planning have been viewed as separate activities, but in today's world they are of one fabric. In today's climate with more service providers, fewer resources, and a growing need for programs, effective planning and marketing for lifelong learning is more important than ever, and more challenging.

Guide to Practical Action

The model that I am proposing for developing and promoting lifelong learning for ministry is distinctive in three ways: (1) the role of learning in the planning and marketing process, (2) the inclusion of both program development and marketing in the process, and (3) the emphasis on practicality. The model has four key elements for developing a comprehensive approach to program development in your institution or center or in a particular course, workshop, or event: (1) identity, (2) context, (3) plan, and (4) results. Although each represents a distinct and important aspect in planning and marketing a lifelong learning program, these four elements are not sequential, are interrelated, and often overlap. Based on my experience at the Center for Lifelong Learning at Columbia Theological Seminary, as well as the experiences of other adult education professionals in nonprofit settings, the purpose of this chapter is to describe a practical and effective guide for action in planning and marketing lifelong learning programs for ministry in a rapidly changing world.

Identity

Even in times of change, a clear vision of your overall program or center is foundational in any planning or marketing effort. In a changing environment this can be difficult. Knowing your program includes clarifying your program's vision, accomplishments, and capacity. It identifies publicity methods and effective financial models. Being able to clearly describe your program to participants, institutional governing boards, funders, and other constituencies strengthens how others understand and, therefore, support it. Written materials help. This chapter suggests developing two documents, a mission statement and a fact sheet for publicity. Both of these have proven helpful in describing our lifelong learning program at Columbia Seminary to participants, groups, and organizations.

Mission Statement

A mission statement is an organization's vision translated into written form. It makes concrete the direction and purpose of the organization. The process of working on the mission statement has proven invaluable to the seminary in clarifying our program's purpose and aligning the staff in not only supporting the mission but also communicating it to others in a consistent way.

The mission statement answers the question, "What is our reason for being?" Mission statements often have a noble and even visionary aspect, and it is this aspect that often inspires and anchors the program during periods of intense change. Actions backed by a sense of mission are often more effective and more satisfying. Most institutions find it beneficial to update periodically their mission or vision in a brief statement.

Each person involved in your setting probably has ideas about the program's mission. If you are writing your mission for the first time, it is helpful to involve the key stakeholders. Stakeholders are important because they have a "stake" in the program's success. These can include participants, staff members, board members, facilitators, teachers, and other constituencies. Each group may have a different stake in the program or institution, so understanding their perspectives contributes to a broader view of what matters to others.

Mission Statement Questions

In reviewing your program's mission (its purpose or reason for being), a focused reflection is often very helpful. The following questions have been useful in guiding such reflection.

- In general, what ministry needs does your institution or program address?
- How does your center or seminary respond to these needs now?
- Where do you see the center moving in the future?
- What values are important to your institution as you meet these needs?
- What are some of the long-term benefits participants might expect from participating in your programs?

- What do participants say about you? What would you like them to say about you?

Defining Your Institution's Mission

Your institution's mission is best described by the people who are involved in the program—the stakeholders. The following activity can be done with any number of people.

1. Plan a meeting to work on your mission statement. Reproduce a copy of "Mission Statement Questions" (above) for each participant.
2. Prepare a sheet of newsprint with each Mission Statement Question at the top. Post on walls around the room.
3. Introduce the purpose of the meeting. Ask each person to write an answer to the questions on note paper.
4. After participants have completed their answers, invite them to report their answers to the group. Write answers on the newsprint. Try to consolidate similar answers so there is little repetition. The answers to each question will cluster together.
5. Ask the group to identify key words or phrases that speak to them by underlining those words using colored markers.
6. On a separate sheet of newsprint, list the underlined words or phrases.
7. Ask a small group of three or four participants to take the words and phrases and write a draft of the mission.
8. Invite all participants to review the draft and give feedback to the small group.
9. Ask the small group to revise statement.
10. Group decides whether to adopt and support mission.

At Columbia Theological Seminary our mission went through several drafts, finally arriving at the following:

Lifelong Learning at Columbia Theological Seminary
is a center for vibrant learning

where Christians are strengthened and transformed
for ministry in the 21st century.
By the leading of the Holy Spirit, we grow in faith and understanding
As we
Explore practices, ancient and contemporary, and confront new
challenges;
Discover energy and encouragement to be disciples of Jesus Christ;
Equip ourselves and others for the up-building of Christ's church; and
Engage God's transforming Word and work in the world.

After developing a statement of mission or vision, sometimes it is useful to identify a shorter phrase that can help potential participants get a sense of your program. We identified four words from our statement that we often use to summarize our goals in lifelong learning: "Lifelong Learning at Columbia Seminary: Explore, Discover, Equip, Engage."

Fact Sheet

A mission or vision statement represents an important general summary of the overall program. A fact sheet is a succinct summary of it at a glance. It includes your track record or accomplishments and is often valuable in conversations with potential partners or funders. An up-to-date fact sheet can also form the basis of a program brochure. A fact sheet generally is a one-page document that answers questions about the program such as:

- How long has your program been operating?
- What particular events do you offer (subject, audience, format, frequency, denominational emphasis)?
- Who has participated in your programs? How many individuals have you served?
- What results have you achieved?
- What makes your work distinctive?
- How much does your program cost and how is it funded?
- How can someone get in touch with you?

Participant evaluation responses can sometimes help to strengthen a fact sheet. Often in their written evaluations participants comment on how the program has benefited them. Their comments can be very compelling. Inserting one or two of these comments can powerfully underscore a program's effectiveness and the difference it made to those who participated.

In addition to a mission statement and a fact sheet, keep files that include copies of articles about the program that have appeared in publications, photographs of participants and program events, and testimonials from participants about their experience in the program. These items represent important aspects of the identity and history of the program.

Context

Context is the set of circumstances or facts that surround and influence a particular program. Every lifelong learning program has a context. For example, most lifelong learning programs are a part of a larger institution and draw participants from particular religious traditions, geographic areas, and cultural groups. Understanding one's place in the larger community can help in planning future events as well as identifying the distinctness of a program. This section highlights two important aspects involved in knowing the context, gathering data related to the community where the program operates and developing a marketing plan that represents an analysis and strategic plan for communicating important aspects of the program to the community.

Gathering Data

Gathering data about the community can take many forms. This section describes four activities that we have found particularly helpful: environmental scanning, personal conversations, participant evaluation surveys, and using the SWOT analysis.

Environmental scanning involves intentionally examining the materials used by other lifelong learning program providers, such as seminaries, retreat centers, and denominational offices in order to gain insights and ideas that can help improve your program. Widely used in educational program development and marketing,[5] scanning is very useful in planning new programs and deciding how best to communicate your programs to potential audiences. Scanning can be done by reading magazines and papers; being aware of what is going on in the arts, in politics, and in social life; becoming involved in professional and civic organizations; examining websites of other noncredit programs; and engaging in partnerships that provide the opportunity to learn from others. At Columbia we have found scanning helpful, although it can be time consuming. Without an intentional data-gathering process, it is all too easy to simply assume that we know what programs would be helpful to potential participants and that we are in fact communicating that knowledge effectively. In environmental scanning all staff are involved and use a common form to document our efforts. The form simply identifies the data source, author, key ideas, and possible applications of the information for our program. Periodically we review completed forms as a staff. In the scanning process it is also important to look at secular educational providers. The Internet is a great resource for program planning and marketing, as are advertisements and articles in journals and publications such as *Christianity Today* and the *Christian Century*.

Personal conversations can be a very effective way to gather data for program planning. Conversations can be in person, by telephone, or by e-mail, and invariably provide opportunity for learning and sometimes lead to important partnerships. Conversations are a way to introduce your program to others, inquire into what others consider important, and build relationships that can lead to future partnerships. Although the use of conversations in understanding the wider community is common, what is often overlooked is documenting key information. An ongoing file documenting your conversations with other lifelong learning providers can identify trends and be an important resource for planning.

Gathering data about your own program through *participant evaluation surveys* is vital. One of the most effective ways to gather data about participants is by including questions on the registration and evaluation forms for each learning event. Data can be stored electronically and analyzed to identify who is participating in your programs and their characteristics, such as geographic region, denomination, age, and any other information that describes the groups who are participating. Although they cost more, larger surveys of former participants or potential participants often are valuable as data to understand an important part of the program's community. In addition, financial data, trends in participation based on program enrollments, and small informal focus groups of former participants that come together to talk about program experiences and future needs can be very helpful in the planning process. No matter how good the data, integrating and interpreting

Figure 19.1. SWOT Analysis

Inward Focus	Outward Focus
Strengths: • What are we good at doing? • Where are we growing? • What are our capabilities, capacities, and resources? • What are our assets in terms of people, systems, finances, knowledge, organization, reputation, and so forth?	*Opportunities:* • What is changing in the community and world? • What resources are becoming available? • What issues, needs, concerns, or demands are emerging that could affect our work?
Weaknesses: • What are we not doing well? • Where are we not growing? • What weaknesses do we have in terms of people, systems, finances, knowledge, reputation, and so forth? • What are some of the frustrations that people have with our lifelong learning program?	*Threats:* • What do other lifelong learning programs have that ours does not have? • How difficult is it for people to participate in our education programs? • What changes are occurring that could negatively impact our lifelong learning program?

community and program data is foundational in planning. O n e way that has proven very effective in integrating these insights is through the use of the *SWOT analysis*. SWOT stands for strengths, weaknesses, opportunities, and threats and is widely used in organizations to better understand or evaluate the potential programmatic effects of internal factors such as program strengths and weaknesses and external factors such as opportunities and threats.[6] Once these are identified, strategic actions can be taken to increase the strengths and opportunities and reduce the weaknesses and threats. The SWOT analysis is a way to focus the thinking of those involved in the planning process.

Every lifelong learning program has strengths and weaknesses and faces opportunities and threats. A challenging question is to determine whether there are ways weaknesses can be seen as strengths or strengths as weaknesses. For example, if a weakness is that fewer funds are available for print publicity, this could be a strength in that it causes staff to increase their knowledge about electronic communication tools. The goal in developing an effective program is to build on strengths and to minimize weaknesses. To do this, it is often useful for a lifelong learning program to develop a plan for communicating with those who have already participated in programs and also with potential participants. In business circles this is called a marketing plan. An effective marketing plan for communicating the learning program makes the program even more efficient and effective.

Marketing Plan

A marketing plan intentionally documents practical lessons learned and applies the results gained from the ongoing data-gathering process, focusing on the program, participants, and the larger community. Marketing is intentional and systematic communication about programs, products, and services directed at potential participants to increase effective communication, resulting, it is hoped, in increased support and enrollment. Marketing and sales are often misunderstood as self-serving attempts to manipulate people into doing things they would otherwise not do. Marketing does have important ethical dimensions. Fundamentally though, it is communication—a way to accurately communicate learning opportunities so potential participants can make informed decisions about their participation. Good marketing requires good information—data about your program, the context of your program, the audience, and the likely benefits.

All organizations have some kind of marketing plan. Some are written and some are not. Some plans are broadly shared; some are not. Written marketing plans can take many forms. Essentially marketing plans answer the following questions:

- What is the nature of our lifelong learning program?
- What products and services are we providing to those who participate?
- What are the special features of our services or products?
- Who are our potential participants or customers?
- How will potential participants benefit?
- How can we publicize our services, programs, or products?
- How much are our services, products, and programs worth?

In a sense, a marketing plan is a summary of the ongoing knowledge that planners have gained through intentional program development and implementation, evaluation, record keeping, and data gathering in the community and among participants. A marketing plan is a communication strategy to reach those who might want to be involved in your efforts. An effective program plan is foundational to marketing and communication.

Plan

Effective lifelong learning program planning matches the needs of potential participants with the resources that the program has available—all within the context of the sponsoring organization and its mission. Resources represent a critical aspect of the planning process.

Resources can include facilities, financial assets, staff and faculty, location, and partner relationships. Resources energize a program; they set boundaries and offer opportunities. For example, when an organization receives a large grant, these resources can actually drive or form a lifelong learning program. When thinking about important resources for lifelong learning programs, financial resources are usually among the first identified. Human resources include the people who are involved in lifelong learning—staff, participants, faculty, administrators, board members, and volunteers. One of the ongoing challenges in planning is to match educational resources including teachers with the needs of a particular audience. Program staff and volunteers who have been program participants are important resources as well.

Instructional materials and methods are also important resources. Because people learn in different ways, it is also important in the present planning environment to look beyond traditional classroom methodologies. The unique materials and methods afforded by the community are also important resources. For example, educational events for individuals whose primary language is not English represent a rapidly emerging need in many communities. Whatever resources, methods, and techniques are used, it is essential that they match the learning objectives for any program or event.

Every lifelong learning program utilizes some kind of facility. Some are associated with educational campuses or a particular retreat center. Others conduct programs using a variety of sites. Given that every facility has its strengths and weaknesses, the goal is to take advantage of the unique strengths and minimize the weaknesses as much as possible.

Technology is a key resource for planning and marketing successful lifelong learning programs today. The capacity to gather, store, retrieve, and analyze data is a fundamental activity for program planning staff. Producing print documents, developing graphics, communicating the program using a website and e-mail are all important in an effective program. Since technology is changing quickly, a proactive plan for training staff and up-grading equipment will keep the program operating at a level that promotes efficiency. For example, numerous software programs are available for keeping track of registrations and fee payments; however, learning to use them takes time. Many programs hesitate to introduce new technology because of the cost or the time it takes to learn how to use it effectively. This is where judgment plays a key role. Is the reward for learning the technology greater than the investment of time and other resources?

Institutional affiliation is often a strong program resource, providing a host of practical benefits such as support for many direct program costs including staff offices, utilities, telephone, and copying. Not-for-profit institutions with a 501(c)(3) IRS designation can receive grants from most foundations and public and private agencies. Finally, the broad range of skills, knowledge, and leadership within an institution can be a tremendous resource in developing effective lifelong learning programs, even if lifelong learning is not the institution's major role. Even a single institution has multiple goals, different perspectives, and a variety of procedures used in planning. Although capturing the resources in one's organization seems self-evident, many programs overlook how these resources can benefit those who engage in noncredit learning.

In a rapidly changing environment, partnerships between and among institutions represent a special and often-overlooked resource for learning programs. A partnership might be described as a relationship that involves two or more distinct organizational entities that gather at regular intervals to intentionally engage in unnatural acts. The unnatural acts consist of collaboration instead of competition. Partnerships represent one of the most effective resources for lifelong learning. In a partnership, distinct entities bring valuable resources to accomplish a common goal. Successful partnerships are based on shared goals and values and require ongoing skillful communication. A key to skillful communication in building partnerships is documentation, since it captures the common agreements of those involved. One effective way to strengthen partner relationships is through a "Memorandum of Understanding" that documents and summarizes the details of the partnership. This document often includes the goal of the partnership, activities, resources committed by each partner, roles, timeline, and process for evaluating and continuing the agreement. Partnerships can bring important efficiencies in resource utilization, but also take a lot of energy and can be challenging for those involved who work to manage differences in their organizations. The bottom line is being clear about the relationship, in terms of who will do what, how, when, and where.

In an effective lifelong learning program, resources must be matched with the particular mission of the organization and the context of the wider community within which the organization functions. In secular marketing approaches this is termed "finding your niche," matching who you are as a program with where you are and the resources you have. In religious organizations this is often termed "hearing your call," a form of discernment. As with discernment, often collaborative relationships can strengthen the process. Whatever the process for discerning the effective interplay between the organization, the community, and the resources available, the concrete outcome of the effort is called a plan for a lifelong learning program.

According to the dictionary, a program is "a plan of action to accomplish a specific end."[7] Planners sometimes use the term *program* to refer to a specific learning event and sometimes to refer to a group of events. Planning programs and learning events are the flesh and bones of the lifelong learning enterprise. As one practitioner has said, "Everyone has a plan. Some are intentional and well thought through. Others are unconscious. Some remain a mystery even to the planner." Planning is a special challenge yet essential in an environment of fast-paced change, given the scarcity of resources devoted to lifelong learning for many programs, and closely related to marketing. A basic planning process includes these elements:

- Goal—answers the question, why are we doing this?
- Outcome desired—addresses the question, what do we want to see happen as a result of this program?
- Objectives—what we need to do to accomplish the goals and outcomes.
- Action steps—specific activities that must be done to accomplish them.
- Timeline—outlines what steps will be completed when and by whom.
- Measurements—how we will know what has been accomplished.
- Resources—what it will take to accomplish this.
- Budget—what the program will cost and the revenue it might produce.

These essential aspects of the planning process do not happen in a linear way but might occur simultaneously. Because the world is changing quickly, it might be necessary to revisit a step that planners thought was already completed.

Plans are not stagnant, but are often adapted over time through ongoing stakeholder conversations. As nationally known professors of adult education Ronald Cervero and Arthur Wilson argue, "People solve problems," and they do so through negotiation with various program stakeholders.[8] These conversations often enable planners to build on what other planners have done and are doing. They also broaden perspective, enable programs to share risk, and increase available resources. Collaboration involves learning to speak clearly about one's position, to listen carefully, and to give and take and allowing the time necessary to learn to work together effectively, persevere, and be open to new and unexpected developments.

Whatever the plan, results are critical in determining program effectiveness.

Results

Thomas Sticht and Larry Mikulecky observed that "if there is one point at which most program developers fall short, it is determining the value of a program."[9] One of the results of learning through continuing education programs should be improvement or positive change of some kind for the individuals who have engaged in the learning and for the organization that has sponsored the learning. These are two different types of results: one focusing on the participant and the other on the program. For example, in an event on developing leadership skills, the goal might be that participants will develop three key leadership skills and be able to show how they would use these skills in their home parish. An evaluation form at the end of an event can help determine whether participants achieved their goals. The program might have had as its goal to engage more dynamic speakers and to have at least twenty participants.

Planners must decide how they will measure and communicate results. Measurements can take many forms: observations, conversations, surveys, written papers, or e-mails. In effective program planning and marketing, periodically measuring and documenting results is foundational. Tracking outputs, or the direct consequences of participating in the learning event, is an important step in determining results. In individual classes this might involve informal conversations or sometimes a more formal midcourse survey of participants to see how the class is meeting their needs. Evaluation surveys at the conclusion of an event give participants a chance to reflect on what they have learned. These evaluations are necessary learning for the program planners. To the degree possible, tracking outputs should be based on specific data, measured, descriptive and not judging, and documented so that the data can be used in future planning. Often Likert scale measures are useful because they allow one to compare means over different groups. For example, if all evaluation forms ask the question, "How satisfied are you with what you learned?" the planner can evaluate the group and then compare one group with another. This helps identify trends over time.

Progress measures are what those who do educational research call "formative evaluation." Formative evaluation is measurement and communication that helps to form the program and improve the effectiveness of learning. Closely related to this is another form of evaluation often termed "summative evaluation," knowing the overall results and effects of a learning program after it is completed.

Effective programs, those that accomplish what they set out to accomplish and make a difference in the lives of participants, often lead to increased registration, funding, and the development of other effective programs. *Outputs* are products produced or events that take place as a result of participation in learning activities, while *outcomes*, or impacts, describe what happened to the people by virtue of their participation in project activities.[10] This provides a long-term way of understanding what lifelong learning really is. Outcomes answer the question, so what? Outcomes can be measured in a variety of ways, including a before-and-after measurement using a survey. If the program is designed to be a catalyst for spiritual renewal, the before survey might ask participants to rate their perceived level of spiritual well-being before the program, perhaps using a five point Likert scale with 1 being low and 5 being high. Participants would complete the same question after the course. An increase could be an indicator of their sense of spiritual renewal. Often participant comments are solicited as well, which help evaluators better understand participant responses. Sometimes participants are surveyed perhaps a year following the program in order to assess the long-term effects of their learning experience. One of the most effective forms of program evaluation involves lessons learned. Useful in a wide array of settings, this type of informal evaluation involves a gathering of representative stakeholders to identify the things that were learned in conducting the program, including items they might change in future programs. Because different stakeholders have different perspectives, the process is often a rich resource of insights.

Whatever the progress or the outcomes of the lifelong learning program, effective communication is critical in disseminating these data to funders, participants, and evaluators. Communicating progress and results can occur in individual conversations, group discussion, or written reports or newsletters. Programs often utilize newsletters and e-mails to do this, along with occasional papers based on research that highlights some aspect of the program. A summary of results is often captured on the program fact sheet.

Putting It All Together

Traditionally, planning involved developing an educational program. Marketing focused on how the program was communicated to others. This chapter has suggested an integrated model for planning and marketing under the rubric of learning. In a rapidly changing world, it is difficult to know ahead of time what needs to be known. Learning has a trial-and-error quality to it that is often referred to as heuristic; that is, we must "make the road by walking." Those engaged in planning and marketing have to learn through their experiences in planning and marketing what needs to be known in order to plan and market effectively. Because the stage on which continuing theological education is set is globally broad and moves at warp speed due to technology, for any one person or program alone to learn what needs to be learned is virtually impossible. Collaboration is a necessity. And collaboration itself is a new and challenging process for many, requiring additional learning. Learning requires data gathered from experience, and that data must be documented. Learning also requires reflection where puzzles can be explored and insights gained. In times of diminishing resources and increasing workloads in lifelong learning, adequate time for reflection and documentation is becoming more scarce. Without time for learning, programs can lose effectiveness and become stale and pointless. Building and communicating an effective program of lifelong learning for ministry takes commitment, persistence, and passion.

The kind of learning necessary in today's world is intentional, systematic, and ongoing—for individuals, groups, and organizations. Organizations developing lifelong learning programs for ministry will need to become more like what Peter Senge and others have called "learning organizations," organizations that continuously learn new ways of responding and adapting to the environment.[11] What is needed in today's challenging environment are networks of lifelong learning providers, formal and informal communities of practice, focused on developing and communicating programs of lifelong learning for ministry. This chapter has suggested four important elements in developing a learning model of program planning and marketing: identity, context, plan, and results. Addressing these elements is a way to focus and systematize the learning process; it can help program providers develop and market effective programs as well as build a clear and effective case for their efforts to communicate to governing boards, funders, potential partners, and potential participants.

Whatever the system used in an age of change, learning will only increase in importance. Learning in organizations whose ethos is spiritual is essentially a form of discernment, a way for a group or organization to learn its spiritual calling and direction for the future. In this sense, both planning and marketing lifelong learning for ministry are holy work, holding great promise for strengthening the practice of ministry and, as such, demanding our best efforts.

Notes

1. Jackson W. Carroll, *God's Potters: Pastoral Leadership and the Shaping of Congregations* (Grand Rapids: W. B. Eerdmans, 2006), 214.

2. Ibid., 215.

3. Myles Horton and Paulo Freire, *We Make the Road by Walking: Conversations on Education and Social Change* (Philadelphia: Temple University Press, 1990), 3.

4. Matthias Finger and Jose Manuel Asun, *Adult Education at the Crossroads: Learning Our Way Out* (New York: Zed Books, 2001), 1.

5. James L. Morrison, "Establishing an Environmental Scanning System to Augment College and University Planning," *Planning in Higher Education* 15, no. 1 (1986–87): 7–22.

6. Robert W. Bradford, J. Peter Duncan, and Brian Tarcy, *Simplified Strategic Planning: The No-Nonsense Guide for Busy People Who Want Results Fast* (Worcester, MA: Chandler House Press, 2000).

7. *Random House Unabridged Dictionary*, 2006, s.v. "Program."

8. Ronald M. Cervero and Arthur L. Wilson, *Planning Responsibly for Adult Education: A Guide to Negotiating Power and Interests* (San Francisco: Jossey-Bass, 1994), 191.

9. Thomas G. Sticht and Larry Mikulecky, *Job-Related Basic Skills: Cases and Conclusions* (Columbus, OH: ERIC Clearinghouse on Adult, Career, and Vocational Education, 1984), 36.

10. Kathleen A. Cahalan, *Projects That Matter: Successful Planning and Evaluation for Religious Organizations* (Herndon, VA: Alban Institute, 2003).

11. Peter M. Senge, *The Fifth Discipline: The Art and Practice of the Learning Organization* (New York: Doubleday, 2006).

CHAPTER 20

Welcoming the Whole Person

Carolyn Henninger Oehler

From first contact through final evaluation, a welcoming environment can be intentionally created to appeal to adults serious about
their continuing theological education. Marketing, registration
procedures, facilities, and learning ambiance may be designed intentionally to attract and satisfy adult learners. When body, mind,
and spirit are considered as integrated parts of the whole person,
adults are more likely to learn at their maximum capabilities. Often, the intangibles and peripherals make the difference between
an okay experience and an empowered learner who will want to
return for more.

Both Hebrew and Christian scriptures contain stories that dra-
matize the central place of hospitality in communities whose faith
journeys are told there. Abraham welcomed the Lord, in the guise
of three men, by the oaks of Mamre. He saw to their comfort and
refreshment himself, offering them the best he had (Gen. 18:1–8).
On the other hand, to violate the norms of hospitality could result in the death of individuals or even whole cities. Sodom and
Gomorrah were destroyed for the sinfulness of their inhabitants,
the lack of hospitality primary among them (Gen. 18:16–19:29).
In order to share her most profound understanding, Wisdom

prepares a feast and offers a banquet to all who would sit with her to become wise (Prov. 9:1–6).

Jesus and his disciples received the hospitality of many in their journeys. They probably could not have continued their ministries without regular offerings of food and places to sleep. Jesus performed his own act of hospitality when he fed thousands of people. He showed "compassion for the crowd, because they have been with me now for three days and have nothing to eat; and I do not want to send them away hungry, for they might faint on the way" (Matt. 15:32).

Today, the eucharistic meal is still characterized as a feast, God's gracious act of hospitality and welcome in the name of Jesus Christ. Those of us who plan and offer continuing theological education can do no less than reflect that hospitality in our offerings to those who come hungry for knowledge, for nurture, and for self-respect.

One continuing education program presents itself in this holistic manner. Its brochure characterizes the program as one that "provides a creative, nurturing, welcoming, and empowering environment for the people of God along their journey. . . . A sacred place where refreshment of the spirit, care of the soul, renewal of the mind, and rest for the body may be experienced through retreats, worship, prayer, the arts, and hospitality." With this as a goal, this program has laid the foundation for welcoming the whole person.

The process of learning is emotional as well as intellectual. The power of place can be an ally in creating a positive learning environment, or physical surroundings can be a distraction in the learning process. Attention to them can make a critical difference in participants' feelings of satisfaction regarding the program.

The single most important ingredient in the learning environment are the people with whom the potential learner interacts, from the first contact through registration, meals, class, housing, and other contacts. The place and the people will work together to create a positive learning environment.

Staff trained in hospitality and customer service are an essential ingredient in a welcoming program. The first contact is a key person in the process and should be gracious and welcoming, as well as knowledgeable. Housekeeping, maintenance, and food service personnel may have more contact with guests than so-called executive staff. All need training in hospitality and service.

Becoming User-Friendly

Who is seeking continuing theological education these days? What will attract them to your program again and again? What does the whole person expect from the experience? Answering these questions from the standpoint of your specific context can set you on the path to becoming a growing program with repeat learners.

Often, it's the little things, done well, that add up to a worthwhile experience, even before the leaders have opened their mouths for the first time. Taking care of details such as the registration process, parking, signage, and accessibility can signal respect and welcome, preparing participants for a positive experience. When some details are omitted or done poorly, event leaders must work harder to overcome a negative first impression.

Easy advance registration, whether on the Internet, over the telephone, or by mail, will set the tone for the experience. Before they spend their precious continuing education dollars and time, learners often have many questions. Potential registrants may call several times, trying to decide if the program is right for them. Questions need to be answered promptly, patiently, and accurately so that potential learners feel they will be nurtured and respected in the program.

The younger and more targeted the learners, the more likely they are to respond to, and even demand, a technology-assisted registration process. Registration via the Internet, or at least a registration form available on the Web, will attract these individuals and allow them to register while they have the motivation to do

so. By the time they wait for that brochure they requested to arrive in the mail, they may have cooled off or have found another
program with an easier registration process.

Telephone registration, including 800 numbers, also attracts
those who want to take action immediately. Capturing that first
phone call and routing it to someone who is knowledgeable and
welcoming is essential; the potential registrant may not make a
second call. Providing the option of paying by credit card benefits
the program by receiving immediate payment and offers the registrant the convenience of completing the registration by telephone.
Careful, confidential handling of checks and scholarship requests
are additional aspects of sending a welcoming, respectful message
before the learner ever arrives on site.

Parking availability can affect a program's attractiveness to
potential learners. In urban and university settings, occasional
visitors may find themselves uncertain where to go or unable to
park in lots or facilities reserved for daily parkers. Clear instructions about the possibilities and problems of parking may forestall
exasperation and frustration that gets directed toward the entire
program. Be honest about what your guests will face; suggest public transportation or alternatives, if that is feasible. Getting a ticket
or having one's car towed can ruin the entire experience!

Reading the "signs of the times" may be easier than finding the
way to a meeting room or a registration table. When we become
familiar with a process or a place, we may tend to assume that everyone knows what we know. It may seem so obvious that it needs
no explanation. Ask someone for directions to a place familiar to
them, and you may get the response that they know how to get
there, but don't remember the names of the streets to turn on or
how many blocks to travel. Familiarity can breed lack of awareness, as well as contempt. Try to look at the meeting site with fresh
eyes, and ask where signs need to be posted—temporarily or per-
manently—to guide the occasional guest to places that the regular
finds without thought.

Don't assume that everyone who will attend the event has been to your facility before. Even if alumni are your main attendees, others may be interested in something you offer. If they are made to feel like outsiders and they feel as if they are the only ones who don't know where to go and what to do, they will not return. In addition, signs can alert staff and faculty that something important is going on. Even people not directly involved in the continuing education program may be called upon to provide directions or other information. Make sure they are informed as well.

Do not forget to visit the sleeping rooms occasionally and ask if you would want to sleep there. Are they clean, well lit, and supplied with necessities? Are bathrooms clean and towels of decent size? If you use empty dorm rooms, think about how they can be made more inviting to adults. A treat for the pillow, a mug for water and other beverages, and personal products in case of emergency can communicate welcome. If you are recommending hotels, check on their accommodations periodically. Do not recommend anywhere that doesn't meet the basic test: Would I like to sleep here?

More and more often now, participants in continuing education want to use computers as part of their learning process. Taking notes during a day meeting or writing reports or papers for a longer course may call for a computer. Easy access to power for notebooks and a printer for documents sends a message that you are up-to-date, not only in technology but also in other aspects of the program. Being able to send and receive e-mail, and even surf the Internet, either through their own phone lines or at computers made available for guests, is rapidly becoming an expectation for a quality educational experience.

Make the safety and security of your participants a top priority. Be clear about what precautions need to be taken for personal safety and for security of belongings. If you have concerns about general security at your site, work with your administration to address these concerns. Feelings of safety and security, which may be subliminal, will affect the program in positive and negative ways and affect the return rate.

Creating and Sustaining an Optimum Learning Environment

The process of learning may be described as an experience that occurs inside the learner and for which the learner has responsibility. The adult learner is one of the richest resources for learning, as she or he cooperates and collaborates with the leader in the learning process. This learning process is the precious gem at the heart of any educational enterprise. The setting in which this gem is placed can make a great difference in whether the experience is productive or whether it is less successful and forgettable.

The conditions that sustain a positive learning environment and facilitate learning, when working together, create an atmosphere in which learners thrive and in which the continuing education program has maximum impact on learners, leaders, and the program developers. Some of those conditions are respect, acceptance, openness, and valuing difference of opinions and learning styles.

Creating a Respectful Atmosphere

Respect is that overarching ingredient that makes possible all the rest. Respect is present when the potential participants' needs and interests are taken into account in developing the courses and the program. Even in situations where clergy and lay professionals are required to earn a certain number of continuing education units (CEUs) to remain in good standing, they have many choices. Including potential participants in planning communicates respect for what they know and what they believe they need.

One way to help assure this is through involvement of potential learners in planning or in focus groups. In a planning group, the potential learners will have the opportunity to shape a particular offering, knowing what will appeal to people in their situations. Once involved, they are also likely to become participants in the offering and to recruit others for it. In a focus group, planners can gain more general knowledge about what kind of program and program offerings will appeal to the people they are targeting. Listening to the customer and then acting on that information is a key way to communicate your respect for the learners as well as develop viable programs.

Respect for the learner who decides to take the class includes offering a setting that communicates that this class and these learners are important to the institution and to the program. Adequate space, an appropriate level of heat or air conditioning, comfortable and adequate furniture, resources ready and available to all, faculty chosen with care and fully briefed on the nature of the class and the needs of the participants—all convey respect for the learner and for the program itself. Their absence conveys a lack of respect for both the learner and the program.

The Role of Faculty and Other Leaders in Setting a Climate of Respect

Respect for the learner must also be a high priority for the leaders and faculty in the program. Those who engage in continuing education for ministry, even in systems that include requirements, are almost always motivated to choose specific courses and classes by their own curiosity and interest. They are readied to learn by their situations and the problems or tasks they are confronting. They are usually self-directed and responsible for their own learning path. Faculty who assume pedagogical approaches that tend to be only expert or subject centered and authoritarian can affect the climate of respect the program is attempting to achieve. Trusting the learner, and what the learner brings to the table, is an essential posture for the faculty or leader to take in setting a climate of respect.

To sustain and extend the atmosphere of respect essential for effective learning, faculty who know their subjects must also know their learners and something about how adults learn. Qualities desirable in faculty include openness to opinions and ideas different from and even in conflict with their own. Faculty should be able to come out from behind a lecture format and model vulnerability and a learning posture. Lectures are usually the easiest way to deliver material and the least effective method for retaining what is delivered. Respect includes willingness to expose ideas and conclusions to debate and discussion, and even to conflict. Faculty who are well prepared and who believe in continuing education and lifelong learning are more likely to communicate respect and enthusiasm for this learning situation.

Learners who experienced traditional degree programs may need to be empowered by the leader to take responsibility for their own learning. Offering them respect is a key way to generate self-respect in the learner. If learners leave with greater respect for their own experience as a resource for learning, and for themselves as learners, they will have learned an invaluable lesson.

Creating an Accepting Environment

By the time people reach the status of adult learner, they have usually acquired certain attitudes about their ability to learn, particularly in structured situations. Even a successful academic career can leave them with feelings of inferiority and anxiety about what kind of learners they are. If they didn't like their formal educational experience or struggled with certain courses or ideas, they may need reassurance before they can give themselves permission to learn up to their capacity.

Acceptance by faculty can make a difference in the amount of learning that occurs and the chances that the learner will want to return another time. Aspects of an accepting attitude include a nonjudgmental approach to ideas and questions from learners and a realization that individuals learn in different ways and at different paces. Creating an accepting environment includes providing a learning experience that appeals to various learning strengths.

Some are more comfortable and effective learners through personal involvement with people in everyday situations. This learning from feeling rather than through a systematic approach places an emphasis on learning from specific experience, relating to people rather than to ideas, and being sensitive to feelings and people. Others may prefer to learn by watching and listening. They observe carefully before making judgments, like to view issues from different perspectives, and look for the meaning of things.

Still others prefer to learn by thinking, by logically analyzing ideas and doing systematic planning. Then they are ready to act on an intellectual understanding of the subject or situation. And yet another group learns best by doing. These are the hands-on learners. They have a great ability to get things done, are risk takers, and try to influence people and events through action.

Most people are able to learn in any of these four modes; they just prefer and probably learn best when one is emphasized more than the others. An ideal learning experience will provide something for each of these learning styles. This may not be practical in a short or confined offering, but it is an important goal to place before faculty and program planners. At another level, continuing education experiences are excellent venues for strengthening less-preferred learning styles, and learners can be encouraged to widen their comfort zone by participating in and learning in other modes. Learning to learn is an important yet usually invisible part of continuing education. Faculty, then, must be skilled in *how* to teach as well as *what* to teach.

Planning for Spiritual Needs

Welcoming the whole person includes attending to spiritual needs. To do this well, worship must be a forethought, not an afterthought. To make the experience truly continuing education for ministry, the experience should include the opportunity for worship, for meditation, and for prayer. It would be unwise to generalize too strictly on what brings people to continuing education experiences, yet many will come from busy, stressful situations. If they have been sent by a supervisor or a congregational committee urging them to address some deficit of skills in ministry, they may be feeling some pain and anxiety as well. Worship experiences designed to offer healing, hope, and a time apart will minister to the whole person. Without them, there is less chance that individuals will be ready to turn their attention to learning. More important, without worship done thoughtfully and well, the program misses the opportunity to provide nurture and care for the souls of those who come. Choose worship designers with as much care as faculty are chosen. What they offer is as important.

For an extended program, consider making a spiritual director available for conversation and guidance to those who wish to pursue this avenue. We, both learners and educators, need to ask the old question of each other: How is it with your soul? Not only will participants learn at their highest capacity but they will also recognize in yet another way that educators care for the whole person. This added value to a program expresses the importance placed on each person and communicates respect for each one's unique spiritual journey and needs.

Worship experiences and attention to the spiritual needs of the learner are part of a larger emphasis on community. The opportunity to be with peers is a key reason why learners choose a program. Talking with someone who is having similar experiences and struggles, laughing about the aggravations and stumbles of ministry, and sharing concerns about family and future are invaluable parts of the continuing education experience. To facilitate community, time and space need to be provided. People will probably seek each other out, no matter what the situation. A well-run program gives opportunity and comfortable space to enhance the experience. In a classroom, introductions, personal storytelling, even name tags, can be part of intentional community building. Meals arranged so that conversation is encouraged also enables community. For those experiencing loneliness in ministry or in high stress ministries, this aspect of the program may be more vital than the content of the course.

Remembering the Body

In addition to the comforts mentioned above, a program that welcomes the whole person will make provision for physical activity and attention to the body as well as the mind and spirit. If there is a place for recreation on site, allow time for exercising, swimming, and running. Develop a schedule that acknowledges the need for physical activity and realize that such activity aids the learning process. If nothing else is possible, consider board games, jigsaw puzzles, team competitions. Make play a part of the learning experience.

If the program and situation allow, consider teaching basic tai chi or other exercises. Perhaps the opportunity for massage would give stressed-out participants a new lease on learning. Even a foot massage or a back rub can change perspective and get tired bodies ready to learn.

A break for the group to attend a play or a concert, a dinner out together, a visit to a place of historic or natural interest—each can serve multiple purposes of learning, community building, and getting bodies off chairs and moving around.

Producing a Well-Rounded Program and Well-Rounded Learners

Remembering that the whole person is involved in any continuing education for ministry will help planners keep in mind the wide variety of needs they must meet. Processes that need to function well each time a program or class is offered can be systematized to assure quality. Registration, parking, signage, sleeping quarters, and quality of space can be designed to communicate a welcome to those who participate. Creating and sustaining an optimum learning environment includes choosing faculty who will use empowering teaching methods. Faculty and leaders who are comfortable with diverse opinions and respectful of the uniqueness of each learner are key parts of creating an accepting learning environment.

Attending to spiritual needs through well-planned and executed worship, time and space for prayer and meditation, and, perhaps, even providing opportunities to work with a spiritual director will nurture and support learners and communicate care for the whole person. Space and time for community building and physical activity—even fun!—will produce a well-rounded program and well-rounded learners. Welcoming the whole person makes continuing education for ministry a true ministry of hospitality.

CHAPTER 21

Through Many Dangers, Toils, and Snares: Risk Management in Continuing Education Programs

Eileen Macholl

Every organization needs a person whose function is to ask the question "What could go wrong?" and to protect the institution from risk and potential problems. Some organizations have a person or department whose sole function is risk management; often, however, this is by necessity a shared function of many people who are all charged with caring about, identifying, and protecting against events that could irrevocably harm staff, students, programs, or the institution as a whole.

Because educational institutions have complex programs and relationships with the broader society, they face a wide array of potential risks. Risk management means being aware of potential exposures and actively communicating, with problem solving in mind. The goal is to maximize the areas over which you do have control and to minimize potential hazards in the areas that you cannot control.

This chapter reviews the basic process and tools used to help manage risk and focuses on contracts, personnel and employment risk, reputation risk, financial risk, technological risk, and general liability and insurance issues. This chapter does not attempt to lay out all the answers for a particular school or situation but presents an outline of the iterative process of evaluating and protecting against risk in various forms. It is a process of awareness and of communication, of asking the right questions to shield the institution from potential liabilities that could cost the organization its existence. Taking steps to prevent serious consequence for a continuing education program frees a director of continuing education to be more creative and to spend the majority of time on the fun parts of programming without having to worry about the inherent uncertainties.

Basic Definitions

Risk is simply the potential for economic loss, human suffering, property losses, income or revenue loss, financial losses from third-party claims, and loss of reputation, among others. Risk is an impediment to accomplishing an institution's mission or goal. The basic definition of *risk management* is "the process of making and implementing decisions that will minimize the adverse effects of accidental and business losses on an organization."[1] Risk management is simultaneously a science and an art; it is about addressing uncertainties.

A *risk manager* is a steward and caretaker of resources. The risk management function is not just to bear bad news; rather, it is also a role of support and creative problem solving. Taking the role of risk management seriously is important, even if that role isn't the primary responsibility of a continuing education director. This requires awareness of potential problems, proactive efforts to eliminate or reduce the conditions and practices that could cause loss, and insurance against risks that cannot be avoided. A risk manager is a planner, communicator, and educator.

Keys to a Successful Risk Management Program

The number one goal of risk managers should *not* be to prevent all mishaps (that is impossible), but rather to reduce as much as possible any surprises. All major contingencies should be anticipated and planned for.

The hallmarks of successful risk management are strong support from the school's or organization's board, chief executive, and senior administrators and shared responsibility for protecting the institution. Proactive risk management should be a shared commitment at all levels of the institution.

The best risk management plans are refined by the use of feedback and helpful suggestions. Listen to the concerns of others and seek solutions to address these concerns. Consider all workers who play a role in helping students have a successful experience, whether or not they might directly interact with students. Have conversations about risk plans with senior administration officials and their advisors, insurance agents, accountants, legal counsel, technical experts, and business officers. Listen to the needs and concerns of desk attendants, janitorial staff, bus drivers, mail delivery staff, administrative assistants, cashiers, database managers, marketing professionals, graphic designers, and advertising people. These conversations will pay many rewards, not the least of which is mitigating potential risks for students and the institution. An important benefit of listening to many different people is the sense of importance and excitement it conveys about the continuing education program, which will encourage a sense of commitment, buy-in, respect, and inclusion that will add to the smooth experience for participants overall.

A critical element of successful risk management is the existence of written policies, procedures, and guidelines. Institutions should have a written sexual harassment policy, emergency evacuation and fire procedures, policies about racism and tolerance, a code of ethics, and guidelines for appropriate behavior on campus. These must be actively communicated and shared with relevant parties. Therefore, one responsibility of the continuing education director is to orient seminar faculty and participants regarding relevant policies and procedures.

Process and Tools of Risk Management

Risk can be categorized into one of four major areas: operating risk, legal and personnel risk, political and reputation risk, and technological risk. *Operating risk* encompasses slip-and-fall accidents, safety and security concerns, campus construction hazards, transit or travel operations, special event risks, and student housing issues that affect life, safety, and security. *Legal and personnel risk* encompasses contractual agreements, employment practices, and compliance with governmental regulations. *Political and reputation risks* are usually intangible but can be some of the most costly to an institution's existence; examples of these include bad publicity and conflicts of interest. *Technological risk*, including protection of intellectual property, Internet exposures, and distance learning issues, can also pose extraordinary threats to an organization's effectiveness.

The process of risk management is both self-reinforcing and repetitive. Reduced to its most basic level, the risk management process traditionally has five stages: (1) identify, (2) analyze, (3) select, (4) implement, (5) monitor and update.

Identify

It is vital for leaders of institutions and continuing education programs to be aware of and to actively list specific unexpected losses and potential accidents. Work collaboratively to identify potential political, reputation, legal, personnel, operating, and technological risks. Identify and assess all potential risks so that institutional decisions can be made regarding which of those to insure, which to retain, what can be controlled, and which risks should be avoided altogether.

Analyze

Analyzing a risk typically means measuring the risk. In school settings this step is sometimes difficult because formulas that can be universally applied are not readily available. Parts of this step are necessarily evaluative, somewhat subjective, and open to interpretation. The objective, however, is to give priority to establishing policies to avoid loss.

Select

Selecting risk management options means deciding on the best tool or combination of tools that best address an identified risk. The options for managing risk are varied. Some are based more on common sense than others. Be creative and resourceful. The tools need to be appropriate to the risk. The tools of risk management can be categorized into one of four general areas: avoid, transfer, mitigate, and accept.

Avoiding risk is the ideal, but not at the expense of choosing not to run a program. Avoiding risk is never guaranteed; risk cannot be entirely eliminated. Nevertheless, examples of risk avoidance tools include the strict enforcement of safety standards, cautioning participants in writing to not leave their valuables unattended, and communicating clearly regarding emergency procedures. It is possible to prohibit the use of candles in programs to avoid the risk of fire, communicate sexual harassment and tolerance policies to all faculty and independent contractors to avoid legal liability risks, implement extra security for library resources to avoid theft and loss risks, and provide ergonomic desks and chairs to prevent potential worker compensation insurance claims.

The key to the tool of *risk transfer* is to literally transfer the risk from the institution to another party, either to an outside agency or to student-participants themselves. The key is to *not* do it yourself; for example, ask program participants to sign a waiver for off-campus events, post signs notifying participants that the institution is not responsible for lost or stolen items.

Review contracts to ensure that appropriate language regarding the responsibilities of each party with regard to personal or property losses is included and in the best interest of the institution. Indemnification language and insurance clauses are critical tools of risk transfer that specify who is responsible legally and financially in the event of a loss.

Several strategies exist to lessen or *mitigate risk*. One is separation. Examples of separating risk from the institution include storing important original papers in a safe deposit box, the use and regular implementation of computer backup systems, and storage of historical documents in archives off-site. Use two cars instead of one to transport key staff and participants to an off-site location or require senior administrators to fly on separate airplanes (if a flight is delayed or cancelled, at least someone will be likely to arrive to make a presentation).

Another important risk-mitigation strategy is to attempt to reduce the severity of loss during or after something has already gone wrong. Examples of this include the use of smoke detectors, policies to close fire doors in the event of a fire, having backup electrical generators on campus, and hiring food service suppliers in the event of emergency.

The purchase of insurance is the classic mitigation strategy. This area is discussed in more depth later in this chapter.

Some risks are too great to insure or fully mitigate. In some cases an institution will decide to *accept* the risk and offer a program anyway. For example, unavoidable political risk may be inherent in offering a sensitive but important program. Because many risks can be lessened, transferred, and avoided, the key is to make sure the decision to accept risk is an informed decision and not one made because the risks were not identified and thought-out in advance.

Accepting risk is okay. The existence of risk does not mean that creative programs must be eschewed. If an institution chooses to assume risk, make sure it does so with awareness and has documented why the decision was made. The reasons an institution might choose to accept known risks include a sense that the risks are extremely remote and unlikely, a decision that the risks are too expensive to purchase outside insurance, or strong political or reputation reasons to go ahead with particular programming.

Implement

Implementing risk management options involves an integrative and collaborative approach that includes the entire organization and continuously raises consciousness about risk.

Monitor and Update

Because risk management is a continuous, repetitive, and self-reinforcing process, the effectiveness of decisions must be continuously monitored and administrators must be ready, flexible, and willing to update, review, and change their decisions as needed and as more information becomes available. Administrators may, for example, find the need to purchase additional insurance or to implement seminars to train staff on various areas of potential risk. Ongoing or periodic monitoring and continuous updating of risk management techniques and strategies are necessary as the circumstances of continuing education programming change, grow, and evolve.

Contracts

When all is going well, it is easy enough to operate on a handshake or "gentleman's agreement." Thankfully, in many situations verbal agreements work out perfectly well. At the point when a miscommunication causes an agreement to go wrong, however, it is too late to try to create a written contract. Agreements always begin verbally, in conversation, but the process of solidifying plans and ideas as they move into action almost always entails both financial and political implications and potential risks for an institution. The risk of miscommunication and lack of clarity is, fortunately, relatively easy to remedy by insisting on written contracts before any work begins.

A contract or letter of agreement must be signed at or before the beginning of the term of service. Do not begin work or allow someone to begin work for your organization before a contract has been fully negotiated, agreed upon, and signed by both parties. Attempts to be expedient by going ahead with the performance of services without tending to the contracting greatly increases potential risk for an institution. It takes only one misunderstanding to create litigation that can derail a continuing education program and threaten the institution as a whole.

Write contracts carefully. Think through all the provisions to be included and send a draft to the other party for their review. Sometimes the other party will want to make changes to particular clauses. Consider these requests and know that this negotiation process is an integral part of the conversation to clarify expectations and essential to good risk management. Do not feel bound to incorporate these requests unquestioned; there is often room to work toward a negotiated solution that is positive for all parties. Be aware that contract revision (especially if and when it needs to go through institutional attorneys) is not always speedy. Make sure that the contract process has been initiated well in advance of the anticipated start date of actual work.

An attorney should be consulted to review any document that binds the organization to another party and to ensure that it does not contain any provisions inconsistent with existing institutional values or rules. Be sure to attach relevant written policies and guidelines, as appropriate.

A contract is not considered to be fully valid until both parties' signatures are affixed to an original document. The ideal arrangement is to generate two original signed copies of each contract: one for your institution and one for the other party. Send two unexecuted copies (originals) to the other party, ask them to sign and return both, and then have your institution's authorized representative countersign both originals. Make sure one fully executed original is kept in your institution's master file (often held by the business office), and return the other original to the outside party. Keep a photocopy of the executed original for your working files. You may need to reference this as your program unfolds, to model other agreements on its language, or to make additional copies to attach as backup documentation with check requests.

Contract Template

The contract template will need to be customized for each situation. It can be in the format of a letter of agreement in standard business English or it can be based on a more formal contract. In either case, these are the important areas to be covered in most contracts in order of most to least priority:

Obvious items to specify include the following:

- Date(s) and time(s) that service is to be performed
- Duties and services to be performed
- Expectations (for example, arrival time, seminar schedule, minimum number of students or participants required, photocopy policy, permission expectations)
- Compensation and amount of pay
- Reimbursement of expenses (within thirty days, upon submission of receipts, no later than four months after end of program, and so forth)
- Travel restrictions and considerations (economy or coach airfare, not first class; ground transportation costs; current mileage rates; and so forth)

Less obvious items to specify include the following:

- Terms and timing of payment (often: half due upon signing, final half at the end of service—usually to be delivered in person on the final date of service)
- Cancellation and termination clauses (how far in advance cancellation can be announced by either party with and without financial ramifications)
- Notice (in writing and delivered to formal addresses)

Items sometimes overlooked include the following:

- Financial ramifications of cancellation (prorating of amounts due)

- Indemnification or hold harmless clauses
- Confidentiality (and the extension of confidentiality provisions in the event the agreement is cancelled or terminated for any reason)
- Explicit statement that the independent contractor is not an employee
- Other rules and policies (attached sexual harassment policy, for example)
- Return of property provisions
- Copyright and ownership of intellectual property
- Governing law, appeal, and adjudication clauses (make sure they conform with the institution's home state)
- Statement that signature acknowledges receipt and agreement to the terms of the contract and to the attached written policies (for example, sexual harassment, ethics, worship inclusive–language policies).

Contract Categories

The major categories of contracts common for seminary continuing education programs are the following:

- Independent contractors (individuals providing services to the school who are not employees of the school)
- Outside institutional parties (joint programming in which other institutions are providing services to your program, or outside vendors, such as graphics design firms, providing services to your program)
- Consultancy arrangements (if your program or institution is providing services to another institution)
- Employment agreements (These are not technically contracts but rather letters of agreement and are discussed in the section below under Personnel and Employment.)

Because the area of contracts carries with it considerable risk and confusion, the specific categories of contracts are each discussed in the following paragraphs.

Independent Contractors

Guest lecturers or workshop leaders are key components of most programs of continuing education. In addition, a program might engage the services of musicians, photographers, coaches, trainers, preachers, graphic designers, consultants, attorneys, writers, or editors. At Auburn I have even had occasion to review independent contractor contracts for koshering a kitchen as well as for caterers and clowns. These individuals are considered independent contractors unless they are employees of the institution. Refer to Appendix A, "Hiring as an Independent Contractor or an Employee," on page 383 for further details about the classification of independent contractors. Note that classification of the individuals working for you is a critical decision. Tax law places the burden of proof that an individual is an independent contractor rather than an employee on the institution making the payment for services. Misclassification of individuals as independent contractors can result in large fines and penalties. When in doubt, consult your attorney.

Outside Institutional Parties

Third party agreements, coproductions, or joint programming with other institutions and relationships with outside vendors are all areas that pose considerable potential legal and reputation risks for institutions. This includes agreements with other schools or institutions for space usage, property rentals, or leases; joint programming; and consultancy arrangements. Refer to the contract template section above for an outline of areas to be addressed and included in contracts with outside parties.

Sometimes the outside party will have generated the first draft of the contract and will present their standard template, expecting your institution to sign a document with prewritten language designed to primarily protect their institution. Be cautious in these instances. Read the fine print carefully and ask your institution's attorney to review it. Be prepared to go back to the other organization to negotiate modifications to make the wording more reciprocal.

The indemnification, or hold harmless, clause is a significant risk-related section in the written contracts between two institutions. Particularly in instances in which the contract was initially generated by the other party, look carefully at the wording of the clauses in this area and know that it is absolutely within the rules of fair play to insist that the language of the indemnification clause be fully reciprocal. The clause should say, in other words, that if they do something negligent or illegal they will take responsibility for the financial ramifications of any legal actions that might ensue from their mistakes; likewise, if it is found that you or members of your institution do something negligent or illegal, your institution will take responsibility for the financial ramifications of any legal actions that might ensue from your mistakes. Never agree to burden an institution with responsibility for an outside party's potential negligence.

Consultancy Arrangements

These are not dissimilar to contracts between outside parties; the difference is simply your program providing services to the other institution instead of the other way around. Again, refer to the bullets above in the contract template section. The consultancy contract will have similar sections but may be more expansive, detailed, and individualized in its construction.

Continuing education programs sometimes require contracts with multiple parties: to provide consultancy to another institution or individual on your institution's behalf, independent contractors may need to be engaged. In these instances, mapping out clearly the relationships and the contractual obligations involved is important. Attempting to write a complex three-party contract is not wise. Keep it as simple as possible. Write one contract between your institution and the party to whom the services are being offered. Write separate contracts with the individuals engaged to do the work that will be provided to the other organization.

This approach is simpler and lessens the risks of potential misinterpretation and future litigation.

In all written contracts with outside parties, be they independent contractors, outside institutions that are providing services, or outside institutions to whom services are being provided, the same basic principles hold true: be clear, be proactive, and spell out the expectations and responsibilities in advance and in writing to as full a degree as possible.

Personnel and Employment

A corollary to the area of contracts is in the area of personnel or human resources. This is another area in which risk is potentially high and clarity is exceedingly important.

Recruitment and Retention

Recruiting and retaining employees is an entire field of specialization. Be aware that the methods used to search for employees, hire them, orient them, and help them adjust to the culture of the institution form an important process that can affect the success of continuing education programs. Be clear about the necessary qualities and skills so that a thorough and specific job description can be developed. Although it may take more time at the front end, wait to find an employee who is the right fit for the program and position. Staff turnover can be disruptive and expensive: the standard rule of thumb is that it costs an institution on average 150 percent of one year's salary every time a position needs to be refilled.[2] Be sure to conduct thorough reference checks (get final applicants' written permission to check both named and unnamed references). Take the time to thoroughly engage in conversations with people who know the candidate well. If careful, deliberate, and persistently optimistic, you can be rewarded with the right employees in the right position that have been well mentored and that will serve you well for a substantial period of time.

Background Checks

Conducting background checks is an area of risk management that has grown in church-related institutions over the past decade. In addition to criminal and sex offender registry checks, a wide variety of background checks are available, including department of motor vehicles records and credit checks. Especially for programs in which minors participate, background checks have become very common.

Continuing education programs' frequent use of independent contractors that interact directly with students poses a broader potential pool of individuals whose backgrounds must be checked than may be realized. Note that having a policy of conducting background checks is not in and of itself adequate protection for an institution.

Legal Requirements and Privacy Protections

State and other laws may establish legal protection and privacy rights for individuals who are subjected to background checks in the hiring process, including the requirement that written permission be obtained in advance of conducting any type of background check and that written notification be given to anyone not hired as a result of a check. This is an area in which consulting your institution's attorney is essential.

Jurisdictional Constraints

Currently, no single centralized database can be checked that will pull up all the criminal arrests and convictions of a particular individual. Records have to be checked on the federal level and then on a state-by-state basis. Typically records are checked in any states that an individual has maintained a legal residence during the previous five years. Unless an institution is willing and able to pay for a full fifty-state search, this standard protocol does not ensure that other arrests or convictions for the individual will be revealed. Furthermore, there is currently no effective method of checking foreign nationals or U.S. citizens for criminal or sex offender records that might have occurred outside the United States.

Expense

While many churches and seminaries are choosing to conduct comprehensive background checks on all employees, this can be costly. The basic per person costs go up with each additional jurisdiction that needs to be investigated, depending on the individual's address history, and these fees can range from fifteen to one hundred fifty dollars (or more) per person.

Although background checks are popular, and probably necessary, this area of personnel and legal risk management comes with heavy administrative burdens and to be fully effective must be applied in concert with other best practices.

Employment Agreements

Employment agreements are simple letters stating the intention to employ, or to continue to employ, an individual at an institution. These letters typically specify rate of pay, anticipated start date, and benefits. The initial letter given to a newly hired individual should be accompanied by a copy of the institution's employee handbook. Refer to Appendix B, "Personnel Handbook Guidelines," on page 385 for further details about the recommended contents of this important institutional document.

Regular Employee Feedback and Performance Reviews

It is sometimes easy to let busyness and uncomfortable feelings get in the way of providing written employee feedback and regular annual performance reviews. This is an area of significant institutional risk, because it can lead to issues of performance problems that remain unaddressed and make subsequent disciplinary action more difficult; conversely it can lead to unrewarded professional growth that can frustrate morale and employee turnover. Remember the number one goal for risk management is to have no surprises. Failing to provide regular employee feedback and failure to conduct regular written performance reviews can come back to surprise you in several difficult and unexpected ways.

Sexual Harassment and Misconduct

Disputes over sexual harassment tend to be costly. The definition of *sexual harassment* as "unwelcome sexual advances, requests for sexual favors, and other verbal or physical conduct of a sexual nature"[3] leaves behavior open to interpretation. The Federal Equal Employment Opportunity Commission resolved 11,936 sexual harassment complaints in 2006, resulting in payment of $48.8 million to the employees who brought the charges.[4]

Note that sexual harassment is usually interpreted as conduct between individuals of hierarchically different rank, such as boss and subordinate, teacher and student, and so forth. Sexual misconduct is also a risk that is difficult to control. Technically, sexual misconduct is interpreted as conduct between individuals of hierarchically equal rank, such as between two students or between two employees at the same level. In addition to a well-publicized written sexual harassment and misconduct policy, make it unequivocally clear that no forms of sexual advances, verbal or physical, are welcome on your property or in your programs, not even seemingly innocent play between partners, spouses, or friends. Friendly touch, hugs, and teasing may be misinterpreted by people from different cultural, religious, socioeconomic, and psychological backgrounds. It is in the institution's best interests to have a no-tolerance policy for any types of verbal or physical behavior that could be even remotely misconstrued. Frequently communicated expectations that everyone be treated with courtesy, respect, and strict professionalism in all contexts and swift attention to even the suggestion of impropriety will set a tone that can help reduce the risks of costly allegations and extremely painful situations.

The larger institution should have a process for dealing with allegations, and all such allegations should be forwarded to the designated person so that the matter can be dealt with in an appropriate and sensitive way to protect the institution as well as the individuals involved. Make sure never to sweep a potential sexually inappropriate situation under the rug or try to cover it up, as it may cause further risk in the long run.

Institutional Memory and Succession Plans

Other common personnel risks for institutions are unwritten institutional memory and lack of succession plans. Some institutions have individual employees who have been around a very long time and therefore hold vast stores of institutional history and knowledge. While this may seem like a great asset, it can also prove to be a significant liability if that employee were to become suddenly ill or incapacitated. It is important to get information out of the heads of key individuals and written down, codified, and systematized so that there can be clarity and consistency about the organization and its history, policies, and procedures, and new employees can be brought into the environment quickly and efficiently.

The institution should have succession plans in place for senior level administrators (including continuing education program directors). Continuing education programs are often created with the force of exuberant and persuasive personalities, but if they are to be successful in the long run, they need to live on without dependence on any particular person. Although succession planning may seem like strategic work of the board of directors, you can aim to create programs today that will live on beyond your tenure. Plan to mentor potential successors. Even if mentoring takes place with associates that come and subsequently leave, you are building lasting relationships in a relatively specialized field. It is a small world, and careers often interweave in mysterious ways. Act responsibly toward all peers and subordinates with an eye toward continually training others to continue the work of your program.

To summarize the best-practice risk management techniques for the areas of contracts and personnel and employment practices: PUT IT IN WRITING. Doing so will protect your programs and your institution against multiple legal, reputation, operational, and personnel risks. It is worth the effort.

Reputation Risk

Negative publicity is the kind of risk of which nightmares are made. The media are capable of taking bits and pieces of a story out of context, emphasizing the negative or sensational, and magnifying a small misstatement. Weigh potential programs, speakers, events, and institutional affiliation, always keeping the institution's reputation for integrity and consistency with its high values at the forefront of your awareness. Vet guest speakers, employees, and independent contractors well before bringing them on board.

Get training in media presentation for yourself, senior administrators, even midlevel and junior administrators. Specialists can give you specific techniques for dealing with the press that can help you keep the focus on the messages to be conveyed without succumbing to attempts to find a sensational angle that might be negatively misinterpreted.

There are times when a program on a potentially controversial topic is current and important to your students or educational mission. Presenting these types of programs could run the risk of negative publicity and be potentially problematic for key funders. One way to address such situations is to actively forewarn certain major donors.

In the unfortunate event that a program or institution does experience unexpected negative publicity, it is critically important that the school be ready to meet the media promptly with a response that is open, forthcoming, and honest and presented by the most media-savvy senior professional on staff. Communicate quickly and as fully as possible with your institution's designated spokesperson so that he or she has accurate answers to all possible questions. Let that spokesperson be the sole public representative for the institution during the crisis and for some time after the crisis has passed. Refer all media requests to that person and make sure to instruct staff to do the same.

Financial Risk

Budgeting and bookkeeping decisions fall under the umbrella of financial risk areas relevant to continuing education directors. Budgets are a planning tool, another method of telling a story. Well-made budgets are reflections of programming dreams and concrete projections of how to bring these plans into reality. Poorly constructed budgets can be a significant source of financial risk for an institution because costs may be incurred without adequate offsetting revenues being generated or a broader institutional awareness of the liabilities being incurred.

During program and budget planning, think clearly about the anticipated number of participants, appropriate price points for the workshops or seminars, expected revenues, and, therefore, the projected funds available to be used toward expenses. The management of petty cash and oversight of other employees and contractors' expense reports is an important area in which careful double checking can be important to protect the institution from unnecessary over expenditures.

If the program area is supported by foundation grants, budgeting may need special attention. Likewise, interim and final financial reports will need to be presented to the granting organizations in addition to any narrative reporting. Note that asking for and studying regular budget-to-actual reports for both the continuing education department as a whole and particular programs is important. Don't wait until financial reports are generated;

initiate and maintain regular channels of communication with the business office staff. These colleagues can be extremely helpful in guiding the budget planning process, making models or projections of risky areas, and fleshing out the full array of potential expenses applicable to particular program initiatives.

Another area of important financial (and potential reputation) risk for an institution is the dissemination, storage, and disposal of papers that contain student social security or credit card numbers. Continuing education directors need to be aware of where the records for their programs are kept, the generation and distribution of duplicate copies, and the regular disposal techniques (shredding, please) of any papers with critical identity or financial information.

Technological Risk

Technology is changing extremely rapidly. This is a time of exploding digital-technology advances that have forever changed the very nature of the world we live in. The types of technology that have direct impact on continuing education programs include websites; e-mail; computer network security (firewalls and password protections); the use the Internet for researching (downloading) and publishing (uploading) information; audio, video, and media files (and related copyright, permissions or releases, and intellectual property issues); and the growing and competitive need to incorporate distance learning components into continuing education programming; among others. These areas present considerable rewards and potential technological risks to an institution.

It is well beyond the scope of this chapter to address these technological areas in depth. What is important to note, however, is that even the most knowledgeable computer experts are only themselves able to specialize in particular, relatively discrete areas of these overlapping fields. While even ten or fifteen years ago, it might have been adequate for an institution to have one or two tech-savvy people on call to help out with whatever hardware or software needs might arise, today this is no longer sufficient. It is a tremendous benefit to an institution's technological health to have a cadre of experts available that can be called upon to consult or advise as needed when any number of potential issues arise, and that someone on staff is able to ask educated questions to assess the level and particular areas of each potential consultant's expertise. Because of constant innovation and change, the area of technology, more than any of the other areas of risk management, is one where the adage "Just when you think you have thought of it all, the world surprises you" holds true.

Insurance

Insurance is the original tool of risk managers and the field of insurance is broad and complex. Institutions usually have one or more agents or brokers that work to interface with insurance companies to obtain competitive bids and to ensure the most appropriate types and levels of coverage for the particular needs of the school's programs and activities. Many organizations share a basic degree of common activities, and typically insurance brokers or agents specialize in clients from specific industries (not-for-profit organizations, educational institutions, or churches and religious organizations, for example). Continuing educations programs, however, frequently represent the newest, most creative and potentially irregular areas of an institution's activities. It is essential, therefore, to be in close communication with the administrators who work with the insurance agents and brokers to make sure they are fully informed about the full scope of the continuing education program's current and planned activities. It is imperative to report any incidents or accidents without delay in the event that a claim might need to be processed—insurance claim payments can sometimes be reduced if lapses or lags in reporting time occur.

This is a partial list of some types of insurance that are available for institutional purchase: property; general liability (slips and falls, accidents, negligence); pollution and environmental impairment (governmental agency regulations); workers' compensation (injury on the job); disability (injury off the job, both short and long term); special events (off-campus venues); professional liability (covers institution against claims that a professional [for example, counselor, minister, coach, consultant] gave bad advice to a client, student, or participant that then had a negative impact on that individual's life or circumstances); directors and officers insurance (commonly referred to as D&O, protects the institutional assets as well as the personal assets of the board of directors and senior administrators against lawsuits that might claim negligence or wrongful acts); travel, auto liability, non-owned aircraft, international transportation; employee behavior, dishonesty, crime, bonding insurance; sexual misconduct; and Internet liability; among others.

Insurance is not the be-all and the end-all. Although an important and traditional element of a risk management program, it is not in itself sufficient. A sound risk management program reduces the cost of insurance through effective risk control practices.

Best Practices

As the world continues to change, risk management grows in complexity and importance. Inevitably, things will go wrong! Some general points to remember when thinking about best practices in risk management include:

Communication is key. Risk management is about planning, participation, and clear communication. While planning programs, remember to ask the important questions: What could go wrong? What are the risks? What are the possible worst-case scenarios to reputation, legal, personnel, technological, and operational areas that could happen in this situation? What can be done to help mitigate these potential exposures? Create and strive to maintain open communications with all levels of the seminary community. Involve administrators early in the planning phases before launching any new programs. Each initiative comes with unique associated risks that need to be identified and analyzed; risk management tools need to be selected, implemented, monitored, and updated. Remember to be inclusive by communicating with all coworkers and engaging in a collective process of problem solving to help minimize risks, avoid potential losses, and leave room for powerful educational experiences for students.

Trusted advisors are essential. Make and maintain good relationships with experts that can help the organization as a whole, including

- attorneys (preferably with either a good pro-bono rate or with exceptional expertise in particular areas needed by the institution)
- insurance agents and brokers
- human resource or personnel specialists (who understand the labor laws in your state, can help review the language in your independent contractor and employee letter templates, and advise you on any implied liabilities)
- financial experts, such as investment advisors, outside independent auditors, accountants, and bookkeepers
- computer, Internet, network, website, and other technical experts
- board members with particular areas of expertise (can be wonderful allies in the risk management process)
- colleagues and confidants both within the institution and, sometimes even more important, outside the institution (Having a network of counterparts from other schools can be invaluable when unusual questions arise that can only be understood by someone with similar direct experiences. These colleagues can help think through complex problems with relative ease. They can help with benchmarking or answering comparative questions such as, "What do other seminaries do about x, y, and z?")

You are not alone. Risk management is shared problem solving in which all members of the team contribute to the implementation of decisions that help protect the institution. Even in large institutions that assign a specific institutional risk manager, that individual or department is neither solely responsible for all the risks of the institution nor responsible for managing them alone. The job of an effective risk manager is to work collaboratively to ensure that someone at the institution is appropriately taking on each area of concern (for example, the human resources department might be where the personnel risk management responsibilities primarily lie, whereas the facilities department might be charged with managing responsibility for property and environmental types of risk). All members of the team should be encouraged to accept a share of the responsibility and to identify and report potential risks and dangerous incidents.

Good risk management provides powerful positive benefits. When done well, thoroughly, and properly, good risk management allows institutions and the programs they support to survive and thrive. Employee retention and morale are known to be better in institutions with strong risk management and prevention practices. Good risk management helps to minimize expenses and allows an institution to be more creative in the pursuit of its mission and programmatic activities.

If you have anticipated and planned for the worst, you will be in good shape to survive the inevitable mishaps with good cheer and a positive attitude. It is perhaps ironic, but generally true, that institutions and individuals that have done a less than adequate job of evaluating, planning for, and mitigating risks end up being the most limited in scope. A commitment to strong risk management allows for measured and aware risk taking with creativity and optimism. Good risk management allows peace of mind and freedom to enjoy the rewards of creating powerful, dynamic, and innovative continuing theological education programming for clergy and laity.

Appendix A

Hiring as an Independent Contractor or an Employee

Independent contractors are usually individuals in business for themselves and available to the general public to perform services. Defining whether an individual should be hired by the institution as an employee or contracted with as an independent contractor can be a complex determination.

Misclassifying an individual as an independent contractor rather than as an employee entails the risk of incurring IRS tax liabilities and potential fines and penalties for both the institution and the individual. The reverse mistake could likewise be costly for an institution: classifying an individual as an employee rather than an independent contractor could lead to misstatements on the institution's disability and workers' compensation insurance records. If any doubt exists as to an individual's status with respect to the institution, a judgment call may have to be made. It is best to leave these decisions up to senior administration officials in consultation with the institution's attorneys.

There is no single rule or test to determine the difference between an employee and an independent contractor; the total activity or situation controls the determination. If the individual meets most or all of the following criteria, they are appropriately classified as an independent contractor and not as an employee:

- Employed elsewhere
- Services available to the general public
- Not directly supervised by your institution's employees
- No set hours or set schedule

- Able to refer or provide another individual in the contractor's place (at no additional cost) to provide the same or a similar service
- Duties not required to be done in-house
- No required regular progress reports
- No utilization of in-house clerical or support staff
- Business travel expenses are reimbursed
- Duties will not continue indefinitely
- Not permitted to supervise your institution's employees or to lead projects.

Factors such as whether the individual holds a license by state or local government and the time or the mode of payment are not relevant indicators of an individual's independent contractor status.

An individual cannot be simultaneously considered an independent contractor and an employee of the company. There are occasionally instances when one individual might legitimately serve an institution in different capacities at different times during the same calendar year, but these are extremely rare. Make sure that the school is clear and consistent in the distinction between independent contractors and employees.

Appendix B

Personnel Handbook Guidelines

Personnel communications is an aspect of the work setting having a strong (almost inevitable) risk that what one person says and thinks they have clearly communicated will be different from what the other person hears. There are always various interpretations to the same communication, unless it is very clearly spelled out in writing and in advance.

Following is an annotated list of basic areas that need to be covered in an employee handbook.

Acknowledgements and Disclaimers

This section of the handbook should include a place where the new employee signs that they acknowledge receipt of the employee handbook (this page should be removed and filed in the individual's personnel file). In addition, include a paragraph stating that the handbook is subject to changes at any time, does not constitute a binding contract, and that the employee is hired on an "at-will" basis. Detail in this section policies about any introductory or probationary period, institutional privacy policy, and the maintenance of employee records.

Nondiscrimination and Equal Employment Opportunity Policy

Having a written institutional policy prohibiting discrimination against any employee or applicant aligns with the values that most seminaries hold, and it is good risk management practice to mitigate against potential litigation. A nondiscrimination policy will typically apply to all phases of the employment process: recruitment, hiring, compensation, assignment, training, promotion, performance evaluation, discipline, and discharge. It bans discriminatory harassment and agrees to provide reasonable accommodation for disabilities and with regard to needs related to religious observance or practices on a case-by-case basis. Discrimination on the basis of race, color, sex, religion, creed, national origin, age, sexual orientation, disability, gender identity or expression, marital status, partnership status, genetic predisposition or carrier status, military status, or any other characteristic protected by applicable federal, state, or local law, except when a bona fide occupational qualification requires otherwise, is prohibited and should all be specified in writing.

Categories of Employment

The federal Fair Labor Standards Act entitles workers to overtime pay at the rate of time and a half for all hours over forty worked per week, except workers with managerial level responsibilities who are considered "exempt." The differentiation between "exempt" and "nonexempt" employees needs to be explained in this section of the personnel handbook and made explicit. This section also explains any other institutional categorizations of employees (for example, administrative officers and managerial staff, teaching staff and staff researchers, adjunct teaching and research staff, clerical and support staff) and provides definitions of each of these categories, as well as any specific distinctions with regard to terms of employment, evaluation of performance, or policies requiring notice of intention to resign or retire that may be required for these different categories.

Standards of Behavior

An employee handbook also details the institution's policies in regard to excessive tardiness, attendance, and the reporting of absences. In addition, the handbook should state clearly the institution's sexual harassment policy and any policy regarding drug and alcohol use. If the institution has an employee assistance program (EAP), information about the program would also be detailed in this section. (Note: Having some sort of EAP, whether formal or informal, is important. Having procedures set up in advance to help employees and their families deal with various life crises [physical illness, elderly parents needing assisted living or nursing homes, mental illness, and so forth] is a wonderful risk management tool that can help guide the institution in both humane and legally responsible actions in the event of inevitable work disruptions because of individual employee's personal life problems.) This section of the personnel handbook should also address the institution's policies regarding regular performance evaluation policies and any grievance procedures in place to address differences of opinion regarding performance evaluations.

Compensation and Increases

State clearly the frequency and method of pay; the frequency, method, and policies related to pay increases; and any policies related to reimbursement of business-related travel and other expenses.

Benefits

A majority of the employee handbook should be dedicated to the various benefits offered your employees. These may include some or all of the following: health insurance coverage, short-term disability coverage, workers' compensation coverage, life insurance, pension contributions (employer's contribution or match amounts), tax-deferred supplemental retirement contributions, pretax plan for payment of medical insurance premiums not covered by the institution, salary reduction plan for unreimbursed health care costs, and dependent care. In addition, include a discussion of the various kinds of time off offered by the institution, such as vacation time, paid holidays, sick leave, study leave or sabbatical time, bereavement leave, jury duty, medical disability leave, maternity and paternity leave, and leaves for other purposes, such as leaves of absence.

Termination of Employment

The handbook should conclude with a section dedicated to the various ways in which employment at the institution might end and detail the policies related to these various areas. These include retirement; resignation; termination by the seminary because of work reductions due to financial exigency or for reasons other than financial exigency; or termination for cause, such as inadequate performance. Finally, the handbook should list what, if any, severance policies apply, depending on how or why employment at the seminary was terminated.

Notes

1. George L. Head and Stephen Horn II, *Essentials of Risk Management, Volume 1*, 3rd ed. (Malvern, PA: Insurance Institute of America, 1997), 16–18.

2. William G. Bliss, "Cost of Employee Turnover," *The Advisor*, http://www.isquare.com/turnover.cfm (accessed July 21, 2008), 1.

3. Janet Willen, "How Do You Measure Risk Management Success?" and "Preventable Claims: Hugs Can Be a Touchy Problem," in *Reason & Risk* 16, no. 1 (Spring 2008), 6. *Reason & Risk* is the newsletter of United Educators Insurance.

4. Ibid., 6.

Additional References

Adair, Rebecca L., and Elizabeth J. Carmichael, Junes C. Jacquin, Glenn Klinksiek, Joseph D. Murphy, John E. Watson. "Risk Management and Insurance." In *College and University Business Administration*. 6th ed. Washington, DC: National Association of College and University Business Officers, 2000.

Bernstein, Peter L. *Against the Gods: The Remarkable Story of Risk*. New York: John Wiley, 1996.

Collins, Jim. *Good to Great: Why Some Companies Make the Leap . . . and Others Don't*. New York: HarperCollins, 2001.

Friedman, Thomas L. *The World Is Flat 3.0: A Brief History of the Twenty-first Century*. New York: Picador/Farrar, Straus and Giroux, 2007.

Kahn, Jeffrey P. and Alan M. Langlieb, eds. *Mental Health and Productivity in the Workplace: A Handbook for Organizations and Clinicians*. San Francisco: John Wiley, 2003.

What Might the Future Be?

Robert E. Reber and D. Bruce Roberts

As the preceding chapters indicate, the continuing education movement among clergy and laity is a vast and complex one. Barely sixty years old, it is loosely organized and reflects the vagaries of North American church life. Although at a considerable disadvantage in the church's educational ecology, the movement has demonstrated considerable creativity and growth. The two of us are confident that it can grow and become even more important in the coming decades. Whether this growth will prove fruitful will depend, however, upon those of us who are committed to lifelong learning and developing programs of quality. To foster the professional development and personal growth of religious leaders, we must answer affirmatively seven key questions.

First, in a society where participation in professional continuing education and commitment to lifelong learning is growing every year, will religious institutions provide attractive and expanding opportunities for lifelong learning for their leaders, congregations, and communities?

Denominations and congregations lag behind the rest of society in recognizing the importance of serving their constituencies on a lifelong basis. Given the priorities of most churches today, there is a possibility that the gap will continue to widen. If this happens, churches and religious organizations will become increasingly irrelevant in meeting the educational needs and interests of their members, which will likely result in the further privatization of religion and the abdication of religion's role in public life. The future of the religious traditions depends upon the ongoing education of its leadership and members so that they may give leadership within congregations, religious institutions, and the larger society. Congregations need a learned clergy and a learned laity to meet the demands and challenges of local congregations and communities of faith in being God's people in the world. Lifelong learning should pervade the entire culture and ethos of religious institutions and be valued, supported, and undergirded with resources in every way possible.

Second, will we shift from a dominant emphasis on education for children to a commitment to lifelong learning for all church members?

In many congregations, the educational emphasis is on children. Great amounts of energy, not to mention anxiety, are consumed in recruiting teachers, reviewing and purchasing curricula, constructing and maintaining buildings, and organizing and running Sunday schools for children. Recruiting teachers for these enterprises is often difficult precisely because adults do not feel adequately prepared to teach anything about their faith.

Not only are we losing youth and young adults, adults are also leaving "old-line" denominational churches in droves, in spite of evidence that people in this society have a high degree of religious commitment. We have ample data to conclude that our educational efforts with children and youth do not take and do not result in lifelong commitment to discipleship. No matter how high quality our curricula, youth leave congregations during their high school or college years because they say, "It's boring!"

The two of us suggest that the key to reversing this trend is not simply to improve youth programs but also to implement quality adult education. To retain members across generations, leaders must create and lead innovative, engaging, relevant, and energizing programs for adults of all ages. Parents must receive training and encouragement to become the primary religious educators for their children. There is an urgent need for continuing educators to prepare clergy and lay leaders in knowledge and skills of lifelong education so that people of all ages may share in the excitement and life-giving vibrancy of a faith community committed to lifelong learning.

Third, will we engage the vast number of people with religious and spiritual interests who do not currently participate in educational programs because of economic, social, political, religious, theological, or racial barriers?

Congregations remain segregated by race, ethnicity, and class. We in religious institutions and continuing education programs have thus far made little effort to reach out to those who are different from ourselves. We have rarely been creative or committed to working with those who have been turned off and even bored by our educational endeavors. Our rhetoric about being inclusive has not changed our reality of division and conflict.

To move beyond the current situation both inside and outside religious institutions, careful study and experimentation will be needed. Delivery systems will have to change and we will have to involve people from many different sectors in planning processes with us. If every seminary, conference, retreat center, or congregation would take on just one educational project a year, short or long term, that addresses explicitly the needs of those who might come but who are not yet a part of the community, what a difference it would make.

Fourth, will we respond to the pervasive hunger for the spiritual life that so many North Americans express and often explore outside the confines of established theological institutions and local congregations?

The Gallup organization conducted a study in the late 1990s on the "Spiritual Pulse of the Nation." Quoting from that study, sociologist D. Michael Lindsay, in an address to the Princeton

Consultation on Spirituality and Congregational Life, sponsored by Princeton and Auburn theological seminaries, said their data suggest that 82 percent of the U.S. public reports wanting to grow spiritually. In a similar study done in 2005, 80 percent of 112,000 college freshmen reported wanting to grow spiritually.[1] That is rather phenomenal growth in the last five years. Yet, the figures cohere with casual observations. For instance, bookstores have greatly expanded sections dealing with spirituality, particularly in areas dealing with meditation and contemplative prayer. In addition, a group of management and planning consultants with whom the two of us are familiar draws its members from those who work primarily in business and not-for-profit institutions. Each of these individuals thinks of himself or herself as a change agent for good in society and as engaged in a spiritual activity and quest. Yet, not one of them belongs to a congregation. They perceive it as an institution with an agenda not conducive to their spiritual development and irrelevant to their quest.

Continuing educators must help congregational leaders, lay and clergy, find ways of engaging people in spiritual quests that are at once novel and appropriate to their faith traditions. While the Christian tradition has many resources for the spiritual life, many other religious traditions have resources that are helpful and informative for Christians as well. We must take the risk of leading people in spiritual practices that help them discern and participate in the will of God in this time.

Fifth, will we persuade religious leaders to respond to the extraordinary and multifaceted challenges to the quality of life on this planet, whether ecological, economic, technological, religious, or political?

The content of much professional and adult education today avoids these concerns. Yet public awareness is increasing and many congregational members also belong to the numerous citizen groups and organizations concerned with plant and animal life, global warming, protecting the environment, recycling, building bridges of peace around the world, eliminating hunger, providing health care, defending human rights, and so forth. The awareness of the interconnectedness of the planet and all forms of life continues to grow. At the same time, violence plagues society; it saturates television screens and movies and political, religious, and ethnic relationships, and it permeates family and community life. However, such issues remain at the periphery of much continuing theological education. We must engage these critical issues of justice, peace, health, and ecological wholeness in educational contexts if we desire to make qualitative differences in the lives of individuals and the places where they live and work and worship.

Sixth, will we foster and support innovation and experimentation in continuing and professional education that will make a qualitative difference in congregations and in the preparation of future church leaders?

It is increasingly clear that there will not be one right answer to any of the questions that face congregations, communities of faith, and continuing theological educators. We must keep reminding ourselves that there are as many right answers to the issues and problems that face us as there are contexts in which we work. Ronald Heifetz challenges us to focus on the adaptive work in our organizations, continuing to pose the questions that require changes in our values, beliefs, and behavior, while resisting the technological or quick-fix solutions.[2] Not having one right answer available to us is frightening on the one hand, but freeing on the other; we know that solutions must be invented in our various contexts, through innovations and experiments that are evaluated and mined for new insights.

Continuing educators are challenged not only to be innovative in their work but also to help clergy and lay leaders learn how to learn through reflective practice, experimentation and evaluation, and trial and error. Congregations need to find new ways to do ministry in this culture or be prepared to be considered irrelevant, if not quaint. Similarly, Rabbi Edwin Friedman once suggested that what is needed in times like these are explorers who risk going against the prevailing worldview to seek new paths and new directions. As continuing educators and lifelong learners to-day, who face an uncertain future, we too will need to become explorers, finding new ways to deliver our programs, forging new partnerships and alliances, allocating funds in new ways that encourage innovation, while maintaining sustained focus on given audiences and issues over time.

Numerous emerging models are being developed in seminaries, retreat centers, congregations, and other religious centers. Some examples are residential centers focused on specific issues (hunger, peacemaking, sustainability of the planet, ecumenicity, interreligious dialogue), coaching for individuals and groups, local and regional peer learning groups, study and travel seminars and cross-cultural experiences, online and distance learning, and alliances and partnerships among organizations in the public, private, religious, and governmental sectors. Undoubtedly, others could be mentioned and new ones created. There is truly a plethora of opportunities for all of us!

Seventh, will we make use of the burgeoning technology and digital revolution, the exponential growth and accessibility of knowledge, and the multiple possibilities of designing and offering educational opportunities that bring the world and its people face to face with us and we face to face with them, whether next door or the most remote places on the planet?

Many complex and ethical questions come to the fore. Who will have access to computers, the Internet, and future technology? Given the energy crisis worldwide and the larger global warming crisis, will only the rich and middle class in industrialized nations have electrical power to run them? How do we build trust and encourage the capacity to think critically, promote fairness, speak truth, develop more collaboration, and build sustainable educational projects and communities?

The chapters in this book on peer groups and coaching provide some answers and clues to what makes a qualitative difference educationally in the practice of ministry. The research that has been done is promising. We know something about what goes into qualitative change. More experimentation is required, as are a strategic use of resources, a commitment to sustained educational programs over time, and careful evaluation of our work.

The two of us believe that the contributors to the chapters in this book indicate the enormous possibilities and challenges for lifelong learning and continuing theological education. What is required is a willingness to take risks, to get involved in new ideas and partnerships, to experiment, and to communicate what we are learning in our educational experiments and innovations. The health of our institutions, whether they be local congregation, judicatory, seminary, college, or conference center, will depend on our willingness to think and act systemically and creatively. More choices, not fewer, will be the future of lifelong learning and continuing theological education. Those of us who give leadership to many kinds of educational programs are surely challenged ourselves to be lifelong learners. Never has there been a time when ongoing education is more needed!

Notes

1. Sonja L. Cohen, "Student Survey Reveals Distinctive Unitarian Universalist Traits," *UU World*, Fall 2005, http://www.uuworld.org/life/articles/1834.shtml (accessed August 31, 2009).

2. Ronald Heifetz and Marty Linsky, *Leadership on the Line: Staying Alive through the Dangers of Leading* (Boston: Harvard Business School, 2002), 13–15.